"Before you can become an advertisement for positive anger, you must first acknowledge the private anger within. . . .

"For many of us this is no problem, as evidenced by a nineteen-year longitudinal study which found that anger was the *predominant* emotion associated with important events in women's lives. Why predominant? Because anger involves us at every level—physically, emotionally, socially and culturally.

"The challenge for us is to take charge of these levels and galvanize our anger into action. It is the only way we, as women, can transcend the many environments and relationships which have squashed female anger in the past and move toward a future in which the healthy, positive side of this emotion empowers and enriches our lives. You, too, can take the first step toward empowerment and enrichment. . . ."

—Sandra Thomas, Ph.D., R.N.,
from *Use Your Anger*

USE YOUR ANGER

A WOMAN'S GUIDE TO EMPOWERMENT

Sandra Thomas, Ph.D., R.N.

AND

Cheryl Jefferson

POCKET BOOKS
New York   London   Toronto   Sydney   Tokyo   Singapore

The information in this book is intended to make the reader a better informed consumer and more knowledgeable about the choices available to her or him. Where it offers guidelines for decisionmaking, these are meant as guidelines only; they are not intended to replace diagnosis and treatment recommendations by competent professionals, nor to provide personal psychological, psychiatric, or other professional advice. For such advice, the reader must seek the service of a qualified health professional. The authors and publisher disclaim any liability arising directly or indirectly out of the reader's use or misuse of the information contained in this book.

While the case histories in this book are those of real people, the authors have changed the names and certain characteristics of certain of those people to disguise their identities.

An *Original* Publication of POCKET BOOKS

POCKET BOOKS, a division of Simon & Schuster Inc.
1230 Avenue of the Americas, New York, NY 10020

Copyright © 1996 by Sandra P. Thomas

All rights reserved, including the right to reproduce
this book or portions thereof in any form whatsoever.
For information address Pocket Books, 1230 Avenue
of the Americas, New York, NY 10020

Library of Congress Cataloging-in-Publication Number: 95-42439

ISBN: 0-671-51973-5

First Pocket Books trade paperback printing May 1996

10 9 8 7 6 5 4 3 2

POCKET and colophon are registered trademarks of
Simon & Schuster Inc.

Cover design by Joanna Riesman
Text design by Stanley S. Drate/Folio Graphics Co., Inc.

Printed in the U.S.A.

This book is dedicated to the
courageous women who took part
in the Women's Anger Study
and shared their feelings so the rest
of us might grow.

◇ <u>ACKNOWLEDGMENTS</u> ◇

We are deeply appreciative of everyone who has supported us during this project—you know who you are. In particular, we want to express our gratitude to our husbands, families, and friends; our editor, Tom Miller, for recognizing the potential of this book and for giving us the opportunity to present this important information to women everywhere; to our agents, Ling Lucas and Ed Vesneske, Jr., for their support and guidance; and Marge Pilot, for her invaluable assistance. We also want to thank the generous, compassionate women who participated in the Women's Anger Study and the Study team members including Kaye Bultemeier, Gayle Denham, Madge Donnellan, Patricia Droppleman, June Martin, Mary Anne Modrcin-McCarthy, Sheryl Russell, Pegge Saylor, Elizabeth Seabrook, Barbara Shirk, Carol Smucker, Jane Tollett, and Dorothy Wilt. In addition, we want to acknowledge the other principal investigators in the current phase of the study, Patricia Droppleman and Carol Smucker, along with Janet Crooks, Janet Deese, Lucy Gasaway, Mary Pilkington, Donna Saravi, and Marilyn Smith. Thanks to you all.

—SANDRA THOMAS, PH.D., R.N.
CHERYL JEFFERSON

◇ CONTENTS ◇

A JUST ANGER

Anger shines through me.
Anger shines through me.
I am a burning bush.
My rage is a cloud of flame.
My rage is a cloud of flame
in which I walk
seeking justice
like a precipice.
How the streets
of the iron city
flicker, flicker,
and the dirty air
fumes.
Anger storms
between me and things,
transfiguring
transfiguring.
A good anger acted upon
is beautiful as lightning
and swift with power.
A good anger swallowed,
a good anger swallowed
clots the blood
to slime.

—Marge Piercy,
Circles on the Water

THE WOMEN'S ANGER STUDY

The Women's Anger Study. Do the words make you think of studying women who go to their respective corners, take off the white gloves, and come out punching? Of documenting quiet types who sit and steam until their eyeballs fuse together? Or, if you're more analytical, maybe you believe it means speaking softly and carrying a big statistic. But the Women's Anger Study is more than statistics, much, much more. It's the true stories of six hundred women sharing their everyday anger and facing its brass-knuckle pain. By identifying with these women and validating our emotions, we too, can share our anger; we too, can face its pain.

But you won't learn about this in very many places. Few books deal with angry women because almost all the research is focused on the crash-and-burn anger behavior traditionally associated with men. It is also the behavior associated with high blood pressure, coronary heart disease, and stress, which is why the ongoing Women's Anger Research Project at the University of Tennessee (Knoxville) was born.

Sandra's interest began during a longitudinal study of midlife health factors that she conducted at the 1982 Knoxville World's Fair. There people ages thirty-five to fifty-five were asked about their behavior, the stresses in their environment, and various psychological issues. As the study progressed, it was obvious that for coronary-prone, type A personalities, anger was a big health factor, so Sandra began asking people about their anger experiences. The answers showed major, significant differences between men and women, but when Sandra tried to find additional studies specifically on women, she came up empty—a scary proposition when you consider that we women, in rapidly increasing numbers, are going down in flames as fast as our male counterparts.

And the more Sandra thought about this, the more these flames spread. She began to do a slow burn. Why was there virtually no research information on women's anger? Why—since our angry emotions are so powerful that they trigger a greater cardiovascular response than any other emotion—was *women's* anger being ignored? And ignored it was. In many male-dominated ivory towers and halls of medicine, there were no brownie points for researching female anger, and since there were no brownie points, the research wasn't done. That's when Sandra decided to do something: she formed an all-female research team and kick-started the Women's Anger Research Project, the first large-scale, comprehensive empirical investigation of everyday anger in women's lives. And what do women think about this work? Most women we speak to about the research respond with a knowing look. Their eyes meet ours and they say

> *Fascinating! Every woman I know is sitting on a ton of rage. I'm so glad you're studying this.* —**Monique**

But we learned that it's hard for us to admit we're angry. Did we say "admit"? Some of us aren't even sure what anger is or if it's anger we're actually feeling. That's because we aren't always mad at a specific event or family member—it's just a life thing, a general resentment of our day-to-day circumstances mingled with guilt and self-blame. Also, we aren't glowering at the world or kicking dogs and picking fights with old ladies. Instead, our anger is hidden, simmering away deep inside until, on occasion, it boils up to the surface. And when it does boil up, we feel like pot scum, even if our angry emotions are totally justified. Worse yet, we feel alone, but we're not, not anymore.

In this book we have access to the emotions of hundreds of women, women who share their own feelings in their own words. And what do these women tell us? That we frequently have the same anger triggers, the same anger targets, and just as commonly, we hit the same marks.

Unfortunately, we have plenty to aim at. What's plenty? Mates and ex-mates who drive us to distraction, lazy teenagers who make us apoplectic, and bosses who royally screw us, not to mention parents, friends, siblings, and assorted significant others who let us down in many ways. In our roles as wives, mothers, and career women, we experience a universe of angry feelings including righteous indignation, subtle or stinging sarcasm, smoldering resentment, and the occasional intense desire to send our mates out for brain transplants. Sometimes we're just mad at ourselves, and this anger contributes to food binges, substance abuse, low self-esteem, and big-time physical health problems.

Speaking of problems, let's defuse one right now: Although this book is about the everyday anger of average women, we are not making flimsy generalizations. We know that once you get beyond textbook biology, there is no such thing as an "average" female human being. However, our research shows that there is such a thing as the "average" anger reaction, and that reaction is discomfort—sometimes intense discomfort because anger makes us feel so inept. In fact, regardless of our diverse marital, educational, social, economic, religious, and occupational backgrounds, our discomfort with anger is much the same.

Indeed, as you read about other women's anger experiences, a lot of them will sound familiar, so familiar that they spark high-voltage emotions. Suddenly you may feel like tongue-lashing a couple of kids, firing your spouse, or telling the boss to go to hell. But don't. Don't use your anger to take an eye for an eye, because your goal—and ours—is not to get even, it's to get ahead, and the only way we can get ahead is to use our anger productively.

Productive anger is healthy and empowering. It does not trash relationships or jobs or endanger our own physical and mental health. And let's say this right up front: Angry women are not sinful, weak, or mentally deranged—they're inspired, inspired to challenge injustice, defend highborn values, and make brave choices for the future.

But we must make these choices with knowledge, patience, and care. For this reason, *Use Your Anger* is based on up-to-the-minute scientific studies and cutting-edge research data—data that dispels anger propaganda, ends old wives' tales, and terminates misleading folk "wisdom." We also clear up the confusion and misinformation about anger, frustration, hostility, and aggression, four terms that have been used interchangeably and erroneously for years. Why is this important? Because a lot of books about "anger" aren't about anger at all—and if these books aren't about anger, their advice can't solve anger problems. This is especially true if the authors used old research or no research, or if they based their suggestions on male scientific models that don't apply to females. For these reasons and more, *Use Your Anger: A Woman's Guide to Empowerment* is a major breakthrough.

For the first time, female anger research is used to give women advice and to fill the shocking information gap we've wallowed in till now. This research examines private, subjective experiences scientists once considered too elusive to measure and quantify. Yet here we acknowledge these experiences as a valuable source of personal insight, insight you can develop through our highly reputable, well-validated questionnaires. In addition, to help you get more of a handle on your own anger, we suggest a host of proven techniques drawn from the very best contemporary social, medical, and psychological literature.

And while we're on the subject, let's say a word about psychology, psychiatry, and getting our heads examined. Although this book is a useful tool for therapists and their clients, it is not a substitute for professional psychotherapy. It is an invitation to explore your anger and other emotions through dream analysis, your journal, and answers to questionnaires. Now some of your answers may convince you to seek professional help. If you do, be sure to shop around (see Parts Four and Five). Look for a therapist who's right for you, and remember, a female counselor may be especially good with anger—after all, she's probably had her share of it too.

We certainly have, and our first-hand experience has convinced us that each woman chooses her response to an angry situation. That's where responsibility comes in. We believe each woman is responsible for her own angry reactions—and these reactions are not based on blind instinct or a return to our primitive cavewoman genes. No, reacting with anger is a choice, a choice that can be controlled.

In fact, choosing to be angry is a reason for optimism because it means you're feeling alive. You want to improve yourself, your family, health, profession, society, or whatever, and you are not willing to settle for second best. You are also not willing to live with one foot in the grave because of your past. Anger over ancient issues and childhood traumas can be overcome, and every day new studies reinforce this point with information on our resilience, strength, and powerful ability to adapt, grow, and change.

> *One changes from day to day . . . every few years one becomes a new being.*   **—George Sand**

So if you are ready to become a new being, to ditch ineffective anger myths and habits, to forswear crippling pain from your past, and to discover—as we did—that your anger is a source of power and enlightenment, you are ready to use this book. All you have to do is turn the page . . .

PART ONE

DEFINING YOUR ANGER

1

_____

MYTHS ABOUT ANGER

Are you a prisoner of the reign of errors? Like these participants in the Women's Anger Study, do you mistakenly believe your anger will sink the love boat?

> _I get mad at him over sex. He could be almost dead and want sex . . . and there are some times I don't want to . . . it makes me feel like shit._ **—Margie, married nine years**

Doom you to a lifetime of soup for one?

> _I've always tried to suppress my anger and not become explosive—because of the fear of rejection from people, you know, they won't like me or they won't include me or they won't understand me . . ._ **—Babs, age thirty**

Or perhaps you think it's not right to get angry, that anger is uncontrollable and people can just see the snakes coming out of your head:

> *I just rant and rave and my kids cringe in the corner . . . They were afraid of me . . . afraid of making Mom angry . . .*   **—Moira, now in counseling**

Maybe you know how Moira's kids feel, especially if you're in a worst-case scenario where expressing your anger is not an option:

> *I married very young . . . When I was pregnant with my first child, my ex-husband would beat me. Just before delivery he kicked me in the stomach and I thought I had lost it [the baby] . . . And I grew real angry then. I hated him but I continued to live with him because I didn't have anyplace to go.*
>
> **—Meg, survivor of two abusive marriages**

or if you're convinced your anger could be harmful to you or anyone who gets in your way:

> *I was . . . aware of how much anger was there and it terrified me. I just thought, man, there's no way I'm going to ever deal with all these things and . . . if it gets out . . . it could really hurt somebody, almost to the extent of killing somebody . . . I could just do like those people that get up in a bell tower and start taking shots . . .*
>
> **—Violetta, once hospitalized for depression**

But it doesn't have to be this way. As Violetta, Moira, Babs, and you will learn, anger doesn't have to turn into aggression, it isn't uncontrollable, and it won't damage relationships—not if you learn to manage it effectively and abort these and other negative myths about anger and human emotions.

What are the other myths? "I'm not responsible." "It was instinct." "Blame my heredity, my environment, *da-dat-da-dat-da-da.*" You've heard them all before. Maybe you've even said them all before. But if this is your idea of emotional currency, you're being seriously shortchanged. You're cheating yourself of one of the most powerful, dynamic, potentially positive feelings of all—anger. Why would you do this? Because like many of us, you were probably spoon-fed some deep-seated mental mythology, mythology we have to rewire right now.

First, you were likely told that anger is a destructive force, a sin, or a sign of mental illness. It's not. Anger is a natural, all-too-human feeling that can be healthy and empowering for women who learn to manage it effectively—which leads us to Myth #2. To many of us, managing anger effectively sounds about as likely as turning straw into gold. Why? There's a widespread misconception in our culture that emotions can't be managed, that our feelings are involuntary and when we're angry, we're possessed or seized by demons. Why else would we say: "I don't know what got into me," "I'm not myself!" or "The devil made me do it!"

But this kind of attitude—

- "I'm struggling with my anger."
- "She's battling her anger."
- "He fought back his anger."
- "She's lost control over her anger."
- "He surrendered to his anger."
- "I was overcome by anger."

—makes anger an opponent, not the valuable ally it was meant to be. So to start making anger your ally, learn to recognize the following:

Myths About Anger and Human Emotion

MYTH: Emotions are instinctive, they just "come naturally."

TRUTH: Both "good" and "bad" emotions are learned; you can choose which emotion you allow yourself to feel during any given incident.

MYTH: You aren't responsible for your emotional actions; emotions are uncontrollable.

TRUTH: Americans excuse crimes of passion due to their "involuntary" nature; as a result, the United States has five times the number of violent crimes per capita as Japan, a society that believes anger can and should be controlled.

MYTH: Adult emotions are determined by childhood experiences.

TRUTH: Although early experiences are important, emotional development continues throughout life. As an adult, you can acquire the knowledge and skills to handle your emotions more effectively.

MYTH: Anger is an appendix—left over from the Stone Age and no longer necessary in the modern, civilized world.

TRUTH: Western civilization has retained anger for over twenty-five hundred years because it serves a valuable social function.

MYTH: The causes of anger are universal.

TRUTH: Anger is highly individualistic. The causes vary greatly from person to person depending on your values, perceptions, self-esteem, and other factors.

MYTH: Men are angrier than women.

TRUTH: Women experience anger as frequently as men, but we are not as free to express it. One nineteen-year longitudinal study showed that anger is the predominant emotion associated with important events in women's lives.

MYTH: Anger leads to aggression.

TRUTH: Typical, everyday anger seldom leads to acts of physical aggression.

MYTH: It's great to "let it all hang out."

TRUTH: Although we are sometimes encouraged to vent our anger to achieve "catharsis," there is no proof that screaming and cussing actually help. In fact, these behaviors usually increase our angry feelings and make us feel worse. As one expert, Carol Tavris, puts it, "Letting off steam is a wonderful metaphor . . . but people are not teapots."

MYTH: Anger causes health problems.

TRUTH: There's been a rash of publicity on the link between anger, coronary heart disease, and other health problems. Articles with scare tactic titles ("Is Anger Killing You?") plus simplistic media advice ("Avoid getting angry") make us nervous about expressing anger, but it is the extreme forms of anger that are linked to disease. Common, everyday anger can be healthy, especially if you handle it in a productive way that uses rational, problem-solving discussion and avoids the unhealthy extremes of indiscriminately dumping on others or being totally inhibited.

MYTH: Anger is a knee-jerk reaction to external events.

TRUTH: There's nothing knee-jerk about it. Anger only occurs after your brain has processed enough information about a situation to interpret it as an obstacle, a slight, or a wrong. This interpretation is based on your belief system and is crucial to determining your response.

MYTH: Anger always damages relationships.

TRUTH: Wrong! Often relationships with the angry person are strengthened, not weakened—and check this out: In James Averill's research, 76 percent of those who were on the receiving end of someone else's anger said that they learned to recognize their own faults as a result of the anger incident.

Now being on the receiving end of someone else's anger may be all well and good, but the important thing here is to recognize our own angry emotions, a real trick when you consider that this mythology has left us confused—very confused.

2

UNDERSTANDING
YOUR ANGER

*Anger is such a tricky emotion for me . . . In my life it is
often mistaken for fear, weakness, embarrassment,
shame, regret, guilt and/or remorse, and many other uncomfortable feelings.* **—Gloria, age forty-five**

*I think . . . a lot of women . . . are very hesitant about it. I
don't think a lot of us feel worthy of being angry and even
when we are angry, we're more afraid of it, we want peace
more than we want to actually express our anger and
have somebody have to deal with it because then we have
to deal with it too. It's a lot easier just to suppress it, not
make anybody unhappy, and not have to deal with confrontation which bothers me and makes me angry at myself.* **—Connie, age twenty-one**

A lot of us are with Connie and Gloria on this one. Although we use different words, we really mean the same
thing when we say: "It's not worth making a scene over," "Go
along to get along," "It's better to stay out of things," "I didn't
want to hurt his feelings," "There's no sense arguing," or "I'm
not angry, I'm just upset."

But why do we do this? Why do we deny our anger even
if we're pretty sure it's anger we're feeling? In part, it's a cultural thing. While most men have long been allowed and even
encouraged to express their anger, most of us women—
practically from conception—have found our anger invali-

dated, trivialized, and forbidden outright. As young girls we pay a high price for expressing our anger directly to parents, teachers, and various authority figures. Television and the movies reinforce these negative consequences by branding angry women as bitches, battle-axes, and shrews. Even the psychiatric establishment gets in its licks with descriptions such as "hysterical," "neurotic," and "castrating." And to rub salt into the wound, this same society rewards us for being nice, docile girls, for selflessly serving others, preserving harmonious relationships, and keeping our anger to ourselves.

And if we don't keep our anger to ourselves, things get even more complicated. First, we discover that we're working without an emotional net and when we're mad, we're frequently swamped with pain and guilt. Then we find that angry displays extract a high price in terms of our self-respect, our jobs, and even our lives. This is particularly true if you work in an environment where you're zapped with a daily dose of racism or sexism but can't complain to your boss. Or if you're in a marriage that saps your spirits with continual criticism. Or maybe you simply fear that your anger will force you to speak some damning prose that will come back to haunt you one day:

> *I don't do anything . . . cause . . . I might say something I didn't really mean or that I'd regret later and I know that I don't like to be yelled at and so I don't yell at other people . . . I just internalize it.*   **—Mary**

Many of the rest of us internalize it too, and with divorce, job loss, and other potentially devastating consequences waiting in the wings, why would we do otherwise? Why would we risk identifying our anger and expressing it? Quite frankly, most of us wouldn't. Instead, we opt for silence. We perfect the pissed-off pout, seethe quietly, suck on a cigarette, or soothe ourselves with sundaes, all of which can create a new species of trouble further down the line (see Parts Four and Five). After centuries of such behavior, we women have become experts at hiding our anger and denying its power to ourselves. In fact, many of us have denied this feeling for so long we're not even sure we can pick it out of the emotional lineup. But now it's time to be sure, to define our anger and acknowledge it for the incredibly positive, potent tool it is.

What Anger Really Is and Why It's Sometimes Not What You Think

To appreciate your anger and use it effectively, you must first make sure that it's anger you're really feeling and not one of the big three emotions commonly mistaken for anger, otherwise known as hostility, aggression, and:

Frustration

Being frustrated, irritated, or annoyed is not the same as being angry, nor does frustration automatically mean that you'll knock someone's block off as the old frustration-produces-aggression theory suggests. Although a tardy companion, a rebellious appliance, or a husband who channel-surfs are all a pain in the ass, such minor incidents pose no real threat to our personal integrity and they don't violate our trust or morals. Sure, these events are momentarily inconvenient or disturbing, and some women with poor frustration tolerance get very upset over them, but in the long run they're small potatoes compared to the serious matters that provoke true anger.

Still, frustration is part of everyday life. When your friends call just as you're stepping into the tub; or you're already late and traffic's moving at glacial speed; or you're dead tired, the kids are crabby, and the only one who takes you seriously is the family dog, it can really stick in your craw. But that's okay. We all overreact to trivial irritations now and then, and feeling frustrated is only temporary.

Often, the solution to our temporary frustrated feelings is a simple stress-reduction technique—like taking time out to rest our shredded nerves or injecting some humor into the situation. This is especially important if you overreact to frustrating events and need help remembering not to sweat the small stuff.

> When the little things start to get to me, I remember Ruchert's law: There is nothing so small that it can't be blown out of proportion.   —**Denise**

It will also help if you remember that the emotional fault line of frustration is much more likely to crack open if you're hungry, physically exhausted, or short on sleep. If this is the case, you need to do some preventive maintenance by getting more rest, eating right, and pacing yourself to reduce stress and irritation. Unfortunately, all the rest, proper food, and great pacing in the world won't help if you're feeling:

Hostility—An Enduring Attitude of Ill Will Toward the World

Some of us see the world as an enemy camp. We believe other people are intentionally selfish, dishonest, and downright mean, not to mention untrustworthy and unfair. When we feel this way, we're filled with hostility, a mental attitude that is more pervasive, long-lasting, and antagonistic than mere anger could ever be. As hostile women we carry a perpetual chip on our shoulders, are very verbal about our dissatisfaction with life, and practically spit fire as we blame everyone else for our own chronic discontent. Others of us are less vocal, but are continually on the lookout for:

> *Incompetence! It's all around me. That's why no one has recognized how good I am at my job and why I got passed up for that last promotion. I work with idiots and they know I know it! I hope they all get fired."*
> **—Toni, age forty, programmer**

> *I've been waiting for an elevator for twenty minutes. Some inconsiderate bitches have been holding it up and when I finally get on . . . I plan to give them the evil eye because they made me late.*
> **—Overheard at a national writers conference**

> *My younger sister is the executor of Mom's will. She doesn't know it, but I've hired an attorney to double-check everything she does because I just know she'll screw things up.* **—Jay-Ann, age thirty-eight, chef**

Screwing things up is exactly what hostility does to us. Instead of being clear minded and able to separate the truly important issues from the flotsam and jetsam, the hostile woman (or man) sees everyone else as incompetent, crazy, inconsiderate, dangerous, and worse. Alas, this attitude seems to be on the upswing. Psychiatrist Willard Gaylin says these are paranoid times and increasingly, people spy danger everywhere they look.

While many women feel this way, nationwide studies consistently show that hostility levels are higher among men. Why? Because hostility is actually fostered by the way many men are socialized to compete, to engage in one-upmanship, and to constantly be on red alert for someone trying to take advantage of them. This is especially true for business types with mottoes like "Winning is everything" and "Get them before they get you" tattooed on their brains.

Unfortunately, it isn't just the brain that suffers from this attitude. It's the heart, the lungs, the blood vessels, and life itself, because hostility has proven links to coronary heart disease and premature death—and this doesn't apply just to men, it's true for women too (see Part Five). But even if you are occasionally mad enough to pop a blood vessel, this doesn't make hostility the same thing as anger, and aggression—also higher among men—isn't the same thing either.

Aggression—Taking Intentional Action to Hurt or Destroy

Some of us are purveyors of pain. We're quick with a cruel retort, a nasty put-down, or a vengeful action. In other words, we're into aggression, which differs from anger in both its intention and its effects. Aggression involves an actual, or impending, physical or verbal attack. The intent of the attack is to hurt someone, to belittle them, or to take revenge, and the aftereffects are sad to behold—especially the profound damage to relationships and the senseless destruction of property.

Sometimes the attack takes the form of a physical assault including hitting, punching, slapping, or injuring other people with weapons. Even though there are severe penalties for these actions, sadly, they are on the increase in America today. So is verbal aggression. Sarcasm, nasty insults, and rudeness can be heard on every street corner of every city and in numerous small towns and private homes as well. Following a pattern set by shock radio and TV, many of us have perfected vocal assaults that could kill a rose in water.

While there is a widespread belief that aggression is a characteristic we're born with, many people—actually, entire cultures—get along quite nicely without it. In fact, the whole concept of an inherited predisposition toward aggression was soundly debunked in 1986 by a prestigious group of scientists who met in Seville, Spain. They concluded that there is no scientific basis for believing humans are naturally aggressive. Quite the contrary. Aggressive behavior is learned and when it's rewarded, it's repeated over and over again. Just ask the nearest schoolyard, office, or factory bully.

He or she will tell you that aggression is often a deliberate attempt to intimidate or control others. Frequently, aggressive acts are planned well in advance and performed in a relatively cool, calculating manner compared to the heated arousal of a genuine anger episode. It's like football. In football, athletes "calmly" tackle, pommel, and wrestle each other in a deliberate, planned, and profitable manner that ritualizes aggression. Of course, sometimes the rituals of agression can go too far and suddenly, it's war.

War is a carefully organized, deliberately aggressive action to defend national pride, secure territory, or "avenge" old ethnic grievances against our enemies. It is the ultimate form of ritualized aggression and from time immemorial, war has been a man's game. So is war reenactment. The popular restagings of D-Day, the Civil War, the French and Indian War, the Revolutionary War, etc., all appeal more to men than to women. In fact, a recent reenactment in Virginia drew over ten thousand Civil War buffs (most of them men) who enthusiastically cheered the simulated mutilating, maiming, and killing, begging the questions:

Do reenactments give macho men who missed out on the thrill of war the chance to do it in a safe and tidy fashion?
—A female newspaper columnist mystified by the appeal of the event

And if there isn't a war—or a reenactment—handy, what do men do with all that agressive energy?
—Regina, age twenty-five, teacher

Some use it to turn a profit. Throughout history, men have been more attracted to and more rewarded for warlike activities. In the boardroom, the back room, in politics, economics, and anywhere else you can name, research evidence shows that men are more likely than we are to use aggressive behavior because many of them think it feels good. The big question is why.

Author Anne Campbell, who has studied the subject for twenty years, contends that aggression feels good to some men because it rewards them with power and control over others. By contrast, aggression feels bad to us because it means our self-control has cracked. In addition, we hesitate to behave aggressively because it can put us in the dangerous spot of "asking for" retaliation in the form of verbal abuse, sexual assault, or physical battering. Plus, we women often feel guilty about causing another person distress—even the person we've singled out for our attack. Compared to many men, then, we see aggression in a different light. We can also see now that anger is different from aggression, but if anger is not the same thing as aggression, hostility, or frustration, what is it?

Anger Defined

Anger is a strong, uncomfortable emotional reaction to another person or event that offends our beliefs about the way things should be in a particular situation. You can identify it more easily if you remember that anger applies to events of greater significance than the trivia that cause frustration, is less long lasting and mean-spirited than hostility, and is not as destructive as aggression. Unfortunately, because society doesn't differentiate between anger, hostility, and aggression, they are all tarred with the same brush and branded as equally dangerous, destructive, and immoral:

Remember . . . Anger is only a d away from danger.
**—A local minister, as reported by a member of
the Women's Anger Study Research Team**

Yet, no less an authority than the Bible provides examples of anger that is righteous and justified:

And Jesus went up to Jerusalem and found in the temple those that sold oxen and sheep and doves, and the changers of money sitting; and when he had made a scourge of small cords, he drove them all out of the temple, and the sheep and the oxen, and poured out the changers' money and overthrew the tables. And said . . . "Make not my Father's house a house of merchandise." And his disciples remembered that it was written, the zeal of Thine house hath eaten Me up.
—The Holy Bible, King James Version, John 2:14–17

Be ye angry and sin not, let not the sun go down upon your wrath. **—The Holy Bible, King James Version, Ephesians 4:26**

Many of us, like many of the participants in the Women's Anger Study, have experienced justifiable anger of biblical proportions, and this anger moves us to do something. In fact, the word *emotion*, from the Latin *exmovere*, means "to have the experience of being moved." In the case of anger, you are literally moved to take action because anger is a powerful source of physiological arousal that involves your cerebral cortex, sympathetic nervous system, adrenal medulla—which secretes adrenaline and nonadrenaline, the adrenal cortex—which secretes cortisol—the cardiovascular system, and even the immune system.

In other words, when you're angry, your heart pounds, your blood pressure shoots up, you breathe faster, your muscles tense, and you clench your jaw or fists as you experience the irresistible urge to move and do something with all that physical energy—hopefully, something positive. And yes, it can be positive. Although anger is sometimes associated with aggressive action and therefore gets a bad rap, it can have numerous benefits:

The Benefits of Anger

Anger:

- Is a course of personal and/or situational insight
- Gets other people's attention because it is an unmistakably clear form of communication
- Enhances your ego, boosts your personal competence, and increases your self-esteem
- Protects you against domination, control, or being taken advantage of
- Serves as a warning signal that your stressors are exceeding your resources
- Lets you know when your rights are being violated or your values are being compromised
- Alerts you to key relationship problems, like when a significant other is doing too much or too little

- Encourages you to explore new approaches and try new options, from job changes to divorce
- Helps you fight disease (Really! Research shows that women who openly express their anger over having cancer live longer than those who don't.)
- Gives you the courage to correct injustices, to improve your life and the lives of others

In particular, anger can help you improve your life because it compels you to make a judgment. It forces you to acknowledge that there's been an unwanted offense to your values, morals, beliefs, or dignity; that someone or something is to blame; and that you deserve a more positive outcome. But before you can become a poster girl for positive anger outcomes, you have to acknowledge your own private anger, and there is no better way to do this than through your new daily anger journal.

3

YOUR DAILY ANGER
JOURNAL

jour-nal—1: a brief written account of daily events 2: a record of proceedings 3: a service book containing daily hours —**The New Merriam-Webster Dictionary**

Anger often leaves us so rattle-brained and confused that it's hard to sort out the issues. Keeping a daily anger diary or journal is one way to work these issues through. The journal is a system for collecting information on your individual anger triggers and responses. It helps you cut through any mental fog so you can zero in on the real issues and identify the source of your angry feelings—the first step in changing your behavior.

Your journal is also the "write place" to call it like you see it and name the emotion of anger for what it really is. This is important because naming anger (even if you only name it to yourself) is a giant step toward self-affirmation and self-protection. In fact, anger is actually a kind of psychological immune system that protects us from emotional danger just as white blood cells guard us against colds and the flu. When you don't name your anger, you weaken this system and increase the chances that you'll come down with something, or maybe just come down . . .

When there is a noticeable absence of a whole set of feelings . . . we know that the psychological immune system

is out of balance. For instance, if we never feel anger or
hate, if our view of the world is that all is love and sweet-
ness, then we suffer from an underactive psychological
immune system . . . This is psychologically crippling . . .

—Jane Goldberg, psychologist

If you feel psychologically crippled because you can't
name your anger or it's hidden from view, your journal can
help you gain remarkable insights. Not only will it help you
build emotional awareness, but as an extra added bonus it
can allay those nagging fears that your anger is a tiger-by-
the-tail in search of its next entree. Here's how it works.

Exercise: The Daily Anger Journal

Establish your journal in a notebook you can carry with you
or keep in a nearby drawer. Commit to maintaining it in a
serious, professional way to reinforce how serious you are
about changing your anger behavior. This might mean using
a business-style notebook or an organizer you purchase from
a stationery supply store. You should also photocopy the
forms in this section to insert in your journal.

Make a further commitment to write in your journal
every day for at least one month or longer. The best time to
write is while the anger is still fresh in your mind but after
you've calmed down enough to clear your thoughts. By keeping your journal handy and recording anger incidents as they
occur, you will become an expert on identifying the repetitive
themes and patterns in your own anger behavior.

For each anger incident, start by describing who or what
made you angry, including the person's gender and status.
Next indicate your first reaction—what you were thinking at
the angry moment. Was it: "Here we go again!" or "I can't
stand this disrespectful treatment!" or "He's not listening to
a word I say!" or maybe "She is an unbearable bitch!"

Remember to record your thoughts while your anger is
still fresh but after you're calm enough to think clearly. Be
perfectly honest too, because the journal is only helpful if
you tell yourself the truth—and don't worry about what other
people think. This journal is for your eyes only. You never
have to show it to anyone else.

Next, think about the tactics you used to handle the anger incident. Were you:

- Accommodating, but hating yourself for it?
- Aggressive, shouting so you could be heard in the next county?
- Conflictive, taking issue with everything and everyone?
- Confrontational, vowing to chew down pine trees with your teeth and spit the needles at innocent bystanders?
- Victimized, clamming up and doing a slow, silent burn?
- Deflective, an expert at avoidance?
- Sarcastic, sending a little zinger swathed in "humor"?
- Assertive, communicating your anger clearly and effectively?

Whichever tactic you used, check it off on the Anger Tactics Checklist (in The Daily Anger Journal form at the end of this section). The checklist will help you see how you managed your anger, whether you squelched it, vented it, or released it. And keep this in mind—although the tactics will vary according to each specific situation, the ones you use most frequently form your "anger style."

Once you've identified your tactics and style, consider the physical sensations and reactions that accompanied your anger. Did you cry or get a headache? Immediately crave food or grab your cigarettes? In addition, how intense were your angry feelings? Clarifying the ties between anger and your own unique bodily symptoms makes you more aware of how angry behavior impacts your overall health and well-being.

Your health and well-being are also affected by the duration of the anger episode. How long did you stay upset? Did you relive the incident over and over again in your mind? Brood about your grievance for hours? And what about the aftermath of your anger? When it was all over, did you feel tense? Guilty? Embarrassed or depressed? Or did you handle your anger in such a way that you felt proud of yourself and experienced new personal growth? Whatever the aftermath was, write it on the checklist.

The Anger Aftermath checklist is one of the toughest sections of The Daily Anger Journal to fill out, but it's also one of the most important. At first it might seem demoralizing to write about feeling sad or helpless after an anger incident, but by recording your emotions honestly and accurately, you can chart your progress. Eventually, as you develop greater skill in dealing with your anger, you'll check "proud of myself" more and more often.

Finally, analyze the anger incident. What was it that really set you off? What threatened you or trampled your ego? An important part of this analysis is unraveling the legacy of your past. Why? In the Women's Anger Study we found that women's most intense anger is generated in intimate relationships, and many of the conflicts in our current relationships echo those of the past, even though we're not always aware of it:

> *Any close relationship, whether with a mate, a lover or a friend, has the potential to recreate within us some of the same feelings of rivalry we had with a sibling, the same separation struggle we engaged in with a parent, the same dependency needs, the same vulnerability, the same conflicts, the same ambivalence."*
>
> **—Lillian Rubin, social scientist**

This is true of your relationship with your husband

> *I believe in the ninety percent–ten percent rule, which is that the things that anger us are only ten percent the things they appear to be and ninety percent in our history. And so when that happened (the argument with my husband) I spent the rest of the day figuring out "what was that all about?" from my past. It was about some unresolved issue from twenty-five years ago that I'd not fully worked out. I went to my husband and told him that was mostly what it was about. It wasn't about what had happened between he and I.* **—Natalie**

and your friends, especially if your relationship with your friends reflects your past relationship with your siblings:

> *I love Bonnie as much as I've ever cared about anyone in this world, but I've never had a relationship, even with my husband, that's so complicated. I don't think of myself as a terribly competitive person, but with her I can get into what feels like an all-out war inside me. She can make me angrier than just about anyone too, except Dick, of course. I've tried to figure it out because it makes me*

*feel bad, and the best I can get is that it's a lot like I felt
with my sister when we were kids. Only I love Bonnie, I
really do; I don't think I ever loved my sister, not then and
not now.*   **—A forty-three-year-old woman
                              interviewed by L. Rubin**

Once you figure out how "then" applies to "now," make a
note in your journal. With this in mind, ask yourself what
you could have done differently in your most recent anger
situation. Try using your answers as a guide to managing
your anger more effectively next time a similar situation
arises.

As you become comfortable working with the journal and
as you learn to recognize the subtle nuances of anger situations, you can create additional categories or checklists of
your own to describe your unique anger experiences. Just use
the log sheets in this exercise as a guide. You can even make
photocopies of the blank sheets and adapt them to your particular needs. The idea is to do whatever it takes to make the
journal work for you, to make you the expert on your own
brand of anger.

Now one of the things that will make you the expert is
the journal section on dream analysis. Why dream analysis?
Often, anger that's been denied, disowned, and unnamed lit-
ters your dreamscape in the form of violent or destructive
images. To see if this is happening to you, try analyzing your
dreams using the following techniques:

1. Make a commitment to record your dreams every day.
Keep a pen and pad of paper or a tape recorder next to your
bed so you can do this as soon as you wake up. After you've
recorded your dreams for several days or weeks, start looking
for recurring patterns and themes.

2. Remember that the images in your dreams are symbols for other things and it may take you a while to crack the
code. You can hasten the process along if you:

3. Relate your dreams to whatever is happening in your
life right now. For instance, what are the dreams telling you
to pay attention to? Why are you dreaming about this particular thing at this particular time? Think about the way the
figures in your dreams look. Are your dreams pointing out

anger your conscious mind is trying to avoid? How do they compare to the incidents described in your journal?

If you find your dreams are enameled with anger and you want to know more about them, or if you're simply intrigued with the wisdom of your unconscious mind, consult some books that focus on dream analysis. We recommend *Dreams and Healing,* by John Sanford, and *Wisdom of the Heart,* by Karen Signell. Signell's book is devoted entirely to women's dreams, and she recommends that women share their dreams with each other as this can lead to additional insights.

After you've analyzed your dreams and anger incidents for one month, check your journal for common patterns and themes in your behavior. For instance, is there a certain person or topic that always triggers you? Do authority figures affect you in the same way as waiters or salespeople? How about your anger toward men? Is it stronger than toward women? Do you get angrier at strangers or friends? Family members or colleagues? Do you hold on to your anger for hours or manage to get it out of your system pretty quickly? What could you do differently?

The journal entries on anger incidents, first reactions, tactics, duration, aftermath, and analysis provide the information you need to become the authority on your own anger behavior. They not only help you to identify patterns, but over time (especially after you've implemented some of the anger management strategies in this book), they help you to make anger an effective part of your emotional repertoire.

Now at first this might seem like risky business since many of us fear our anger will turn into an uncontrollable juggernaut, but it won't. Why? Because we can control our emotions and if we're afraid of disrupting a relationship, provoking disapproval, or making waves in an inappropriate environment, we can choose not to reveal our anger until we're ready. We can also choose to reveal it, to determine when, where, how, and to whom our angry feelings should be expressed. Your journal will not only help you chart your progress toward this goal, but ultimately, it will be your guide.

THE DAILY ANGER JOURNAL

THE ANGER INCIDENT

I got angry at: _____

FIRST REACTION

When I got angry I was thinking _____

ANGER TACTICS CHECKLIST

My anger was:

_____ Suppressed (kept to myself)

_____ Vented outwardly by screaming, yelling, swearing, or making sarcastic remarks

_____ Released by talking it over with a confidant (spouse, friend, etc.)

_____ Released through vigorous exercise or physical activities

_____ Released by throwing or breaking things

_____ Released through a nasty note or memo

_____ Expressed through pouting or sulking

_____ Expressed in an assertive manner to the person who provoked it

_____ Other

PHYSICAL SENSATIONS AND REACTIONS

My anger was accompanied by:

_____ Crying

_____ A tight, knotted feeling in the stomach

_____ Headaches

_____ A stiff neck

_____ A pounding heart

_____ Clenched fists

_____ Faster breathing

_____ Lumps in the throat

_____ Shakiness

_____ Eating and more eating

_____ Smoking

_____ Drinking

_____ Taking drugs

_____ Other

ANGER INTENSITY

On a scale of 1 to 10, how strong was my anger? _____

ANGER DURATION

I remained angry for _____ (minutes, hours, all day, longer)

ANGER AFTERMATH

Afterwards I felt:

_____ Tense, nervous

_____ Guilty, remorseful

_____ Depressed, sad

_____ Mad at myself

_____ Helpless

_____ Embarrassed

_____ Defeated

_____ Ashamed of myself

_____ Proud of myself

ANGER ANALYSIS

As I think about this incident, I realize my anger was mainly due to:

_____ Unfair treatment

_____ The unfair treatment of someone I care about (family member, friend, co-worker, child)

_____ Unmet expectations

_____ Powerlessness

_____ Offense to my morals or values

_____ Stress and pressure

_____ Threats to my self-esteem

_____ Someone else's thoughtlessness

_____ Someone else's incompetence

_____ Disrespectful treatment

_____ Criticism

_____ Inability to control something or someone

_____ Interference with my goals or plans

_____ Harassment

_____ Delays (traffic, long lines, etc.)

_____ Fatigue

_____ The irresponsibility of someone I depended on

_____ Property damage or destruction

_____ My own stupidity

_____ Other

DREAM ANALYSIS

What I dreamed about at the time of the anger incident was

The symbols in my dream stand for _____
This is how the dream relates to the anger in my life right now

UPON REFLECTION

Once you review your journal and think things over, you may decide you could've handled the anger incident more effectively. Before you write down what you could do better next time, try applying psychologist James Averill's and counselor Elma Nunley's list of:

ANGER RULES

1. You have the right to become angry if the wrongdoing you've experienced is correctable.
2. You should not get angry at events or misdeeds that can be corrected in more standard ways.
3. Your anger should only be directed at those who can be held responsible for their actions.
4. Your anger should begin with an explanation of the harm done.
5. The aim of your anger should be to correct the situation, not to inflict pain on others.
6. Your anger should be proportional to its cause.
7. Your anger should not exceed what is necessary to correct the situation or prevent the instigation from recurring.
8. Your anger should include a commitment to appropriate follow-through.
9. Terminate your anger whenever the target apologizes or makes amends.
10. Do not displace your anger onto an innocent party.
11. Your anger should not last more than a few hours or days at most.
12. An angry person should not be held completely responsible for his or her actions.

But before you decide that rule #12 gives you the license to be Rambo in pantyhose, consider this: You can't get away with murder just because you're mad. You can, however, have compassion for people who bungle their anger expression, and you should also for-

give yourself when you fail to express your anger effectively. With
that in mind, consider what you'll do differently next time.

NEXT TIME

I've applied the Anger Rules and come up with a new, improved
way to handle my anger. What I'll do next time to achieve a more
effective outcome is: _____

You should also make a note in your journal of the things you're
already doing right. And yes, there are some—you just need to
know what they are.

What You're Doing Right

For starters, you've busted your buns for a month to record
your anger incidents, and for that you deserve a big bouquet.
You made and kept an important commitment to yourself
and it wasn't easy. Whether you discovered you're a cream
puff or the heir to Lizzie Borden—in other words, no matter
how dissatisfied you are with your anger behavior right
now—you deserve credit for taking a good hard look at yourself. That takes courage and it is a positive, proactive thing
to do. So is talking it over.

Talking It Over

If your journal reveals that you usually release your anger by
talking it over with a friend or relative, three cheers for you,
because this is no idle chitchat. Indeed, women's willingness
to discuss their anger with a confidant is a valuable and sel-
dom-acknowledged strength. Holding such a conversation in
a safe environment with a trustworthy listener is a healthy
way to get things off your chest.

We females are much more likely to practice this emotional bosom-baring than the average male. In fact, research
shows that compared to boys, girls of all ages are more willing to confide their angry feelings in another person, and this
remains true later in life. Our own research demonstrates
that this is so with adults ranging from eighteen to seventy-
seven. No matter whether they're young or old, the women

in our studies were all more interested in discussing their anger than the men—and these discussions are not an unhealthy sort of displacing or "dumping" on a third party. Rather, they're a healthy way to reflect on what's happened, an effective method for obtaining empathy and feedback, and a good means of solving problems and formulating ideas. However, sometimes, no matter how much you discuss them, your problems can lead to waterworks. When this happens, remember that:

Crying's Okay!

In fact, ironic though it seems, you should actually feel good if you checked "crying" in your anger journal. Why? Tears are a healthy way to release your anger. Unfortunately, American society undervalues them as a safety valve—so much so that "crying" isn't even listed on the standard anger expression questionnaires. We discovered this during the Women's Anger Study when, following normal research procedure, we used established questionnaires so our findings could be easily understood and compared to the findings of other investigators. But we wondered if women had other ways of expressing anger that weren't listed on the structured tests, so we asked participants to write down any additional anger reactions and coping strategies they used. Crying was the number one response.

Unfortunately, we are often ashamed of crying because we believe it indicates immaturity or a loss of control. This misconception is reinforced by social sanctions that restrict crying to children and, after a certain age, to girl children only. What a sharp contrast to other cultures, where the value of tears is not only acknowledged but praised!

> It is the wisdom of crocodiles, that shed tears when they would devour.   **—Sir Francis Bacon,** *Essays*

Likewise, we women have the wisdom to shed tears before anger devours us. These tears are not only cleansing and therapeutic, but have several other positive effects as well. One study that analyzed tears and their physiological function found that emotional tears (which are chemically different from the irritant tears caused by onions, air pollution, etc.) contain chemicals that may strengthen the immune system's response to stress, which raises an intriguing question: By stifling tears are some people—read men—depriving themselves of a natural way of fighting the stress associated with anger? If so, showing this paragraph to the men in your life and suggesting that they read it and weep might be a very good thing to do.

Speaking of good, let's switch gears to another good thing your journal might contain, and that's sweat.

Sweating Out Your Anger

I just go away from everybody. I'll go clean a closet or work in my flower bed . . . it seems like if I go out and do something aggressive like haul mulch, dig some holes or something like that . . . I feel so much better. **—Irene**

What you accomplish by digging holes, cleaning closets, exercise, and other productive, sweaty physical activities is the release of your anger—and the emphasis here is on "productive," a lesson Julie has yet to learn:

I was angry and there was a laundry bag in the hallway and I kicked it. It slid down the hall and hit a fern stand that had this glass globe on it, this expensive globe. It wasn't just a dime store globe, it was an expensive one and I loved it—and it fell off and shattered.

I think it was a release, but in the end I was very disappointed in the results. I . . . feel like that was a really weak and immature and unnecessary thing to do. Anytime I break something or kick something I feel very guilty.

—Julie

If your journal shows that you choose inappropriate physical outlets that leave you grappling with guilt, you need to get off this pro-wrestling circuit right away. Instead, choose an activity that not only helps with the immediate anger problem, but promotes a healthy body and a healthy mind—especially in situations where you can't confront your offenders directly. For suggestions on perspirey, muscle-powered activities that help burn away the physical tension produced by anger, turn to Part Five. There you'll discover some other fringe benefits too. Appropriate physical activity saves you from splitting headaches, upset stomachs, and food binges. In addition, like many participants in the Women's Anger Study, you may discover that the best time to get something useful done is during a mad fury. So give it a try, and then give yourself a gold star for the effort.

However, don't be discouraged if the gold star count is lower in some sections of your journal than others. After all, the whole point of this exercise is to help you identify areas where there's room for growth, as this woman discovered:

> *I have recorded my symptoms every day for ninety days. I don't have PMS. I have a rotten marriage and I'm getting a divorce.*
> **—Bertha, who once attributed her anger to PMS**

Likewise, Judith Anne, a participant in the Women's Anger Study, was stunned at the sheer number of anger incidents she experienced at work and decided a job change might be in order. Now what about you?

Identifying Areas Where There's Room for Growth

As you study a month's worth of entries, what does your journal reveal? Do you see patterns you don't like? Are you angry more often than you're not angry, feeling your anger very intensely, experiencing anger over prolonged periods of time, causing other people pain with your angry feelings, stuffing your anger or shouting it out, or enacting the same scenes over and over with your mate, colleague, friend, teenager, etc.?

If so, your anger may be causing you a problem. In fact, anger is a problem any time it's too frequent, intense, prolonged, or painful. It's also a problem when it's ignited by irrational thoughts like "He made me do it," "She deliberately provoked me," or "They should not act that way."

A sure sign that your anger needs some fine-tuning is if your First Reaction journal entries contain words like *ought*, *must*, and *should*, all of which imply that other people's behavior has to conform to certain rules—your rules.

> *Jan should have written a thank-you note by now. That wedding was weeks ago . . . I don't care if she did lose her job, that should've given her lots of free time to take care of her social obligations!* **—Nikki, age fifty-five, retired**

*We've been married ten years and you'd think he'd know
me by now. If he expects to make it through another ten
he better take mind-reading lessons and quick.*
—Myra, age forty-one, benefits manager

If you expect other people to be prompt, polite, mind-
reading paragons of virtue, you probably have equally high
standards for yourself ("I must not be late," "The house must
look perfect," or "I really should work this weekend so that
my desk will be completely clean") and just as often, you fail
at your own game, setting yourself up for anger and disappointment. If your journal is filled with similar irrational
thoughts and impossibly rigid codes of conduct, you're aim-
ing for a fall. To prevent this personal fallout, first understand that these expectations are as unrealistic for you as
they are for everybody else—and second, they make you
more anger-prone.

Now, if you are more anger-prone, you may be using ineffective anger tactics like becoming a screaming meemie or
turning helplessly mute. Does this describe you? According
to your journal, which anger tactics—screaming, silence,
pouting, etc.—do you use most often? Do these tactics help
you correct situations or leave you feeling worse than before?
If it's the latter, your personal anger style needs some work—
especially if your "style" is donning a fashionable pair of
mental battle fatigues.

PART TWO

YOUR ANGER STYLE

4

THE ANGER PRONENESS ASSESSMENT TEST

Proper words in proper places.
> **—J. Swift, *Definition of a Good Style***

Or just a good, swift kick in the butt.   **—Tina**

Some of us project our anger at a frequency that could hail the aliens. Others clam up and stare at the world through I-told-you-so eyes. Whether your journal shows that you're an ice queen, a raging inferno, or something in between, your anger style depends on your family history and cultural influences including your ethnic background, community traditions, religious upbringing, and social status. In addition, we each have our own ideas about how we should behave toward our husbands, children, relatives, friends, co-workers, and fellow human beings. We also have definite expectations about the way these people should treat us in return.

Anger occurs when our expectations aren't met—when we're confronted with someone or something that offends our values, violates our principles, or legitimately presses our hot buttons. According to your journal, what presses yours? Don't be surprised if your buttons are wired into the same three major themes identified by participants in the Woman's Anger Study, starting with:

1. Powerlessness: When we're unable to get someone or something to change or even to make ourselves heard because others are not listening.

2. Injustice: When we're treated unfairly or disrespectfully, when our trust is betrayed by a loved one who lies or a friend who takes advantage.

3. Irresponsibility: When others fail to live up to their commitments, to pull their weight at the office or at home.

Of these, powerlessness is the most frequent anger trigger. In fact, two thirds of the anger-producing situations described by participants in the Women's Anger Study involve variations on this theme. For instance, some women were angry at themselves because they felt powerless to live up to their own expectations or lacked the authority to change something. Others were angry at their lack of power in dealing with intimates, including co-workers, friends, children, and spouses:

I try to weigh the pros and cons and be logical about decisions. . . . [My husband] just jumps in and decides . . . [what] he wants and that's it . . . which makes me really mad. I think he sees it as a power struggle . . . **—Susan**

Vicki had a very big part in my college years . . . We always did things together . . . She recently got married . . . and I didn't have any part in her wedding. She was in my wedding. She was a bridesmaid and . . . I've . . . really just loved her to death. It just really hurt my feelings that I wasn't in her wedding . . . Normally, weddings have servers and people that keep the books . . . I thought at least she would have me do something like that. But she didn't . . . I'm still angry . . . hurt and disappointed that she doesn't value our friendship like I valued it.

—Melanie

Likewise, we often feel angry, disappointed, and powerless when dealing with groups who have different values than we do including "bigots," "politicians," "liars," "cheats," or just about anyone known as "them."

Finally, powerlessness and anger are triggered by the following all-too-familiar circumstances:

- "People using me"
- "When someone won't listen to me because I'm a woman"
- "When I'm minding my own business and some man says something harassing or threatening"
- "When a person I talk with is always right and I'm wrong, or when I try to tell something that's happened which is really important to me and no one listens"

Not being listened to is the ultimate form of powerlessness. Why? Because it means our views, preferences, and ideas are ignored as if we're mute or invisible, or worse yet, as if we don't exist at all:

I feel restricted, like I can't say what I really mean, and if something does make me angry at work or at home and I speak up, no one listens anyway. I'm not only powerless, I'm voiceless. It's not worth it to get mad. **—Jayne**

I get blown off, or ignored and not taken as an intelligent person. As long as I'm being pleasant and smiling and happy and cooperative then no one seems to have a problem. But when I raise questions or if I get tense or if I don't like a particular situation, then people seem to get uncomfortable. **—Bette**

There are many reasons (see Part Seven) people start squirming when we get bent out of shape. For starters, no one knows for sure how another person is going to react in an anger situation—sometimes we might put a lid on our anger and keep it to ourselves, at other times we might choose to modify or redirect it, and on select occasions, we may even escalate our angry feelings to achieve a greater good. Whatever your individual reaction is, it will be strongly affected by two things—your general anger proneness and the way you express your anger once it's been aroused. Together these form your anger style.

Anger Style

Some of us wear out pair after pair of fashion boots as we go around every day kicking butt:

> *I like to confront and get things out in the open . . . I don't like hidden things, nothing hidden . . . Get it out . . . and over with.*   **—Laura**

Others of us get angry so infrequently that we have to make a special trip to the mental garment bag just to haul this emotion from cold storage:

> *It takes me a long time to get angry . . . by the time I decide I'm mad, the incident is past . . . the offender is out of reach . . . [and] I feel like a fool . . .*
> **—Margie, age forty-one, editor**

Then there are those of us who style our anger somewhere in between:

> *I will either go from just being very tense like kick ass . . . to being very docile and when other situations . . . arise then I will explode inappropriately over the most benign things . . .*   **—Pam**

Finally, some of us prefer to be "indirect." We'll tell a co-worker something "for her own good," preface an unkind remark with "I thought you'd want to know," or make "candid" comments about another woman's hair, weight, clothing, or jewelry. In each case, we're still showing anger, and it's about as subtle as a bop on the noggin:

> *Candor bears little relationship to honesty. It is often another form of anger. It is the closest permissible thing to a punch in the nose.*   **—Willard Gaylin, psychiatrist**

How often do you punch noses? In other words, what is your general anger proneness? Although the frequency and intensity of your anger will vary from situation to situation, you are also relatively consistent over time and over a range of circumstances. Psychologists call these consistent personality characteristics "traits." For instance, some of us have the trait of liking an orderly environment wherever we are—at home, at work, in our cars, etc. Others of us thrive on mess and chaos and leave every place looking like a tornado hit it. In another example, introverts have the trait of turning their thoughts inward and preferring quiet reflection over noisy parties. By contrast, extroverts are energized by the social scene, excited about sharing their opinions, and always ready to join the nearest conga line dancing down the street.

In a similar way, your general proneness to step up to the firing line is a trait. In other words, are you quick on the trigger or slow on the draw? Most people are usually one or the other. If you're not sure which you are, think about the way others describe you. Do they use words like fiery, volatile, short-fused, hot-tempered, mercurial, or the aforementioned quick on the trigger?

If any of these sound familiar, you'll probably score high on the following anger proneness test. If you do, it doesn't mean you're Cruella de Vil, rotten to the core, or anything else. It simply means that you have a tendency to become angry more often and in a wider range of situations than other people do. You also have more intense and prolonged anger experiences.

To see if this characterizes you, take the following test. Remember, whether you score high or low, this test is not a value judgment. It's simply a tool to help you in assessing your general anger proneness.

EXERCISE

The Anger Proneness Assessment Test

Instructions: Occasionally, everybody gets angry. Following are a number of statements people have used to describe these angry moments. Read each statement and using the guidelines below, circle the number to the right of the statement that best describes you.

If the statement is completely undescriptive of you, circle 1.
If the statement is mostly undescriptive of you, circle 2.

If the statement is partly undescriptive of you and partly descriptive
of you, circle 3.
If the statement is mostly descriptive of you, circle 4.
If the statement is completely descriptive of you, circle 5.
Answer every item and remember, there are no right or wrong
answers.

ITEM	ANSWER
1. I tend to get angry more frequently than most people.	1 2 3 4 5
2. It is easy to make me angry.	1 2 3 4 5
3. Something makes me angry almost every day.	1 2 3 4 5
4. I often feel angrier than I think I should.	1 2 3 4 5
5. I am surprised at how often I feel angry.	1 2 3 4 5
6. At times, I feel angry for no specific reason.	1 2 3 4 5
7. When I get angry, I stay angry for hours.	1 2 3 4 5
8. I get so angry, I feel like I might lose control.	1 2 3 4 5

To compute your score, simply add up the total number of points. The
higher your score, the more likely you are to be aroused to anger.

Marcia is one of the participants in the Women's Anger
Study who scored high on general anger proneness. She describes herself as:

> . . . hotheaded, quick-tempered and fiery. I scream, rant,
> rave, throw things and drive my car too fast! When I get
> mad I say nasty things to my husband, my sister-in-law,
> and I all too often yell at my kids when I'm not even angry
> at them. Actually I'll vent on whoever is handy. I can
> sometimes be mad all day—or even for days . . . I get
> angry if my husband is thoughtless or when someone
> does something stupid that interferes with me or my
> family.   —**Marcia**

A variety of things trigger Marcia's anger. Like many of
us, she mentions family and work situations, including the
management of the institution where she's employed and the
insurance companies she deals with in her job. In addition,

criticism and a lack of recognition make Marcia angry. There is also a sense of time urgency and impatience when she says:

I get angry when I'm slowed down by others' mistakes.

—Marcia

Who is Marcia? She's a married thirty-year-old with two young children who works full-time in a stressful health care profession. She is also a woman who only lists two people in her social support network—the same two people with whom she is usually angry. In addition, Marcia has low self-esteem. In fact, one of the most striking aspects of Marcia's performance on the tests we gave her was a low score in the self-esteem category, where she agreed with statements such as "at times I think I am no good at all" and "I certainly feel useless at times." Marcia also told us that she wishes she could have more self-respect, and she volunteered the following rather pessimistic forecast:

I don't think my self-respect is ever going to improve.

—Marcia

When your self-respect is in the negative numbers—like Marcia's—you're usually more anger-prone. We discovered this reciprocal relationship in the Women's Anger Study, the first study to determine that the lower a woman's self-esteem, the higher her tendency to anger easily.

Now that's the bad news. The good news is you can learn to improve your self-esteem and to control your esteem-based anger proneness (see Part Four). Unfortunately, some of the other factors that contribute to anger proneness are not so easy to deal with.

There is not much you can do about the unique, genetic temperament you received at birth (some babies are real howlers early on). Nor can you change the emotional climate and experiences you had in your childhood home, both of which have a big impact on you as an adult. In fact, studies show that children who are angrier are involved in more disciplinary confrontations and experience less unity and warmth within their families. One group of researchers even showed that feelings of hostility and discord actually linked unstable personalities across four generations. (Ill-tempered daughters became mothers who had battle-scarred marriages and lost control when disciplining their offspring; then this unfortunate legacy was passed on through succeeding generations.) The result of this genetic and environmental mix is usually greater anger proneness in adulthood.

You're also more anger-prone if you lack personal boundaries. If you refuse to separate the big things that bother you from the mere minutia, you become hypersensitive to every potentially threatening situation. As a result, you snap a tether over stuff that doesn't even faze someone else. You can also be more anger-prone because of the situation you're in. If you're in the throes of a divorce, an extremely stressful problem at work, or a personal health crisis, you might be angry at everyone and everything for a long, long time. The bottom line here is that any of these factors—or any combination thereof—can make you more hotheaded.

But being more hotheaded doesn't necessarily mean that you're comfortable with your anger or feel free to express it. In fact, it's quite the opposite. Many anger-prone women hold their feelings inside until eventually, these emotions become highly unpalatable

> *I retreat and sulk. Anger just sits there like an uncooked doughnut.* **—Woman interviewed by Carol Tavris, social psychologist**

This is especially true if they—and you—were erroneously taught that those unable to take the heat should get out of the emotional kitchen.

5

WHERE INEFFECTIVE ANGER STYLES COME FROM

*I tried pouting. I tried screaming. I tried shopping. Then
I just decided to ignore him and withdraw . . . It didn't
work. I just don't get what I'm doing wrong.*

**—Caryn, age twenty-four, on fighting
with her boyfriend**

There's no question that practicing emotional coitus inter-
ruptus is unsatisfying—but so are pouting, shouting, and
being afraid to express our angry feelings in a positive, honest way. But where did we learn to be like this? Why do our
journals show that we communicate our anger as ineffec-
tively as we do? Because

We don't see things as they are, we see them as we are.

—Anaïs Nïn, writer

And what we are, emotionally, is whatever we were taught to
be. Unfortunately, most of us were taught to be girls . . .

Why the Learning Curve Led Us Astray

From that bottom-slapping moment when we first enter the
world we all have unique dispositions. Some of us are so
cheerful we can warm hands with our smiles. Others of us

make our parents wonder if the hospital nursery pulled a switch. From placid to fussy, we all react differently. In part, these emotional reactions are inherited from our parents, but human emotions aren't based solely on a swim in the local gene pool. Indeed, most emotional reactions are learned. Unfortunately, the "instruction" we receive in this area is usually gender-biased.

From infancy on, our anger is often treated differently than boys'. For starters, parents teach boys to be generally unemotional except for anger and aggression. Most boys also learn that their anger and aggression will be rewarded—just look at the countless fathers (and mothers) who cheer on their one-and-a-half- and two-year-old sons, encouraging them to be tiny raging bulls! By contrast, we girls are usually instructed to bite the raging bullet and squelch our angry feelings—even when these feelings are a legitimate response to provocation. This is very difficult for us to do, since we're taught to be more emotional than boys in every other aspect of life. In fact, by the time we reach preschool, happiness, sadness, fear, and general emotionality are all attributed more to girls, while anger and aggression are attributed more to boys. As a result, we learn to be emotional but unaggressive, which is why we, as girls (and later, as women), are likely to take on a Judas load of guilt whenever our anger is aroused.

Frequently, our girlish anger is aroused in interactions with playmates and siblings and the response we get from these peers has a profound effect on our emotional development. How so? As girls, we tend to play cooperative games, but quit when there are quarrels or when other girls won't get with the program. Unfortunately, most of us—and our parents—think this is proper feminine behavior.

> When my three-year-old took away my four-year-old's Barbie . . . the older one refused to play anymore. I thought she was being a bad sport, but my husband said no, she was just being a girl. —**Connie, age thirty-six**

Just as "girls will be girls," "boys will be boys"—meaning that unlike girls, boys play competitive games punctuated by numerous arguments. It's also more acceptable for boys to throw or break things and act out their anger in a physical way. By contrast, we girls can't even raise our voices. Ultimately, all this makes our light bulbs go on and we're forced to acknowledge how anger power politics work:

> *Time and again, Maggie grows angry with Tom and expresses her anger by withdrawing . . . but this strategy does not work . . . Tom remains unaffected by her withdrawal, while she suffers acutely from his absence. The bitter lesson Maggie learns is that he who remains oblivious to the other person's anger, while making the reality of his own felt, wields power. The corollary is that anger is worse than useless for the subservient person, for it causes one's own heart to be rent, while leaving the object of one's anger quite untouched.*
>
> **—An encounter between Maggie and her brother Tom, from George Eliot's *The Mill on the Floss***

As girls we get a lot of negative reinforcement that convinces us that female anger is worse than useless. When this happens, we may begin to turn our anger against ourselves, like Maggie:

> *. . . beating the floor with her foot and tightening her fingers on her palm.* **—George Eliot, *The Mill on the Floss***

We also discover that it's equally masochistic to express our anger through direct defiance. In fact, when we, as young females, directly defy the men in our lives, we often can't handle their negative reactions, so we respond with a sense of determination as long lasting as a lit match: We immediately negate our own anger, claim we've been "naughty," and beg our men not to be mad at us!

This is particularly true when our "men" are sporting peach fuzz. During adolescence, the feedback from our first love and our best friend(s) is a key influence on our emotional behavior—especially when it comes to anger. Why? Adolescents have love/hate relationships with everyone around them and the "hate"—otherwise known as anger—is as intense as the love. In fact, studies of adolescents' emotions show that anger is the most prominent negative feeling boys and girls have during this time, yet the experience is totally different depending which side of the gender fence you're on.

Whereas most adolescent boys direct their anger outwardly, we, as adolescent girls, turn it inward. In addition, while boys get angry in situations in which their performance is questioned, the things that cause us to see red are related to interpersonal experience. Indeed, we're much more likely to get mad over unfair treatment or being taken advantage of, and we go positively puce with outrage when the culprit is a friend.

But even if we're enraged, what do we, as adolescent females, usually do with this pent-up purse of emotion? Nothing—because it's during adolescence that the most profound oppression of our anger begins. The worst perpetrators are our parents, teachers, and peers, all taking a hard line on the traditional, gender-based expectations for girls. And this hard line is one we dare not cross, because if we do, our anger (and seemingly, our existence) is invalidated. In other words, it's negated, ignored, or dubbed "inappropriate" by some powerful other who clucks in disapproval:

> *My Uncle Art told me that going to college was a waste of time for girls. He said I would just end up married—squandering all that tuition money. I was so mad I started to cry. I was in the top ten of my high school class and college was my dream. I started to tell him how wrong he was, but my father told me to be a good sport. Then he informed my uncle that I never could take any teasing.*
>
> **—Cheri, age seventeen, class of '94, valedictorian**

> *I found out Rod went out with another girl and I was furious. But then he told me I was cute when I was angry and I just couldn't be mad at him anymore. My feelings were still hurt, but maybe that's not as important as I thought it was since Rod said I was just being silly. Boy, did I feel like a jerk! Next time I'll just shut up about it.*
>
> **—Melissa, age fourteen**

When our anger is invalidated, our feelings are trivialized or denied. In effect, we're being told to "put up and shut up." As a result, we, as girls, feel misunderstood. We question our own judgment and our perceptions of the original incident. This not only undermines our self-confidence, but makes us feel ashamed of our angry outbursts. It's also frustrating because it puts us in a double bind—damned if we express our anger and equally dammed if we don't.

Harvard researchers Lyn Brown and Carol Gilligan documented this "psychological foot-binding" in a five-year study of the transition from girlhood to adolescence. During the study, one hundred girls were interviewed annually. Brown and Gilligan discovered that at younger ages, like seven and eight, girls are clear, honest, and outspoken about their angry feelings—but all are under enormous pressure to be "perfect," that is, to be perfectly quiet, calm, and kind.

By adolescence, this pressure takes its toll, and with few exceptions, girls stop expressing their real feelings—especially anger. Why? Anger pulls the rug out from under us in terms of popularity and personal relationships. Some of us are even confused about whether anger really exists at all and whether we're capable of experiencing such a risky emotion.

In fact, rather than take this risk, most of the girls in the Brown/Gilligan study became brainwashed by boundaries—they denied their emotions, suppressed their self-expression, and put a lid on their true characters to escape social disapproval. In other words, they learned normal feminine behavior. Unfortunately, the rest of us did too. Why "unfortunately"? Because learning "normal feminine behavior" is akin to donning a dunce cap on demand and tipping it with a smile.

> *The smile is the child/woman of the shuffle; it indicates acquiescence of the victim to his own oppression. In my own case, I had to train myself out of that phony smile, which is like a nervous tic on every teenage girl. This meant that I smiled rarely, for in truth, when it came down to real smiling, I had less to smile about. My "dream" action for the women's liberation movement: A* SMILE BOYCOTT, *at which declaration all women would instantly abandon their 'pleasing' smiles, henceforth smiling only when something pleased* THEM.
>
> **—Shulamith Firestone, in *The Dialectic of Sex***

But often we don't even know what pleases us because we're too busy pleasing everybody else. Why do we do it? Because most of us have assumed our "normal," culturally specified gender role, the role that requires us to put everyone else first, value others over ourselves, respond to outside feelings and opinions at the expense of our own, and to silence our individual voices. By doing this, we not only "learn to be feminine," we "learn" to sacrifice our talent, our individualism, and our right to a whole range of fulfilling emotional experiences—and *learn* is the right word. Why? Because self-sacrifice is not an inborn female virtue; rather, it's a behavior that is taught and learned.

Fortunately, our daughters, nieces, and sisters can learn differently if they're taught differently. We, as mothers and teachers, can show them the way by being positive role models and setting better anger examples for the future—and it's up to us to do this, because if they don't learn it from us, they might not learn it at all.

Indeed, one reason many women don't handle their anger more effectively is that we have few good role models to follow. This is especially true in the United States, where there are few rewards for being polite, civil, or restrained—in fact, it's quite the contrary. Not only do we Americans live in a culture where anger is freely expressed by those in positions of power and dominance (Congress, for example), but people actually take pride in announcing, "I told her off," or "I decked the SOB." Worse yet, this attitude is encouraged by the countless acts of physical aggression we see on TV each night and by the indiscriminate, hostile attitude that is common in many business and professional settings.

> *The messenger was a young guy on a bike. He brought over the legal documents we were waiting for and I called my boss to say they were here. My boss storms out of his office, rips open the envelope and reads the first page. Then he turns on the messenger and . . . me! He called us both *(#$% idiots, said we would never understand the situation . . . then stomped into his office and slammed the door. Since when is this acceptable business behavior?"*

> **—Annie, age thirty-three, communications expert**

But troubling expressions of anger don't end with messengers on bikes. We know department heads who've spit on staff members, lawyers who've thrown tantrums and hot coffee at secretaries, physicians who hurled instruments during surgery, and one doctor who actually pitched a bedpan out a patient's window! For the most part, though, throwing tantrums, frothing at the mouth, and giving other people shit is the prerogative of those in authority—and like it or not, most of those in authority are still men. While some of these lords of misrule might get away with expressing their anger in a hostile fashion, culturally speaking, most of us women can't.

This is reinforced in an interesting experiment by psychologists Michael MacGregor and Karina Davidson. MacGregor and Davidson played videotapes of actors and actresses expressing verbal and physical hostility and found that viewers rated the women as more hostile even though their behavior was identical to the men's! The bottom line here is that people's perceptions get highly distorted when we climb out of the box, indulge in behavior to which we are not "entitled," and violate gender role expectations.

> *Women are not entitled to anger. Anger, except in some girlish tantrum, is unfeminine. Direct, bold, eyeball-to-eyeball, confronting, dominating, resisting, insisting anger has been traditionally forbidden to women.*
>
> **—Judith Bardwick**

Although the world will not be any better off if we women confront, resist, and insist like some of the men we know, it's also no better off if we wallow in passive victimization. Once we realize that pouting, sulking, and withdrawing are actually signs of hidden anger, we can take constructive action and learn to express our feelings more effectively. In this way, our anger can become a powerful force for positive change, and the sooner this process starts, the better.

> *How might it have been different for you, if, early in your life, the first time you as a tiny child felt your anger coming together inside yourself, someone, a parent or grandparent, or older sister or brother, had said, "Bravo! Yes, that's it! You're feeling it!"*
>
> *If, the first time you had experienced that sharp awareness of ego, of "me, I'm me, not you" . . . you had been received and hugged and affirmed, instead of shamed and isolated.*
>
> *If someone had been able to see that you were taking the first tiny baby step toward feeling your own feelings, of knowing that you saw life differently from those around you. If you had been helped to experience your*

own uniqueness, to feel the excitement of sensing, for the very first time, your own awareness of life. What if someone had helped you to own all of this . . . to own your own life? **—Judith Duerk,** *Circle of Stones: Woman's Journey to Herself*

Clearly, for us to own our own lives, we must reject some of the blind-leading-the-blind lessons we learned in the past and replace them with advanced anger techniques—the techniques that allow us to improve our styles and empower our lives—and the time to start is now.

6

IMPROVING YOUR ANGER STYLE

I was so mad that when I talked, I started choking. The words literally would not come out of my mouth. But then I started practicing what I wanted to say and finally, I could spit it all out.

—Gayla, age twenty-two, secretary

Many of us rehearse the perfect mental speech, flash dimples of iron, open our mouths, and then say nothing at all. Indeed, one of the most distressing findings of the Women's Anger Study was that only 9.6 percent of the participants said they would speak directly to the person who triggered their anger. Although they found other healthy ways to work the angry feelings out of their systems (including a good cry or a marathon phone conversation with a friend, not to mention access to the cleanest closets in town), these women did not resolve the grievances that provoked their anger in the first place. This lack of resolution is a problem for many of us and for our provocateurs.

When we fail to let the provoking party know that we're angry and why, the other person has no opportunity to reconsider his or her behavior and no motivation to make any changes. For example, if it drives you crazy to pick up your husband's wet towels day after day, you continually refuel your anger until you tell him what you want. And the trick is to tell him in an assertive fashion: "I would appreciate it if you would put your towels in the hamper." Don't assail or blame with statements like "I can't believe how inconsiderate you are. Do you think I'm your personal maid? Even the children have learned to put their towels away!"

Assertiveness prevents you from becoming an attack dog and allows you to communicate your requests directly to whoever can do something about the situation. What's more important, assertive behavior enables you to act in your own best interests, to stand up for yourself without undue anxiety, comfortably express your honest feelings, and exercise your own rights without denying the rights of others. It also allows you to share your feelings in a nonblaming way: "I am angry," "I feel disappointed," "I don't appreciate comments about my weight," etc.

To that end, a good, assertive request is clear, direct and to the point, firm but not hostile, respectful of the other person, aimed at equalizing the balance of power, and delivered without whining, apologizing, or making excuses such as "I hate to bother you but . . ." or "I'm sorry to have to ask you but . . ."

It is also a way you can ask specifically for what you want: "I want you to ask me before you borrow my credit card," or "I want you to tell me what time you'll be home."

However, sometimes an assertive appeal needs more clout behind it, and you can get a bigger bang for your buck by adding a statement about the consequences of disregarding your request: "If you are unable to get the lawn mowed by Friday, I will not be able to give you your allowance," or "I promise you that if you are late, I will leave without you to make the concert on time."

Of course, there are no guarantees that assertive requests—no matter how confident, logical, and articulate—will solve the problem. Your co-worker may still shirk his duties, your spouse may still drain the checking account, and you may still feel angry enough to take no prisoners, but at least

As we become truly clear and direct, other people may become just as clear and direct about their own thoughts and feelings or about the fact that they are not going to change.
　　　　　　　　　　　　　　　　　—Harriet Lerner

Even if the other person isn't going to change, you can improve your own personal situation and feel better about yourself just by taking action and making your wishes known. After all, action always beats inaction, especially when you practice your assertive vocabulary and get it down pat. And that vocabulary will have an even greater impact when it's reinforced by powerful body language, as you'll learn in:

Exercise: Making Your Bubble Bigger

Power and powerlessness are communicated nonverbally as well as verbally. Researchers have found that our strong words are often undermined by our nonverbal body language: language that's weak, vulnerable, and submissive. Compared to men, we take up less space as we walk and sit. We use more restricted hand gestures and avoid direct eye contact when we're uncomfortable or intimidated. This makes it almost impossible for some of us to express our anger effectively. It's like wearing a sign that says OF COURSE I DON'T MEAN WHAT I SAY or KICK ME or TAKE ADVANTAGE OF ME PLEASE! But there is something you can do if you find you're sporting a silent sandwich board. You can strengthen your body language.

One way to do this is by expanding your personal power zone, your private space, your aura, sphere of influence, or whatever you want to call it. We call it making your bubble bigger, and we have used this exercise with hundreds of women who swear by its effectiveness.

The idea comes from the "First Venusian Anthropological Expedition to Earth," by Nancy Henley. In the Henley story, Venusians visiting earth observe that

> . . . all earthlings have a space bubble around them, the amount of space belonging to their own bodies. Dominants have larger space bubbles . . . One need only watch the Earthlings move about in their bubbles of different sizes, approaching bubble to bubble, to know immediately who is the superior, and who is the inferior, in any interaction.   —**Nancy Henley**

You can watch powerful Earthlings—CEOs, doctors, lawyers, or just people with self-confidence and self-respect—

and see for yourself how big their bubbles are. Now your bubble can be that big too.

First, pick a private time and place where you can concentrate, uninterrupted, on expanding your bubble. Stretch out from the tips of your toes up through the top of your head. Focus on this feeling, on what it's like to stand tall, to make huge, expansive arm and hand gestures and walk across the room like you're grand pooh-bah of the world. Why you can actually feel your bubble growing bigger! You can sense the increased power in your body and the surge of confidence that comes when you assume the pose of a great leader—even if you don't usually seek the leadership role.

Now try the same thing in front of a mirror. Do this to make sure that the feelings of confidence and personal power you just experienced are communicated by your body language before you even open your mouth to speak. In other words, see yourself as others see you.

Start with your posture. Are you standing tall and proud with your head high and relaxed, or are you hunched up and trying to hide? Study your body and observe what you do, then work on your carriage. Prime it to broadcast your sense of self-confidence and self-respect.

Next look at your hand gestures. Are they definite and deliberate or barely noticeable? Do you use them to emphasize your points or not? To check this out, try expressing an opinion that you feel very strongly about in front of the mirror. Observe what hand gestures come naturally, then build on them. Try adding some new things too, such as sweeping your hands and arms in an outward arc or dramatically pounding your fist into your palm. You should also observe what other people do and adapt anything effective into your own repertoire.

Now what about walking the walk? Practice walking up to the mirror. Are your movements confident and sure, more like a victor than a victim? Do you move comfortably and with determination? Think about it. Maybe you need to take larger steps or plant your feet more firmly on the ground.

While you're walking the walk, don't forget to talk the talk. Just as your body's got to reinforce what your words are saying, so do the tone and timbre of your voice. Make sure your tone is strong and assertive, not flat or filled with pauses that indicate hesitation or a lack of confidence. Avoid child-like whines and giggles or any timbre that will discredit your message. If necessary, adjust your volume. Is it too soft or too loud? An easy-to-miss whisper or the confident, commanding sound of an intelligent adult? Remember that your voice is part of your nonverbal body language and the whole package should strengthen the intent of your words.

As you work in front of the mirror, be sure to look yourself in the eye. Feel the power of your physical being, the increased confidence you experience when you make your body your ally and use it to add credibility to your verbal messages—and don't confuse credibility with domination. The goal of this exercise is not to establish yourself as dominant, but to level the playing field in situations where you feel powerless, intimidated, and unable to express your anger like you really want to.

Once you've practiced in front of the mirror, it's time to visualize using this technique in real life. Picture this. You're on the twelfth floor of a high-rise office building, finally on your way home after putting in some overtime. The elevator doors open. Four rowdy refugees from a company party join you, joking around, pressing elevator buttons for fun, and inadvertently crowding you into the corner. Automatically you start to move, angry that they're intruding on your space.

But then you stop yourself. Standing taller and straighter, you firmly stick to your position in the front of the car and even place one hand on your hip to create a greater sense of personal space around your body. You relax your neck and shoulders and hold your chin up, the picture of confidence. You even look your fellow passengers in the eye and smile. The other riders fall back or move to the corners because they can see by your nonverbal language that you have ex-panded your personal power bubble and are not going to be messed with. As a result, you're the first person out the door and on your way, and you have the satisfaction of having leveled the playing field in a situation that otherwise might have intimidated you.

This exercise is important because it prepares you for confrontations with superiors at work; conflicts with your spouse, parents, or neighbors; argumentative meetings with colleagues; or any situation in which you need a little extra "oomph" to express your anger in a direct, effective way.

The first time you actually try this exercise out in real life, do it in a low-risk situation, like with a store clerk or waiter who's ignoring you, a mechanic who's giving you flak over a car repair dispute, or someone who cuts ahead of you in line. As you practice and gain confidence, try making your bubble bigger in increasingly complex situations, like those listed above. You can do it, because now you have a powerful ally to add credibility to your verbal message, an ally known as your body.

And with this ally, plus the assertive anger tactics we learned earlier, you are increasingly empowered to act, to

Change the world and change ourselves, to ask what will I do now? **—Robert Solomon, philosopher**

What Solomon suggests we do now is take anger's positive potential one step further. In other words, we should think of anger as a strategy which, if applied on purpose, can correct injustices and improve lives.

Ironically, one of the first injustices we must correct is society's denial of our right to anger. We women need to reclaim this emotion, to acknowledge anger that's been denied, redirect anger that's been diverted into depression or psychosomatic symptoms, and convert our angry energy into empowerment. However, before any of us can cultivate the spring-steel backbones needed to do this, we must first make a thoughtful, conscious appraisal of our individual anger situations. In other words, we each must ask ourselves:

What's happening here? Why is this pushing my hot button? **—Stephanie, age fifty-two, professor**

As you know, a whole range of circumstances can push your hot button because anger is in the eye of the beholder and the three major themes of powerlessness, injustice, and irresponsibility (see Chapter 4) are all open to highly individual interpretation. However, once the button is pushed, all angry women—including you—go through the same process. First, you consider alternative courses of action ranging from "I'll tell her off" to "I won't give her the satisfaction of seeing she got my goat" to something in between.

If you decide that the provoking incident is trivial, you might choose to tone down your reaction because you figure "this isn't worth getting mad about." But some things are worth getting mad about, and after you think it over, there may be no doubt in your mind that getting angry is the way to go: "I can't believe he did that! This is the last straw. I am not going to take another day of this. I don't deserve to be treated this way. I have given that man the best years of my life and he can stuff it!"

Of course, whether a man (or anyone else) deserves to be shot, stuffed, and mounted depends on what took place; whether you believe your reaction is rational; and whether you feel your angry response is appropriate. Obviously, if you judge an offense to be malicious, intentional, or unjustified, it's easy for your anger to escalate. This is why it's so important to do a reality check, to correctly appraise the situation and make sure you're not having irrational thoughts or an inappropriate emotional outburst:

> *When I politely asked the antique dealer what the piece was, she snapped "a vase." The woman was so rude I wanted to slap her—at least verbally. But I held my tongue. She was an older lady and it was late in the afternoon. I figured she might not have made too many sales (could it possibly have been her personality?) or maybe she was tired from being on her feet all day. I also noticed that she was surrounded by empty coffee cups so it might have been caffeine overload. In any case, the minute I thought to put myself in her shoes, my attitude changed and I decided it wasn't worth expending the energy to be angry anymore.*
>
> **—Taylor, age twenty-eight, gallery manager**

The next time you experience an anger power surge, feel trip wire tense, or hit with an emotional lollapalooza, stop a minute and take a 20/20 look within. Carefully examine whatever caused your angry mood. Ask yourself whether it's "nothing" or whether your anger is justified. For example, did your insensitive spouse cut communication off at the knees so you felt ignored or invalidated? Did you mother butt in and rearrange the furniture (not to mention your life) so you felt childlike and incompetent? Or maybe your teenager belched a hole in the wall (much to the delight of his motley crew of friends) and defiantly stormed out of the house, leaving you feeling exhausted and defeated.

When life-with-loved-ones hits us below the belt, we often deny legitimate anger and launch into self-criticism, depression, or even a sense of hopelessness. We may actually believe we'll never "straighten things out" or "get it right." Worse yet, when relationships go sour, we usually blame ourselves even if we've done our best to be a good daughter, wife, mother, sister, friend, or you-name-it:

> *Ron insisted I make the dinner reservation for five o'clock. I wondered how he would make it in rush-hour traffic since he leaves work at four and it's a forty-five-minute drive when the highway's clear, but I didn't say anything because I figured he must know what he's doing. Well, he was forty minutes late and they wouldn't honor our reservation. Then he wouldn't speak to me for the rest of the night, which made me furious since it was our wedding anniversary. Still, I suppose I brought it on myself since I didn't remind him.*
>
> **—Jaemel, age twenty-seven, sound engineer**

What Jaemel and you really need to do in these kinds of situations is to remind yourselves that you're angry. Why? Because the fire and energy of anger can liberate you from self-blame, sadness, helplessness, confusion, and other negative feelings. In fact, when we claim this unmistakably clear, strong emotion, therapist Judith Avis says we've found the "white light."

Now claiming the white light of anger does not mean putting the spotlight on your inner bitch. It does not mean you'll viciously attack your husband, mother, or teenager. What's more important, when you claim your anger as a real, legitimate, and appropriate emotion, you won't attack yourself.

All too often we women compromise our own physical and mental well-being because we abort our anger to prevent someone else from being hurt. But in the process we often hurt or attack ourselves:

- "I could kick myself for behaving that way!"
- "I want to die, I'm so embarrassed over the way I acted!"

- "I'll never forgive myself for getting so mad!"
- "I was so inappropriate, I'll never show my face here again."

But what is "appropriate," really? Robert Bly, leader of the men's movement, says appropriate anger is when no one is hurt. For women, this means when no one is hurt *including ourselves*. When we come to this realization, we're free to say: "I know what's wrong. I'm angry and I have a right to be!"

PART THREE

THE ANGER/STRESS CONNECTION

7

THE STRESS TEST

Take
   1 pint of crushed ego
   ½ cup of job discrimination
   ¼ tablespoon of chauvinism

Add
   1 well-beaten path to the washing machine
   ⅓ teaspoon grated nerves

Plus
   1 pinch from a man on the street
   1 dash from the dentist to home in heavy
      traffic to release the baby sitter

   Mix all the ingredients together and stir
      violently.
   Cook to a slow burn, then add 1 last straw.
   Serves 53% of the population—the percentage
      that is female.

   —The Knoxville News-Sentinel, April 30, 1992

Sometimes the ingredients in life become so stressful that you hit the boiling point and want to serve everyone you know hemlock soup and arsenic entrees. Most of the time it's just a fantasy, but every once in a while you could dish up a banquet and easily find buyers for franchises. Indeed, the Women's Anger Study found that stress is one of the most frequent, most powerful precipitants of everyday anger in women's lives. Is this true for you, too? To find out, try taking the following stress test.

EXERCISE

The Stress Test

Instructions: The following questions ask you about your thoughts and feelings during the last month (refer back to your Anger Journal if you need help remembering). For each question, circle how often you felt or thought a certain way. Be sure to answer all the questions because even though some seem similar, there are important differences between them. For this reason, you should treat each question separately. You should also remember that the best approach is to answer each question fairly quickly. Instead of counting up the exact number of times you felt a particular way, just pick the answer that seems to be the most reasonable and honest estimate. Now go ahead and give it a try.

	NEVER	ALMOST NEVER	SOMETIMES	FAIRLY OFTEN	VERY OFTEN
1. In the last month, how often have you been upset because of something that happened unexpectedly?	0	1	2	3	4
2. In the last month, how often have you felt that you were unable to					

	NEVER	ALMOST NEVER	SOMETIMES	FAIRLY OFTEN	VERY OFTEN
control the important things in your life?	0	1	2	3	4
3. In the last month, how often have you felt nervous and "stressed"?	0	1	2	3	4
4. In the last month, how often have you dealt successfully with irritating life hassles?	4	3	2	1	0
5. In the last month, how often have you felt that you were effectively coping with important changes that were occurring in your life?	4	3	2	1	0
6. In the last month, how often have you felt confident about your ability to handle your personal problems?	4	3	2	1	0
7. In the last month, how often have you felt that things were going your way?	4	3	2	1	0
8. In the last month, how often have you found you could not cope with all the things you had to do?	0	1	2	3	4

	NEVER	ALMOST NEVER	SOMETIMES	FAIRLY OFTEN	VERY OFTEN
9. In the last month, how often have you been able to control the irritations in your life?	4	3	2	1	0
10. In the last month, how often have you felt that you were on top of things?	4	3	2	1	0
11. In the last month, how often have you been angered because of things that were outside your control?	0	1	2	3	4
12. In the last month, how often have you found yourself thinking about things that you have to accomplish?	0	1	2	3	4
13. In the last month, how often have you been able to control the way you spend your time?	4	3	2	1	0
14. In the last month, how often have you felt difficulties were piling up so high that you could not overcome them?	0	1	2	3	4

Add up your scores. (If you want to make a comparison, the average score for participants in the Women's Anger Study was 25, although some women scored as high as 49.)

The higher your total, the more often you perceive that you are stressed or overtaxed, or that your resources are inadequate to meet the demands of the situation, whatever those demands might be, and, who is a better judge of this than you yourself? After all, stress is a matter of perception, and no one can make the determination that you are stressed but you. Consider this example.

Stress researcher Carolyn Aldwin was questioning an eighty-year-old man who denied having any stress problems in the past month. A social worker who happened by reminded him, "Why, Mr. So-and-so, don't you remember? You had a big fight with your wife last week and she threw a knife at you!" The elderly gentleman replied, "Yes, but she missed me, so it wasn't really a problem!" Like the old gentleman, only you know whether or not you're stressed, and if you are, then you know that:

Stress Perception = Stress Reality

Men are disturbed not by things, but by the views which they take of things.
                    —Epictetus, philosopher in ancient Rome

Epictetus could have said the same of us women. The more we see our current life situations as too stressful and difficult to manage, the more likely we are to be angry most of the time. The Women's Anger Study bears this out. In our analyses of the study results, women who scored higher on stress also had higher scores on general anger proneness; on intense angry thoughts; on the tendency to brood over incidents; and on physical symptoms of anger like splitting headaches or tight, knotted feelings in their stomachs. These connections held up statistically even for women who had the support of their family and friends—an important consideration since previous studies show that support is a key buffer in reducing stress.

Unfortunately, this buffer doesn't do squat for some highly stressed women. The more stressed these women become, the more likely they are to vent their anger outwardly by flying off the handle or spouting slurs. As their stress increases, so does their tendency to become queens of the killer sentence and to lash out angrily at others. They are also intensely preoccupied with their own angry thoughts. They brood and ruminate, ruminate and brood:

> *I tell myself over and over again that this situation is unfair. It's become my mantra.* —**Gina, forty, technician**

If this is your mantra, you, like other angry, highly stressed women, may experience a variety of physical sensations including a quicker pulse rate, clenched fists, faster breathing, stomach tied in knots, shakiness, headaches, pounding heartbeats, and choking feelings or lumps in your throat. When you feel this way, your stress–anger connection is in full gear and you're primed for overdrive. Why? First, your escalating stress generates more anger, then your heightened anger fuels more stress. The anger hot-wires your sympathetic nervous system and adrenal gland, increasing your physical, stress-related arousal and keeping your body "keyed up" for an extended period of time.

When you're in this state, it's hard to move on to healthful stress reduction techniques. In addition, if you lash out angrily at family members, friends, and co-workers, you make your own situation even worse since these people may retaliate or withdraw their support, increasing your stress and anger even more.

But there are proactive strategies that interrupt the anger/stress connection and produce more positive results, starting with something as basic as learning to catch your breath.

Proactive Strategy: Deep Breathing

Do you ever forget to breathe? If you're like many of us, you develop respiratory amnesia when you feel angry and stressed. First, your breathing gets rapid and irregular. Then cement blocks seem to be stacked on your rib cage as you take shallow upper-chest breaths, or you even feel like you're "losing your breath" ("apnea" to all you medical jargon fans). By deliberately focusing on deep, slow, regular breathing, you can successfully calm yourself. Plus, you can do this simple exercise anywhere—at home, at work, or at your mother-in-law's, for example.

Start by taking a deep slow breath in while counting 1–2–3–4, then breathe out to the same count, 1–2–3–4. Let your body go limp and hollow. Allow each breath to fill this hollow space with relaxation. If it will help, you can even "see" your breath as a soft relaxing color that gently floods your being, washing away the tension and stress. However you picture it, let your anxiety go, and gradually, when you're ready, return to an alert state.

Now, if your life even remotely resembles the lives of participants in the Women's Anger Study, you'll use this strategy a lot, especially when you compare your stress to that of the men you know.

CATHY © Cathy Guisewite. Reprinted with permission of UNIVERSAL PRESS SYNDICATE. All rights reserved.

Stressors: When Dr. Jekyll Becomes Ms. Hyde

While many men can list all their stressors on the inside of a matchbook cover and still have space left for a short novel, our lists are so long that if we had to write them on one page, there wouldn't be room for the commas. It's a phenomenon every female knows but one which researchers have only recently documented. Quite simply, women are more stressed than men.

From adolescence through adulthood, we feel more day-to-day and long-term emotional distress. We are usually less happy about life and less satisfied with our roles than men, and often we don't know why:

> *No matter how much I delegate, prioritize or whatever, I . . . get more stressed than the men I work with. Either they're much better at this than me or they're taking something stronger than the aspirin I've been gobbling down since I started this job.*
>
> **—Katie, age forty, engineer**

> *All I wanted to do was have a house and kids. I never thought I'd have to work two jobs too. It doesn't seem to faze my husband a bit, but I'm totally stressed out because this isn't the way it was supposed to be.*
>
> **—Holly, age thirty-eight, mother and insurance analyst**

For many of us, life is "supposed" to be better than it was for our mothers. With fewer social restrictions, improved educations, and greater employment opportunities, many of us figured we would get "more" than Mom, and we have—more stress. Today we're confronted with megastress our mothers never dreamed of. Indeed, no other generation of American women has faced the demands of excelling simultaneously in so many roles, including wife, mother, housekeeper, chef, decorator, hostess, community leader, employee, employer, volunteer, and more. But many of us now wonder if less is more, and we think back to a time when things were different.

In the past, a woman took on roles sequentially: Beth worked *until* she had a husband or a baby and then left her work role behind; Hannah didn't get married *until* she finished caring for her elderly parents, and only then did she walk down the aisle; and Joyce postponed her own college education *until* her children graduated and could finally make do for themselves.

Unfortunately, today, we women not only "do" for ourselves, we "do" for everyone else too, including our bosses. In the last thirty years, there has been an increase of twenty-nine million women in the workplace, bringing the total number of women currently employed to more than fifty million. That's fifty million of us who have added the responsibilities of paid employment to the duties we already have at home. Although men have always combined these work and family roles, the novelty of large numbers of women doing so has attracted considerable, high-pressure attention.

Part of this attention comes from the popular press, which has put the female image into a free fall with its articles on "jugglers" and "superwomen." Then there's the scientific community with its research on "female role overload," "female role conflict," and "female role strain." That is, having too many duties, too little time, and too much tension, frustration, and anxiety—otherwise known as stress. And with this much stress, no wonder society is convinced that every woman who takes on two or more roles has fried her cerebral hemispheres with electric curlers!

The disturbing thing is that many of us believe it too, and with good reason. Take the stress of role conflict. The necessity of adopting an unemotional, task-oriented, competitive business persona at work, then behaving like a helpmate, tender nurturer, and peacemaker at home often creates intense personal turmoil and confusion:

> *I have two selves—one at home and in the social world I live in, and one at work. My husband doesn't like aggressive women, and if people in my home world had to deal with me the way people in my work world do, it wouldn't work at all.*
> **—An attorney interviewed by L. Rubin, sociologist**

Besides role conflict, most of us find that a lack of time is a severe stressor. In one recent study of female white-collar workers, the total combined demands of paid and unpaid work on women with two children was eighty hours per week; with three or more children, that total rose to ninety hours per week. Whether we are at home, at the grocery store, in the car, or even in the bathtub, time pressure is gnawing at us, urging us to get going, speed up, and do more.

Unfortunately, this sense of time urgency is not a distorted, panic reaction. Rather, it's a clear, realistic grasp of the fact that we have an incredible amount of things to do and very little time in which to do them.

We also have very little help. In previous generations, women could ask the neighbor next door to watch an active (read exhausting) two-year-old for an hour. They could get advice about marital woes from their aunts and other wise, older women or cry on the shoulder of their own mothers, who lived right around the corner. But it's not that way anymore. We modern women are much more isolated. Mother might be two thousand miles away. Extended kin are probably scattered across the country, and the neighbors mistrusted or unknown.

What is known is that this lack of readily available support, plus time pressure, plus role conflict adds up to incredible stress, and for many of us, the emotional reaction to stress is anger. But until now, that stress-related anger was not adequately explored by researchers. Up to this point, most stress studies have focused exclusively on men in the workplace or in artificial laboratory settings where a typical "stress-producing activity" was to solve arithmetic problems or trace the outline of a star for ten minutes while looking at a mirror image of the shape. Sound stressful? Not exactly!

Not for most women, anyway. A simple reality check tells you that these kinds of experiments don't reveal much about dealing with real-world stressors. In addition, since the tests were conducted primarily on men, the study findings don't adequately explain whether or not we women become stressed by the same things or respond in the same way.

One thing we do know, though, is that stress is additive and can eventually turn even the sweetest Dr. Jekyll into Ms. Hyde. This is particularly true if your personal perception is that you're overloaded. Unfortunately, for many of us, this personal perception combined with the dramatic changes in our roles and lifestyles, plus increasing social problems, has produced a level of frustration, tension, and anxiety we are not prepared to deal with. What makes it worse is that the world is unpredictable and few, if any, of us have the kind of life we expected when we were growing up—even those who appear to have it all:

If I'd known this is what it would be like to have it all, I might have been willing to settle for less.

—Lily Tomlin, actress

Do most of us secretly, or maybe not so secretly, agree with Lily Tomlin? The answer is surprising. While results from the Women's Anger Study strongly support the stress–anger connection, some of the data is not what our research team expected. In fact, one piece of information just blew us away, and that is the high cost of caring.

There's not enough of me. Everybody needs so much of me. I constantly feel as if one person or one group of people has one of my arms, and another group has the other arm, and they are pulling in different directions. And then two other groups have my feet. And then the phone rings.

—Julie, as told to psychologist Faye Crosby

When people are pulling at you and everyone wants a piece of you, and you try to oblige them all, you're plugged into the social tradition that says we women should sacrifice ourselves in service to others. But we all know what happens to human sacrifices . . .

The participants in the Women's Anger study know this stressful, emotionally drawn-and-quartered feeling all too well. We discovered this when we asked "What is your greatest stress right now?" In response, the women described specific stress incidents in their lives and the single most striking answer was that they were stressed by the high cost of caring. In fact, when we broke the answers down into categories, the stress of caring ranked number one.

Women's Greatest Sources of Stress

1. Vicarious—caring for others/concern for others
2. Work/job
3. Finances/money
4. Love life
5. Health
6. School
7. Time pressures
8. Existential—worrying about the purpose, meaning, and brevity of life

If vicarious stress is number one on your list, this is not uncommon. In fact, so many women experience stress from the lives of loved ones that before we can cope with our other stressors (covered individually and as recurring themes elsewhere in this book), we must first assess the high cost of caring.

The High Cost of Caring: Assessing Your Level of Vicarious Stress

While many men define themselves as "me, myself, and I," most of us are defined by our connectedness, by our sense of caring and giving to other people. A group of female therapists at Wellesley's Stone Center named this concept "the self-in-relation," and it figures strongly in women's definitions of stress. In fact, it figures so strongly and is so embedded in our views of ourselves that the majority of us actually describe our chief stressors in terms of other people. Examples given by participants in the Women's Anger Study include their daughter's breast cancer, son's divorce, grandson's bad grades, mother's Alzheimer's disease, husband's unemployment, friend in jail, daughter-in-law's mother's illness, etc.

Notice anything unusual? Even though each woman was asked "what is your greatest stress," each answered by identifying someone else's stress, a stress the woman herself was not experiencing firsthand. In every case, these women chose to take on the stressful burdens of others including the trials and tribulations of nieces, nephews, grandchildren, parents, and friends, not to mention their own children, whether those children were nine or ninety.

But that's not all. Complicating the situation is the fact that at every age, more women than men take on the high stress assignment of caring for ill, disabled, or elderly family members. One large study of married couples particularly underscores this fact. The study found that wives are more involved than husbands whenever an acute health crisis arises in their social circle. This is true whether the wives are employed or not. In addition, compared to caregiving husbands, caregiving wives put in far more hours each week.

And single women aren't far behind. Why? Popular mythology promotes the idea that unmarried females have abundant time and energy for family caregiving tasks. As a result, single women end up with a disproportionate share of the responsibility for elderly parents including shopping, cooking, housecleaning, errand-running, and chauffeuring. Indeed, a new study conducted at the University of Michigan found that one-fourth of single women in their fifties care for frail parents. The motto seems to be "if she's single—she can do it."

This even applies to single female senior citizens. More than two in five unmarried grandmothers average a hefty twenty hours a week caring for grandchildren, and married grandmothers put in just slightly less time. Is it any wonder then that the stress of caregiving is sometimes like a bad horror film, turning our best Good Samaritan intentions into "The Samaritan's Stress Strikes Back"?

And what about those of us who are middle-aged and suddenly find ourselves in a double feature—taking on the care of aging parents while continuing to raise our children?

In the past year I've had to start taking care of some of my family members, my dad and my grandmother, which has been a lot of stress, stress on me, stress on my children, and my husband. But sometimes those are the things you have to do . . . I've had the responsibility of doing the grocery shopping and the doctor taking for my grandmother and my dad. My dad developed dementia and he had to be put in a boarding home. I had to go through a big turmoil with him and it's just put a lot of pressure on me. You can't slow down. You're always on the clock, especially if you have children and a family. Then you're trying to take care of somebody else and trying to get ready to go to work.

Some days it's really made me cry, you know, [I] just lose my emotional stability for the day. It makes me angry but it also scares me because I feel like I'm losing control of myself—like everything else is controlling me except me and I'm not even being me or doing anything that I want to do. I'm somebody's mom. I'm somebody's wife. I'm somebody's daughter. I'm somebody's granddaughter and I help to take care of all these people. And I'm a lot of people's friend . . . I get angry at myself because I don't say no, because I always want to try to help somebody.

—Jolene, who works full-time outside the home and cares for her grandmother, father, husband, and three children ages six, eight, and twelve

As Jolene recognizes, helping somebody can take its toll. In our own previous study of stress and anger in middle adulthood, the majority of the women we sampled reported severe daily stress, and their number one stressor was the health of a family member.

Many older women are not only stressed by a family member's health, but by their own. Why? In 80 percent of all cases, relatives decide to care for the frail elderly at home and the caregivers are usually the wives, wives who are typically in their seventies and in fair to poor health themselves:

This is the worst thing I've ever gone through—I look at Mom and she's going down hill fast, I mean she's ninety for God's sake—and here I am at seventy and my arthritis is so bad that I can't help either of us. The whole situation is out of control! I could just scream!

—Marilyn, age seventy, retired

Two characteristics make vicarious stress especially hard to cope with, and the first is lack of control. Indeed, uncontrollability is a key contributor to highly stressful situations. This is why the circumstances described by participants in the Women's Anger Study are so stressful—they're giant sieves—draining control from our lives.

Just take another look at the examples to see that this is true. The women describe other people's divorces, illnesses, and misdeeds, yet what could the women themselves possibly have done to control or prevent these situations? Nothing. For instance, consider the "refilled-nest syndrome" experienced by several women in the study and something that may be a source of stress in your life as well.

This stressor, caused when adult children return home because of a personal or economic crisis, has increased in the 1990s. It is particularly stressful if you're a midlife woman who likes the freedom of the empty nest and if you believe that now it's "your turn." Unfortunately, the return of adult children—often accompanied by *their* children—can send you back to the end of the line, making you wonder if "your turn" will ever come again. It's even worse if you don't feel you can say no, and how many of us can say no to a child who needs help because of a painful divorce or job termination? Not many. As a result, women faced with the refilled nest get angry, and the anger we feel is produced by our sense of powerlessness combined with guilt over our angry feelings. After all, a mother should always be there for her child, shouldn't she?

For many of us, the problem is with those words *should always. Should always* implies serious, long-term consequences, the other crucial characteristic of vicarious stress. If you have an unmarried, pregnant daughter or a son in the process of divorce, you're dealing with a complex stressor that has profound, long-term implications. Worse yet, you're helpless. You can't take away your child's pain or work out a "happy ending." And simply "relaxing your muscles" or using trendy, superficial stress management techniques is about as much help with this kind of stressor as a popgun is against Godzilla.

In fact, taking on a monstrous amount of other people's stress is what does us women in. It happens because we tend to be intimately involved in the lives of many individuals beyond our own families. Although there are certainly benefits to such large social networks (and our networks are usually bigger than men's), this has led to the often erroneous belief that we have more support—but we don't.

Connections to dozens of friends and neighbors doesn't mean that you automatically get the support you need. Actually, it can mean just the opposite because you may be in a caretaking role with these folks just as you are with your own family. In addition, large networks extract a high price in the time and energy it takes to nurture all these people. It's obvious then that when you take on others' burdens you perform a very valuable function for them, but you aren't doing much for yourself except to add to your own stress level.

That level can increase even more if you're married. Why? Both men and women tend to rely on women for support since culturally, women are raised to be good listeners who respond with empathy and compassion. But many of us respond with so much empathy and compassion that often our husbands turn solely to us in moments of stress. This puts a heavy responsibility on us to provide counsel and to shore up our mates' resources, even at the cost of our own. The stress of this responsibility gets worse if your husband doesn't reciprocate. Psychologist Deborah Belle calls it the "support gap" in male–female relationships, and every one of us knows it as getting less than we give. Unfortunately, getting the short end of this stick is quite common. In one large study of middle-aged women, a third of the married respondents didn't even include their husbands as members of their support network.

But to be fair, the husbands may not have been aware of their wives' actual stress levels and need for support. This was the case in a study we did a few years ago, in which we separately questioned husbands and wives in dual-career marriages about the types and severity of stresses the wives were experiencing. It was no surprise that the husbands greatly underestimated their wives' stress.

But how could a man living under the same roof as his wife have such a passing acquaintance with her reality? Easy. Traditionally, we women have tried to protect our husbands from stress by withholding information. When we do this, our spouses can only react to what they think they know. A social psychologist who interviewed husbands and wives separately as part of his study on sex differences in psychological distress explains:

> *We would interview a woman and she would tell us her daughter had had an abortion. When we asked why her husband hadn't mentioned it, she would say, "Oh, I didn't tell him."* —**Ron Kessler**

> *My husband has enough to worry about with work and all. I don't want to add to his load if I can help it. That's what my mother did for my father and that's what I want to do, no matter how tough it is.*
> —**Penelope, age fifty-eight, marketing analyst**

And tough doesn't begin to describe it. When you decide not to tell your husband about major life events, to protect him by withholding information, and otherwise to carry his—or anyone else's—troubles, you start to feel vicarious stress eating you alive. What's worse, because its overbite extends beyond specific roles and ages, vicarious stress chomps away at every level of your existence. The question is, what can you do about it? One answer, ironic as it seems, is to get busy!

Surprisingly, the Women's Anger Study showed that women who are the busiest—those juggling the three-role combination of wife, mother, and worker—were less angry than never-married women and women with just two roles, including homemakers who were wives and mothers but unemployed, married workers without children, and divorced workers with. These findings fly in the face of the "role overload" theory of stress.

This theory says that (1) because there are many stresses in each of the major roles we women play, (2) because stress is additive, and (3) because higher stress is associated with an increased tendency toward anger, women with the greatest number of role responsibilities, time pressures, and competing demands from different parts of their lives would have bragging rights to the most anger. Right? Wrong! So what's the explanation? It's this: How you view your lot in life is much more important than what you have to do.

Call It Like You See It: Multiple Roles and Personal Perceptions of Vicarious Stress

Many of us who take on multiple roles are fully aware that stress "comes with the turf," but just because we're on this turf doesn't mean we'll feel angry and resentful. For instance, women who freely choose motherhood often apply good will and Erma Bombeck–type humor to reduce the stress of child rearing. These women are successful in handling stress because they have chosen their role—in this case, motherhood—voluntarily. The key here is choice. Whether you see yourself as an unhappy wife, a reluctant employee, a nervous mother, or someone who enthusiastically selects and controls the roles she undertakes makes all the difference to whether or not you believe you are stressed.

According to the Women's Anger Study then, stress is a judgment call—a very conscious judgment call—that every woman must make for herself. In other words, if you feel stressed, it's because you judge that your well-being is threatened and that your resources are insufficient to handle the threat. Furthermore, if you don't make this conscious appraisal, you are not stressed.

How else do you explain the turbo-charged wife, mother, and worker who is undaunted and even—gasp—cheerful about her multiple roles and responsibilities? Obviously, she sees herself as far too fruitfully occupied to get hung up on minor daily frustrations or trivial incidents that could become anger triggers.

> *How long does my typical day-to-day anger episode usually last? A few minutes—I'm too busy to let it affect me any longer.* —**Ginger**

> *As I switch back and forth between teaching, writing, and working at a job all week, not to mention being a wife, daughter, sister, aunt, friend, and colleague, I sometimes wonder if someone who stews in her anger may have too much time on her hands and needs to develop more perspective. I, for one, love being busy and having different roles.* —**Angeline, age forty-one**

In all the tabloid talk on angry, burnt-out, mega-stressed superwomen, one important fact is often overlooked: multiple roles can have multiple benefits. That is, each role can be a buffer or resource for coping with the stress of another. A number of studies bear this out, particularly those that examine the emotional benefits of being a paid worker. Among the findings is this: employed wives are less stressed than housewives. This means that when you have a job, you have the opportunity to temporarily shelve your vicarious stressors. In addition, working gives you an increased income, greater social status, more contacts, professional accomplishments, and artistic achievements, not to mention the chance to use your talent, intelligence, and creativity.

However, not every job is this wonderful, and those of us faced with "the career that ate my brain" can balance dissatisfaction in our professions with satisfaction in our marriages and/or by taking solace in rearing healthy, well-adjusted children. The point is that if one area of life is going down the tubes, there are always compensations somewhere else.

But what if you aren't married or don't have enough multiple roles in which to take comfort? The bottom line is this: If you do not have enough alternative sources of gratification, you may find yourself unduly stressed—and angered—by events in one area of your life. Consider this corroborating information. A recent longitudinal study shows that when the quality of their job role declines, single women and women without children experience increased levels of stress. By contrast, women with partners and women with children do not associate a change in job role quality with greater stress levels. This lack of alternative sources of gratification probably explains why never-married women were the angriest, most stressed-out participants in the Women's Anger Study. It also explains why these women—and perhaps, you—need to employ the *stress-busters!*

8

EFFECTIVE TECHNIQUES FOR MANAGING ANGER AND STRESS

*I'm a lawyer and I always believed in being Attila the Hun.
I just don't know if I can turn that into Attila the Hen, no
matter how much stress it relieves.*
— **Nicolete, age forty-seven, corporate counsel**

Converting from Attila the Hun to Attila the Hen is no
easy task, especially when you're trying to find an approach
to stress management that really works. Indeed, the stress
management bandwagon is overloaded with books, tapes,
magazine articles, exercises, and programs. Stress is big
business, and we Americans have been inundated with more
than our share of trendy stress management techniques. Yet
much of this stress reduction information seems bogus because for the average female, it just won't work. Take social
withdrawal . . .

What Won't Work and Why

Social withdrawal is frequently recommended as a short-
term way of coping with everyday stressors and negative
emotions. Although withdrawing might restore you to a
more positive emotional state, retreating to the privacy of

your room is about as likely as retreating to your mother's womb. Why, some of us can't even go to the toilet in peace!

Worse yet, while some men feel free to top off a rough work week with a get-away-from-it-all fishing or golf weekend, most of us top off our rough weeks with even tougher Saturday and Sunday schedules. Frequently we're locked into children's soccer matches, dental appointments arranged months in advance, or pressing household duties that simply can't wait. No wonder participants in the Women's Anger Study said social withdrawal was their least used coping strategy!

And what about the considerable emphasis in stress management literature on coping by solving the problem? Although this is certainly an excellent strategy for problems that can actually be solved, it's not much help if you don't even know what the problem is—which is often the case. Most women's stress situations are so complex, ambiguous, and uncontrollable that it's hard to identify the precise issue that needs to be addressed. In this instance, about the only thing we can do is be stressed in smaller doses, otherwise known as "sequential worrying."

For example, on the first day of class in each new semester, the students look at all the requirements on Sandra's course syllabus and immediately feel overwhelmed. They already have syllabi and assignments from their other professors and combined with what they get in Sandra's class, it's too much. The problem is that these students are in a very demanding professional program and there is no solution to this stressful situation. To help them combat continuous stress throughout the semester, Sandra suggests that they focus on one assignment at a time and worry about everything in smaller, more manageable, weekly or daily chunks.

Now certainly being stressed in smaller chunks beats being stressed in larger ones, but not by much. After all, stress is still stress and sometimes not even advance information about the stressor will help. In fact, knowing in advance can make the situation worse—much worse.

Whenever the steward or stewardess starts demonstrating the oxygen mask . . . I just tune them out . . . all that emergency stuff makes me . . . nervous so I . . . ignore it.

*A lot of other people ignore it too. They're sleeping, read-
ing, or staring out the window. They look everywhere but
at the flight attendant. It's like if you don't pay attention,
you won't need the information and if you do pay attention, it's bad karma.*

—Joan, age forty-one, stage manager

Giving people advance information about a stressful situation is supposed to help them cope, but often this stress
management technique backfires. After all, if you can't do
anything about the situation, what can the advance information do except make you feel more tense and nervous?

This is why "provision of information" usually fails as a
stress management technique for women even though it's
championed by dozens of programs and manuals. Think
about it. How many females joining the labor force appreciate being told that they'll average 15 more hours of work and
3.5 fewer hours of sleep each week than they did as housewives? And what mother wants to believe that her adorable
newborn will someday have the corrosive disposition of a
teenage slam dancer? The point is that no news is sometimes
good news when it comes to advance knowledge of a stressor
we can't control.

But if advance knowledge, solving the problem, and social withdrawal won't help, what will? What stress/anger
management techniques are actually useful and do more
than put a ribbon around a bomb?

Proactive Strategy: Managing Stress/
Anger with Useful Action

Many of us are so angry at the stress in our lives that our
emotional landscapes are potential minefields, but it doesn't
have to be this way. We do not have to remain locked into
the anger that increases our stress, especially when we realize that the final step in the stress–anger chain is behavior:

Stress» Anger» Behavior

Behavior is the key to managing the stress–anger connection, and another word for behavior is *action*. We know this
from personal experience.

Sandra's daughter Shana was in that "worthless period" of adolescence when once-charming children are transformed into lazy, inconsiderate, messy, disrespectful creatures (even though Sandra knew she would emerge as a delightful adult later on). One evening, Shana stomped into the kitchen, surveyed what Sandra was preparing for dinner, and pronounced it unacceptable to her taste. She demanded macaroni and cheese instead. Sandra told her daughter she would start the food, but that Shana must attend to it as it cooked because she had other things to do. Sandra then went about her business in another room and some time later, the odor of burnt noodles filled the house.

Instead of attending to the cooking food, Shana had gone downstairs to her room and was blithely unaware of the smoking pan on the stove. Sandra doesn't recall why she was so stressed that particular evening, but the burning pasta really set her off. It was probably the culmination of a tough day at work, the usual six P.M. rush of dinner preparation and necessary household chores, plus Shana's contemptuous dismissal of the evening's meal, her insistence on something else to eat, and her subsequent irresponsibility in following through.

At any rate, Sandra's response was to grab the pan and furiously hurl it from the deck far into the backyard. Her action was swift and surprisingly effective. By the time the blackened pan clunked harmlessly to the ground somewhere out of sight beyond the cedar trees, Sandra's anger had dissipated. When her daughter and husband appeared in the kitchen doorway, they all started to laugh. Dinner was pleasant and Shana ate what was put before her without a murmur.

Granted, hurling a burnt pan is not precisely what most of us have in mind when we think of action, but the point is that doing something constructive or at least harmless helps to relieve both the physical and emotional symptoms of stress and anger. Besides, the alternative is pretty unappealing—Sandra could have seethed silently throughout the dinner, tying her own stomach in knots. Or, she could have yelled at Shana for her selfishness, thoughtlessness, carelessness, and other sundry faults and shortcomings, leaving her daughter feeling bad. Later on, Sandra would have regretted dealing with her anger in either of these ways. But she really felt good when she threw that pan!

Moving from stress and anger to a place where you feel good is what taking action is all about, and for those of us who decide the cookware discus throw isn't quite our style, there are other options. Suzanne, for instance, chose a very rational approach.

Suzanne and her family had just finished breakfast at their rented beachfront house. It was the first day of a long-awaited vacation and Suzanne was enjoying her coffee as she gazed out at the ocean and idly skimmed a magazine. Suddenly the peace and quiet was interrupted by the arrival of roofers. Not wanting to deal with the stress of pounding all day, not to mention the intrusion of strangers, Suzanne called the property manager and requested that the job be postponed. Unfortunately, she was told it had been scheduled for weeks and couldn't be put off. Furious that the work was taking place at a time when the house was rented to vacationers, Suzanne acted quickly.

She requested compensation for the disruption of her family's vacation and for the inconvenience. This took courage for Suzanne who, although in her forties, is just learning to be assertive (see Chapter 6). Although the property manager stalled for a few days, Suzanne persisted and finally got satisfaction in the form of free maid service. But even before Suzanne knew she would be compensated with money or services, she felt good about the way she handled the situation. Better yet, her anger receded and she enjoyed the rest of her vacation.

While taking action certainly helps with relatively minor stressors (i.e., spoiled vacations and burnt pans), it is absolutely critical to dealing with the major stressors that make you ulcer-conjuring miserable—like your child's failure at school, your husband's job termination, or your mother's decline due to Alzheimer's. How so? Although you don't have direct control over the events affecting others, your anger in these vicarious stress situations can be used productively. It can inspire you to take an action that makes a huge difference to someone you love:

My daughter was born with a congenital anomaly that required highly specialized and life-threatening surgery.

*Not all of the doctors I dealt with were arrogant and un-
feeling, but many of them were. In dealing with the bun-
gled diagnoses and advice of physicians, I had to learn to
be an advocate for my daughter without alienating the
doctors whose help she needed. I had to learn how to be
forceful without appearing to be demanding and how to
appear to defer to their authority while protecting my
child. In this situation, I learned to acknowledge my
anger but not to express it in ways that might place my
child in any jeopardy. It was quite a tightrope to walk, but
my love for my daughter helped me use my anger to get
her what she needed.* **—Lynn**

Using her anger to achieve a positive goal transformed
Lynn into a forceful advocate for her daughter and allowed
her to secure better medical care. Without that anger, Lynn
might have remained passive and compliant—and her child
might have paid a high price for Lynn's inaction. You, too,
can use your anger to achieve a positive goal—to get your
child more assistance at school, to protect the elderly, to
draw attention to a community problem, or to right a national wrong:

Why do you think they call us MADD?
**—Geena, age fifty-one, member of Mothers
Against Drunk Driving**

Anger can also help you make it right when it's about to
go personally wrong. In other words, anger is a clear, strong
signal that your stress level is too high to give any more of
yourself to others. Whether you're "stretched too thin," "have
reached your limit," or are "emotionally tapped out," anger
means that your endurance has been exceeded and you need
a break to recharge your batteries. When this happens, you
must honestly admit to your friends, your family, and yourself that you're going off duty to look out for number one. It's
a strategy that can help you achieve a sense of control in even
the most chronic, difficult vicarious stress situations.

Of course, achieving that sense of control really means
taking control of yourself. It means knowing your own limits
and your own threshold of "interpersonal overload." For
most of us, this threshold is difficult to assess. Why? Since
girlhood, we have been socialized to help others. By the time
we become adults, the helpmate role is not only second na-

ture, but deeply desired, and many of us find that we want to be involved in other people's lives. We're gratified when spouses, children, and friends approach us for advice and good counsel. In addition, we feel guilty about saying no to those who need help. But if we don't say no to our families and friends when we're feeling overloaded, we're saying yes to personal disaster. After all, we can only comfort so many souls before we bankrupt our own—and that price is too much to pay.

This is why we women must relinquish the costly fantasy that we can "be there" for everybody, every time—and this is especially true for those of us in the traditional professions of teaching, nursing, counseling, and social work. We "give at the office" all day and our jobs are already emotionally depleting (read burnout city) *without* the added responsibility of caregiving to family and friends. The same goes for women in nontraditional fields. They, too, fill the roles of nurturer and caregiver in the workplace as they support stressed colleagues, become human buffers between opposing factions, and pour out compassion along with coffee in the course of the daily grind. All of us pay the high cost of caring and we each must learn to deal with the resulting stress and anger by taking action on our own behalf. And don't worry if, at first, other people don't understand this self-action stance. (Witness the encyclopedic 1993 *Handbook of Stress*, which doesn't even mention vicarious stress, let alone how to handle it!) The world will catch up eventually.

Proactive Strategy: Avoiding Stress Carriers

Speaking of catching, vicarious stress can be as contagious as common colds or the flu. "Stress carriers," like other disease carriers, erode your resistance. They consistently drag you down with their sense of eternal pessimism and accounts of crisis after crisis after crisis:

> *I just dread talking to Mimi. Whenever she calls there's always something wrong. Her foot, her eyes, PMS, the IRS, you name it . . . I could dump her as a friend, but deep down I know she's a good person and professionally she's taught me a lot. I just have to continually remind myself that she's a high-maintenance relationship and if*

*I'm feeling bad myself, I avoid dealing with her until I feel
better, otherwise I'll be bummed out for hours.*

—Crystal, age forty

The empathy between friends often causes you to take on
someone else's stress, sadness, discouragement, and anger.
Unfortunately, these negative feelings can linger long after
your conversation has ended, depriving you of precious time
and energy. Now if these conversations only happen once in
a while, if the friendship is basically one of give and take,
then there's no problem. The problem only comes in if there's
an imbalance, if your kindness is being exploited and you're
being taken advantage of. If this is the case, you must limit
your interaction with the stress carrier. After all, life is short,
and you owe it to yourself to spend your valuable free time
with people who lift your spirits and with whom you can
joke, smile, and share mutually satisfying, happy activities.

Proactive Strategy: Activities That Help Reduce Stress

The key word here is *activity*. We each need to find an effective stress reduction activity that suits our own individual
style and can be built into our daily routine. Then we must
commit to participating in these activities on a regular basis.
For instance, shy, quiet personalities might benefit from private meditation in the garden while extroverts might prefer
to rehash the day's frustrations over a pitcher of sangria with
friends. Athletes could choose a vigorous game of tennis
while those of us with an aversion to sweat could select
needlework or reading. There are literally hundreds of stress
reduction activities to choose from, including these cited by
participants in the Women's Anger Study:

- Exercise, especially walking (see Chapter 18)
- Direct action (one woman with two sets of twins wrote
  "get a baby sitter")
- Talking it over with someone or just being with
  someone
- Pleasurable activities (reading, hobbies, music, shop-
  ping)
- Spiritual activities (prayer, meditation, church)
- Relaxation (sleep, vacations, relaxation techniques)

- Professional help (therapy, medication, support groups)
- Outlets (crying, laughing, smoking, drinking, eating)
- Being alone ("Isolate myself for quiet time"—a technique mentioned by a tiny minority of study participants)

The point is that most of us find adaptive ways to cope with our stress. With the exception of smoking, drinking, and eating (see Part Five), we choose healthy activities that suit our lifestyles and are highly proactive. In fact, very few of us "do nothing" or "try not to think about" our stress levels. The Women's Anger Study bears this out with data that suggests that females are not the helpless stress victims portrayed in some scientific literature. Quite the contrary. Many of us fight stress with the savvy of warrior queens, and you can too.

Proactive Strategies: How Warrior Queens Send Stress Packing

There are several action steps you can take to boost your stress resistance, starting with a strategy that increases your sense of personal control. If you believe you can control the course of events in your own life, you will not only be more stress-resistant, but also more successful in deep-sixing any unavoidable stress you have to face.

How can you learn to do this? While there are a number of effective methods for increasing personal control, many women find it helpful to begin with a little introspection, and you might find it helpful too. First, carefully examine the roles and responsibilities that are most important to you. Next, decide which stressful aspects of these roles can be changed. For instance, you may need to dump meaningless obligations and heavy personal albatrosses. You might also need to be more assertive and say no to those who make unreasonable demands on your time and energy.

You can also benefit from increasing your commitment to positive action. For example, Sally gets high stress and few rewards from her monotonous, low-level job. By committing to graduate study, she seizes control of her career potential and increases her chances of getting a more satisfying position in the future. In addition, Sally's action makes her present job easier to bear.

Like Sally, many of us have found that having a goal, a plan, or a dream can sustain our spirits when we're about to be crushed by the daily grind:

> *After being a stay-at-home mom for . . . two very rough decades, I went back to school . . . I had dreamed of doing this for years and . . . this dream . . . kept me going when the kids got into trouble, when my husband went to work for himself and it didn't go so well, and whenever anything went wrong. Now, when I have a bad day at school, I think about my next dream, which is to get a great job and be a respected professional. At age forty-three I finally feel like I'm in charge of my dreams and my life.*
>
> **—Anna, student**

Dreams, goals, and plans put you in the driver's seat of life, and it's not even the specific action you take that makes the difference. Rather, it's your strengthened sense of personal control.

Now an important part of personal control is time control. In fact, time control—or the lack thereof—is directly related to increases in your stress level. But if you develop good time management techniques, if you set a schedule, write out a prioritized "to do" list, and impose some order on routine household and office tasks, you can begin to get control over time. However, keeping control may mean going one step further. Many of us must become minute mavens, hour hoarders, and month misers, seizing every needed second from family members, friends, and colleagues. Why "seize"? Because teaching other people to respect a woman's time is easier said than done.

Everyone from children and colleagues to Fido, the family dog, thinks it's all right to interrupt a woman, and unless you put a stop to them, these continual interruptions will increase your stress level and perceived lack of control. This is why you should hang out a DO NOT DISTURB sign and mean it, providing reinforcement with locked doors, dirty looks, phone answering machines, or whatever it takes to get the time you need.

For about the past six months I've been practicing my violin—maybe a couple hours a week. And when I'm doing that it's so noisy nobody else wants to be in the room. So it's like the only space I have, you know.

                    —Kayla, wife and mother of three

Time waits for no man, and not for any women either, that's why I protect mine. I use my phone machine to screen out calls . . . I say a polite no to unwanted invitations, and I keep a daily appointment book with everything listed neatly in order of priority. Together, all these things make me feel like I have control. Of course, it's control over a three-ring circus, but at least it's control over something.   **—Sherry, age forty-one, teacher**

Tickets to the Circus

Sometimes you go to the circus and sometimes the circus comes to you. If your work space is crammed full of leftover carryout lunch wrappers, vases of flowers that died two weeks ago, and files you haven't used in years but can't quite bring yourself to throw away, you should start charging admission to the circus you call an office.

The same goes for kitchens with dirty dishes breeding in the sink, bedrooms with clothes-eating closets, and counters with stacks of mail awaiting review—when the environment is in chaos, you feel stressed and out of control. Of course, chaos is in eye of the beholder, but most of us know it when we see it, and you should also know that controlling your physical surroundings will help you get a grip not only on home and work, but on life.

A Few Caveats About Getting a Grip

For some of us, getting a grip might be as simple as reorganizing our time and cleaning out a closet. For others, it's a lot more complicated. An increasing number of American women live in poverty or have very limited financial resources. Indeed, more than 50 percent of all adults below the federal poverty line are women and more than half the poor families in America are headed by single females.

Many of these poor families live in public housing projects or deteriorating inner-city neighborhoods where they are besieged by hassles everyday. Not only is the environment unsafe, but crimes against property, assaults, gangs, and drug deals are routine events in this high-stress world. One woman Sandra visited couldn't even put her laundry out on the clothesline because each time she did, the clothespins were stolen. The reality of poor women's lives is truly shocking, and there are no easy remedies. Yet even in these dire circumstances, some women have mobilized their anger to find delinquent fathers and obtain long-overdue child support payments, to run drug dealers out of the neighborhood or terminate abusive relationships.

But whether you're using your anger to change society or to change yourself, combating stress and anger is never easy.

How people react to stressors and how successful they are in overcoming them are a function of deep-seated aspects of the self, complexly reflecting the interweaving of a person's internal and external resources.
—Stevan Hobfoll, psychologist

Whether due to low self-esteem (see Chapter 10) or a lack of coping skills, some of us simply don't have the resources to go it alone. If you're very vulnerable whenever stressful events occur, you may need the assistance of a counselor or support group. Others of us can go it alone sometimes, but not always, and we occasionally require a helping hand. And not even those women who appraise stress realistically and take appropriate steps get off scot-free because:

Life is just one damned thing after another.
—Elbert Hubbard

Unfortunately, one of those "damned things" is the fact that American society is still somewhat sexist and highly individualistic. According to psychologist Faye Crosby, this prevents or at least slows the movement toward programs that would reduce our stress, like national child or elder care:

. . . no amount of thought and individual planning will make women free of stress. To function with less stress, they would need to live in a society that values women and children more than ours does and in a culture that does not impose the burden of individualism on women, children, and men. **—Faye Crosby, psychologist**

What Crosby is really saying is that there's no easy way out. Until our society evolves, the best many of us can do is learn to function adequately despite daily stress, minimize our anger and resentment, and find things to be happy about. But we can learn something else too. We can learn to take advantage of stress and use it to improve life for ourselves, our families, and our world. How? By recognizing:

The Benefits of Stress, or I Work Better Under Pressure!

When we successfully master multiple stressors, we develop powerful abilities. We emerge healthier and stronger for having dealt with disruptive, emotionally painful issues. This applies not only to our minds, but to our bodies as well. In fact, one researcher has collected an impressive amount of evidence showing that physiological toughness can result from repeated exposure to stress. As long as it isn't constant and as long as you handle it well, the stress you cope with now makes future stress easier to bear. Indeed, your physical arousal will be more rapid and efficient, and your body will return to normal more quickly. There are psychological benefits too.

Social psychologist Marjorie Fiske says stress can make us more growth oriented, insightful, and competent. In addition, it can help us mature into complex individuals with broader perspectives on ourselves and on society as a whole. Stress can also serve as a mental alarm bell that warns us that we must take better care of ourselves before we turn up two sandwiches short of a picnic. Just turn the page to see what we mean.

PART FOUR

ANGER AND YOUR MENTAL HEALTH

9

ANGER AND YOUR MIND-SET

I always feel mentally strung out when I'm mad . . . It makes me worry that I'm having some kind of breakdown. **—Phoebe, age twenty-five**

Feeling "mental" when you're mad does not necessarily mean you're having a nervous breakdown—it could mean you're having a nervous breakthrough. In other words, your mismanaged anger might be trying to break through in the form of low self-esteem, depression, prolonged grieving, or other mental health problems. Unfortunately, anger's role as the real cause of or the major contributor to these conditions is often overlooked, especially if your anger is the silently simmering kind so many of us experience. In fact, sometimes this emotion is so closemouthed that no one knows we're angry—not our families, our friends, our therapists, not even we ourselves recognize that aborted or repressed anger is what's really behind our sad moods, tiredness, and feeling "nutsy" enough to be squirrel food. So why do we deny and disavow our anger until it mutates into the emotion from hell? For the social, cultural, and other reasons we've discussed, and for a hidden reason we'll confess right now: acknowledging our anger is a painful, all-expense-paid trip to agony acres.

Indeed, the pain of some women we interviewed for the Women's Anger Study is stunning because their feelings went beyond mere anger to the deepest soul-wringing agony. Several are so miserable in their current situations that they are just a half second from home wrecking as they contemplate running away from their marriages, their jobs, and their day-to-day lives:

> Every morning you get up, fight, fight, fight . . . It's just constant anger . . . it's not the kind of lifestyle I want. It's just a constant nitpick. When we first got married it wasn't like that and then, as the years went on, it's just continually getting worse and worse . . . The anger you feel is not rage. It's more stored anger that one day you know that you're just going to explode . . . or you're just going to walk out. I've thought to myself many, many times like I could just sell everything and just go away someplace where no one could find me.   **—Bonita**

Instead of a lifestyle issue, some women, like Judith, find their mental pain and anger grounded in a specific trauma of mammoth proportions. The trauma? At the age of forty-seven, Judith was raped by a man who came to her door asking to use the phone:

> What I began with during and after the rape was extreme fear . . . I felt anger [when] I was stronger, anger at any human being treating another human being the way I'd been treated . . . How it expresses itself is, I will read about a rapist in the paper who gets off . . . and I just immediately grip my hands and my nails. Just now I dug them into my hands because I feel such outrage and I felt that kind of thing against the man who raped me.
>
> **—Judith, age sixty-six**

Other painful violations take the form of an uninterested, absentee father; a hypercritical mother; a favored sibling who got more affection and lavish material goodies; a first love who dumped us for a rival; a traitorous friend; being denied the opportunity to go to college or to take that great job; or anything else from the past that keeps us mired in anger and resentment. The only way to escape these angry feelings, to move on and keep each experience from becoming an emotional disaster du jour, is to face our feelings and

Unravel Our Big Ball of Anger

It's like you build up so much anger inside . . . without really sitting down and talking about the problem . . . it just rolls up into a big ball and you've not even sure what it's really about . . . then you have to take that ball apart . . . in little sections . . . ask questions and poke places that are . . . deep and hurt you sometimes . . . **—Robin**

And it does hurt. In fact, anger is especially hurtful to our mental health if it's chronic and unexpressed, if old angers fuse with new ones, or hurtful incidents pile up until there's so much bad blood our relationships are jeopardized and the whole emotional house of cards threatens to tumble down. This is particularly true if we feel our parents dealt us a losing hand . . .

I've got so much anger stored up . . . How do you get rid of twenty years of your father . . . and your mother . . . How do I get rid of all this? I don't know. **—Myra**

Whoever invented that word mother—*must have gotten as mad at her mother as I get at mine.* **—Melody**

Residual Anger at Your Parents

For some women, the mother of all anger is born when their parents fall from the pedestal. Indeed, our parents are often the first people we ever get mad at, and sometimes that anger lasts a lifetime. In fact, the interview data from the Women's Anger Study revealed deep pain and anger over ancient parental actions that shattered childhood ideals. This is exactly what happened to Louise, who, as a small girl, believed her minister father was God-like as well as

. . . warm, helpful, supportive, responsive to my needs.

—Louise

But during adolescence, his rules and orders proved too much for Louise, who paid a high price for her defiance when she came in after curfew and her beloved father hit her—hurting Louise's body but causing much greater injury to her soul.

I was very angry and disillusioned about a father who was no longer God. He transgressed his own rule, which is you never hit anybody, you never allow a provocation to be so much that you would harm someone else, [he] preached it from the pulpit. **—Louise**

Louise left for college at age seventeen and never went back. It took another twenty-five years before she finally reconciled with her dad. Like Louise, Peggy has been angry with her father for years, but unlike Louise, they have not made up:

Approximately three years ago my mother and father got a divorce. They had been married for thirty-eight years. That was probably the most anger I have experienced in my life and the anger was toward my father. My father and I had always been real close . . . I had him . . . put upon a pedestal and I did not want to see any flaws or faults in him. The reason . . . they got a divorce was because he was having an affair. To me, my father just wasn't supposed to do that. I became angry at him for doing this . . . because a lot of my image of him was shattered. . . . he was the last male in the world that I had any confidence in and he just destroyed that.

I was angry, too, because my mother was ready to commit suicide, she was very distraught. I had to be strong for her and . . . my father was walking away from the situation, going right back to live with another woman. . . . Here he is walking from one cushy situation into another cushy situation and it was my life and my mother's life and my sister's life that were going to be greatly affected by this.

I still talk with him but . . . very infrequently. I still have anger toward him. He has since remarried and lives in a condominium and just acts like everything's wonderful. I'm angry every time I'm with him. **—Peggy**

Peggy is also angry with her mother because the divorce revealed a hidden side of her mom that Peggy finds hard to accept.

> *She's a good Christian lady and never said anything bad about anybody in her life. I had to witness a side of Mother through all this that I had never seen before. I had never heard my mother use a cuss word. She had never hated anybody before in her life until now. [Now] she hates my father and . . . I still deal with that on a daily basis—her calling him an SOB and saying that he's going out with everybody in town, just things to make herself feel better.*
>
> *But she doesn't realize what it's doing to me. It makes me angry because I think, "Why can't she just let it go and go on with her life?" I get angry with her a lot because I feel like she's just stagnant. She's determined to be miserable. She wishes she was dead . . . the day she and Daddy split up was the end of her life. She won't go places and do things. What I want to do so badly is say, "Mom, get over it. It's been three years. It's time to move on with your life." I've told her that several times but it just doesn't appear to be sinking in at all. She says, "Well, you've got your husband." Well yeah, I've got my husband, but I don't have a daddy anymore. She just doesn't seem to comprehend that. It's like, "You've got your husband and that's all you need in life." Well, that's not all I need in my life. I need a mother and father.* **—Peggy**

While many of us are angry with our fathers, our mothers, or both over a divorce, the majority of us probably had some positive, predivorce family experiences. But other women weren't so lucky. Some participants in our study described childhoods in which the affirmation and security needed for healthy development never saw the light of day and negative, hurtful messages were everywhere.

> *[My father] was an angry man. He said very hurtful things, cutting things, hitting below the belt, cheap shots, and then laughed about it later. I've always detested that. We'd go to church and put on a happy little family smile. We'd go home and he's screaming all week long, screaming and yelling and fighting.* **—Violet**

Ironically, parents who keep silent anger us as much as parents who scream and yell. Pauline had a "silent parent" in the form of a father who was never there:

My dad was never in my life. He wasn't really a dad. He wasn't around like my mother was . . . He didn't really need his children in his life unless he was drunk. Then he thought of things he wanted to tell us. That's pretty much it . . . finally, I had to get angry at him, and then I kind of got over it. **—Pauline**

Some women get over their anger at their parents, others get even angrier when they become parents themselves. For instance, women in our study frequently cited mothers who didn't help out when grandchildren came along—violating the unwritten code that says that each female generation should link arms with the next, passing along wisdom about child care and assisting in the nurturance of new lives. When this assistance isn't forthcoming, anger inevitably is.

My biggest anger that I deal with every day is my mother . . . because my mother wants to be a mother when she wants to be a mother. She wants to be a grandmother when she wants to be, on her terms only . . . If she wants us around, we can come around. If she doesn't, she doesn't want to have anything to do with us. We have friends that have parents that always keep the grandkids, want the grandkids around, do special things . . . my mom doesn't. She stinks as a grandparent . . . it'd be nice if she could pick up the phone once a week . . . call the kids and find out how they're doing . . . but she never does. She's not interested in anything they're involved in. I want her to be a mother . . . someone who's there, who calls . . . is interested in your life and . . . your kids and she's not [unless] she wants to impress somebody or she's in the mood . . . I don't say anything cause it's better to keep your mouth shut with her and accept it the way it is. **—Betsy**

Is it better to follow Betsy's example and "keep your mouth shut" or to express your anger toward your parents?

If you choose to express your angry feelings, you have lots of company because venting resentment is in vogue. Newspapers and magazines are filled with celebrities publicly bemoaning their "dysfunctional" families, not to mention those who confront their parents on sleazy, prime-time talk shows, hoping for a media mea culpa. But is it worth it? After all, angry blaming is not therapeutic, especially if you use it to define your life, as numerous patients of psychotherapist Thomas Moore do. Many of these individuals introduce themselves with a litany of mom and dad's faults and paint their self-portraits with parental blame.

> *My father drank and as a child of an alcoholic, I am prone . . .*
> **—A patient introducing herself to Thomas Moore**

Certainly this blame may seem justified if your parents were cruel and disapproving, or if they neglected you, but as an adult, do you really need—or want—to be defined by your family's dysfunction? The answer is no. After all, every family is dysfunctional to some extent or, as Moore puts it, ". . . a veritable weed patch of human foibles."

So why not mourn the past and, without negating the pain you've experienced, pull the weeds by acknowledging your family for what it is:

> *A sometimes comforting, sometimes devastating house of life and memory.* **—Thomas Moore, psychotherapist**

Along with acknowledgment, there are several other healthy ways you can clean your emotional house and release the festering anger you feel toward your parents. For example, some therapists recommend that you write them a letter. Another option is

Proactive Strategy: Holding Peace Talks

The peace talk, described in *Dr. Weisinger's Anger Work-Out Book*, by Hendrie Weisinger, is a way of getting old grievances out of your system. However, if you decide to try this method, remember that your intent is peace, not the declaration of a new war! The peace talk works like this. First, schedule a private meeting and ensure that you will not be interrupted. Tell your mother or father that the meeting is important for you and you are doing it because you care. Then express your loving feelings. Next, express your anger about the past incident or issue. Explain what you want now—a healing of the wound, an improved relationship, and peace instead of alienation and smoldering resentment. Finally, listen carefully to your parent's perception of and feelings about the incident. Don't dispute them, just listen.

The peace talk may end in hugs and reconciliation—then again, it may not. For some of us, the possibility of healing wounds inflicted by our mothers (and fathers) may be slim because

> *There are mothers living in smothering intimacy . . . who are jealous of the love and attention their daughters give to their children . . . There are daughters who'll always be four years old with their mothers . . . who, having read some child-psychology books in college, have decided that their mother never did anything right. There are distances . . . too vast . . . too unbridgeable.*
>
> **—Judith Viorst, writer**

But even if you are trying to cross a bridge too far, at the very least, you can feel good that you tried, that you honestly verbalized the feelings you've held inside so long. This takes a lot of courage. It also takes a lot of courage to accept the fact that your relationship with your parents may never change and be what you want. Mary Jo has reached this point:

> *I just said, "They're never going to be different . . . there's no point in my being angry!" At that point in time, I thought, "This anger is hurting me more than it is hurting anybody else." Now, things do feel . . . better.* **—Mary Jo**

The main reason things feel better is that Mary Jo has decided to move on with her life, and so should you.

Proactive Strategy: Don't Forgive and Forget, Forgive and Remember So You Can Move On

You can move on with your life when you unpack your emotional baggage, when you liberate yourself from the anger you've been lugging around and forgive the parents who neglected you. But be sure to unpack this luggage piece by piece. Why? Working through major pain and anger is a lifelong process and you may need to revisit some of your anger incidents several times. Fortunately, with each visit, you let go of a few more angry feelings, you lug around a little less resentment, and in so doing, open yourself to greater joy and forgiveness.

And remember, forgiveness is not the wimp's way out. It does not mean you were born to be mild or that you condone the hurtful actions of parents or others who injured you—quite the contrary. Learning to forgive takes courage. In fact, the first step in forgiveness is courageously acknowledging that you deserved better treatment than you got. Then you must make the brave, conscious decision to spurn the role of the wronged victim and choose to be the victor instead. Now victory, through forgiveness, can take many forms:

> *One deep form of forgiveness is to cease excluding the other . . . ceasing to stiff-arm, ignore, act coldly toward, patronizing and phony . . .*
> *Forgiveness is . . . when you fully let go of the prospect for personal vindication and revenge.*
> *Genuine forgiveness does not deny anger, but faces it head on.*

Going head to head with your anger means more than just thinking about forgiveness. Why? Because forgiveness is not just an idea, it's an action, and the action you need to take, according to researcher James Pennebaker, is to talk about what happened, to verbalize your forgiveness, and reach a resolution. Now this conversation does not necessarily have to be with the person who injured you. In fact, many participants in Pennebaker's studies talked to an anonymous listener or to a tape recorder. The traumas they described ranged from humiliation and beatings to sexual abuse by parents and the brutal terrors of Holocaust death camps. Although the topics varied, the research subjects all had one thing in common—none had ever verbally discussed their deepest feelings about these painful, degrading experiences.

Once they did, the floodgates opened, and the cleansing effect of talking it out produced remarkable, measurable improvements in the participants' health. Indeed, a year after the study, Pennebaker followed up and discovered that the more these individuals discussed their horrific experiences, the fewer doctor's visits and illnesses they had.

Why is talking it out and verbalizing your forgiveness toward parents and others so beneficial? Because over time, holding back your feelings requires actual physical effort that puts your body into a state of chronic stress. Talking about your painful, angry emotions can reduce this stress and improve your health, as the participants in Pennebaker's study found. Indeed, discussing the cruel treatment they received provided these individuals with closure, with a way of understanding their personal tragedies and moving beyond them. Many enlightened people do this every day when they talk to counselors, pastors, or friends, and you can too.

Besides sharing your feelings verbally, another effective way to work through your parental anger and pain is to write about them in your journal (see Chapter 3) because your journal is a journey toward peace.

Your Journal Is a Journey Toward Peace

Your journal increases your self-knowledge, it helps you reflect on who you are and who you would like to become. It is also the place to express the emotions for which you have no other outlet, especially your angry feelings toward deceased parents and anyone else who is out of sight but not out of mind. In this safe, private space, you can write whatever you want to say. You can get everything off your chest and put any hurtful chapters of your life behind.

> . . . life can hurt and . . . writing heals and then goes beyond, to make something new from the old.
> **—Suzanne Lipsett, writer**

Making something new of your relationship with your parents is a momentous event. Carol Tavris recommends that you create a "healing ritual" to mark this important occasion and honor the end of your anger. Your ritual should involve signs and symbols that are meaningful to you. For example, you might resurrect old family photos you packed away when you were mad and reframe them, compose a song about your parents, paint a family portrait, or plant a family tree, and if you experience a twinge of pride as you conduct your ritual, you should. After all, you've earned it.

10

WAYS TO IMPROVE YOUR SELF-ESTEEM

No one can make you feel inferior without your consent.
—Eleanor Roosevelt

If you have good self-esteem, you will seldom consent to feeling unnecessarily angry or bad about yourself. Why? Self-esteem is the degree to which you value yourself as a human being. It is the extent to which you see yourself as a worthy, significant individual and believe your accomplishments are meaningful. You base this evaluation on the way your parents treated you as a child and on the appraisals of other people, especially those with whom you have close relationships. If your evaluation is thumbs up, if you have high self-esteem, you are usually better equipped to meet life's problems and challenges. If you have low self-esteem, you are more likely to face verbal or physical abuse (see Chapter 26). You are also more likely to be uncertain and insecure, short on self-respect and long on anger—sometimes very long.

Anger and Self-esteem

As the Women's Anger Study discovered, the lower a woman's self-esteem, the higher her tendency to anger easily. In addition, women with low self-esteem handle their anger more inappropriately by stuffing it or lashing out at others.

Unfortunately, these anger tactics get you nowhere fast. After all, when you stuff your angry emotions instead of honestly expressing them, you usually get mad at yourself for staying silent. And if you lash out, there's often hell to pay in terms of damaged relationships, remorse, and the guilt you feel after your angry outburst. Either way, these reactions leave you feeling misunderstood, inadequate, and isolated because you've violated the laws of self-esteem.

But there is good news. You don't have to remain an emotional outlaw. You can improve your self-esteem. The bad news is that it's tougher for us women to do this than it is for men. Why? The powerful propaganda of gender role socialization (see Chapter 5) makes women more prone to this problem. In fact, a recent nationwide survey shows that one in five women report low self-esteem. In addition, despite the advances fueled by the women's movement over the last two decades, a new survey sponsored by the American Association of University Women found that today's girls still have a poorer self-image than their male counterparts. Worse yet, as girls mature, this image continues to decline. By high school, girls' self-esteem drops three times more than boys'! It's probably no coincidence that this backsliding corresponds to the years girls are under enormous pressure to be "perfect" and to gain popularity by hiding their true emotions. But sadly, perfection has a killer price tag.

As these "perfect girls" move into adulthood determined to be equally perfect wives, mothers, and professionals, they go into greater and greater emotional debt and often end up in the mental poor house. Why? Because perfection is impossible to achieve and the more we aspire to it, the more we end up gnashing our teeth and beating our breasts as we berate ourselves for the failures which surely must—and do—come.

> *I'm a perfectionist. When I do something it's one hundred and ten percent and if I don't accomplish it . . . I batter myself real bad . . . Sometimes I call myself stupid. I . . . sit and contemplate . . . "I could have done it this way, that was really dumb," [or] "I know better than that . . ."*
>
> **—Joni**

The solution is in the words *knowing better* because knowing how to treat yourself better—and then doing so—is what healthy self-esteem is all about. What's better? Feeling sure of yourself, looking and acting confident, and refusing to apologize for making reasonable requests or for stating your opinions. When you make this transformation, some people, especially other women, may give you a little (or a lot) of flak because they mistakenly interpret your healthy self-esteem as a license to be forward, pushy, mannish, or egotistical. But rest assured, a self-confident woman is not arrogant or bull-headed, nor does she does suffer from

Egotism—case of mistaken nonentity.

—Barbara Stanwyck

Indeed, such a woman knows exactly who she is and what she wants. She also knows that the negative feedback she receives will usually be from people in positions of dominance who prefer her as a submissive employee, wife, or girlfriend, or who perhaps just enjoy keeping her down.

In fact, one reason so many of us download our self-esteem is that we don't get any reinforcement from our husbands, friends, employers, or even from our work. Indeed, the nurturing work most of us do—child care, homemaking, and even our paid work outside the home, which is usually just an extension of the wife/mother role to students, patients, and customers—is undervalued and underpaid. The upshot is that because we women are devalued by others, we often devalue ourselves:

I have slighted my own value so often that it is hard to learn to take it seriously.

—Mary Catherine Bateson, anthropologist and author

It's especially hard to take our own value seriously when our life's work consists of:

Years spent scraping shit out of diapers with a kitchen knife, finding places where string beans are two cents less a pound, learning to wake at the sound of a cough, spending one's intelligence in figuring the most efficient, least time-consuming way to iron men's white shirts or to wash and wax the kitchen floor or take care of the house and kids and work at the same time . . . When your body has to deal all day with shit and string beans, your mind does too. **—Marilyn French, author**

Men can make contributions to their fields and to society that are recognized by a large impersonal public. They may be in their offices making their reputations while their wives are at home making the baby smell good. I got that message one morning about twenty-five years ago when it suddenly occurred to me that my lover was in his office writing one of the books that made him rich and famous at the very same moment I was sitting in bed writing him a love poem. In twenty-five years, would he be as dependent on me for his self-esteem as I would be on him? Hardly. So I got out of bed and went to school.

— **Elizabeth Friar Williams, therapist**

But schooling, men, money, or having the perfect body won't give you great self-esteem. Neither will fifteen minutes of fame and fortune. Indeed, no matter how sexy the external validation is, it cannot raise your perception of your own self-worth. Why? Because clichéd as it sounds, it's what's inside that counts—the belief in your own heart that you are a valuable, unique, and precious human being. And no one can give you this gift, which is why you shouldn't pin a lot of your identity on the opinions of others or on the dictates of society.

It was all exterior. I had pretty good self-esteem on the outside but didn't on the inside. I needed approval, followed society's dictates and came up empty.

— **Lynn, age forty-two, career woman with a Stanford degree**

Do you, too, come up empty when you honestly answer the question "how's your self-esteem?" Let's find out.

EXERCISE

The Self-esteem Test

This short questionnaire was developed by Morris Rosenberg in 1965. It has been used in thousands of studies of men and women of all ages, and we used it in the Women's Anger Study as well. When you finish, check your score against that of our study participants and see how you compare.

Instructions: Following is a list of statements on how you feel about yourself. Please circle the number that best corresponds to how you feel.

	STRONGLY AGREE	AGREE	DISAGREE	STRONGLY DISAGREE
1. I take a positive attitude towards myself.	4	3	2	1
2. I feel that I have a number of good qualities.	4	3	2	1
3. I wish I could have more respect for myself.	1	2	3	4
4. All in all, I am inclined to feel that I am a failure.	1	2	3	4
5. I feel that I'm a person of worth, at least on an equal basis with others.	4	3	2	1
6. I feel I do not have much to be proud of.	1	2	3	4
7. At times I think I am no good at all.	1	2	3	4
8. I am able to do things as well as most other people.	4	3	2	1
9. I certainly feel useless at times.	1	2	3	4
10. On the whole, I am satisfied with myself.	4	3	2	1

Add up your answers. The higher your score, the higher your self-esteem. The average score for women in our study who were not in psychiatric treatment was around 32. For women who were psychiatric outpatients, the average score was 28, and for women who were hospitalized in psychiatric units at the time of data collection, the average score was 25.

If you are dissatisfied with your score and would like to work toward a higher level of self-worth, here are some suggestions.

Proactive Strategies: How to Increase Your Self-esteem

1. Do some detective work to figure out how you developed your childhood view of self. Think back to childhood nicknames, interactions with your parents, and early experiences with performance evaluations, like when you brought home your report card. In addition, take a look at old photographs, talk to family members, and reflect on your past. If you were the ugly duckling or the black sheep, close up the menagerie. After all, what's done is done, and while you may have been injured, it's never too late to begin thinking, feeling, and acting differently.

2. Focus on the smart, brave things you did to make it through a childhood that was lonely or traumatic. Dr. Steven Wolin, a psychiatrist who works with the adult children of alcoholics, describes a woman who, as a little girl, had to cook the family meals because her mother was always drunk. To foster the woman's pride, Wolin asked her how, as a child, she figured out that beans go into soup? He wanted the woman to realize that as a youngster she had coped with adult responsibility and coped well. This realization allowed the woman to focus on something positive instead of just the shame and hurt she felt as a member of an alcoholic family. Remember:

Pride drives the engine of change; shame jams the gears.
—Dr. Steven Wolin

3. To help you focus on making changes for the future, try this imagery exercise. First, you need to become deeply relaxed. Find a quiet place, unplug the phone, dim the lights, and sit in a comfortable position. Now close your eyes. Concentrate on your breathing, counting *one* each time you exhale. Imagine that your body is empty and each breath fills it completely. Disown your tension. Smooth out any tight muscles.

When you're ready, become aware of the fact that you are not alone. With you is a wise old woman who cares deeply about your well-being and who is totally trustworthy. In whatever way works best for you—thinking quietly, talking aloud, singing, etc.—make contact with her. Feel her love and knowledge surrounding you. Ask your wise guide anything you wish, such as "What do I need to do to feel better about myself?" Hear her out and keep an open attitude toward her advice.

When your imagery is finished, pause and reflect. What did your wise woman recommend? Are you aware that she is a part of you? That her wisdom and advice are coming from deep inside your soul? And yes, we all have this depth, this ability to know our own true natures and our purpose in life. Some people call it the Center. Carl Jung called it the Self. Here we call it the wise old woman, and if it helps, you can picture her in the context of your religious beliefs. However you see her, the important thing is to gain access to your own inner wisdom and to benefit from its guidance.

4. Expand your sources of self-esteem. Some women fish in too small a pond, seeking validation from only one or two people or maybe just their husbands. The result is that the criticism of this gang of one (or two) becomes extremely powerful. To stay in balance, you need to find time to be with friends, friends who appreciate and enjoy your company and accept you just as you are. You might also benefit from a support group where members validate and support each other.

5. Learn to validate yourself through affirmations and positive self-talk. Do a 180 on the Golden Rule by "doing unto yourself as you do unto others." For example, if it's easy for you to praise and encourage your family, friends, and co-workers, try turning a little of that sunshine on yourself. In addition, give yourself credit for your strengths instead of always focusing on your flaws and shortcomings. Researchers have found that when we women succeed at something, we call it luck, but when we fail, we blame ourselves and say we're stupid. By contrast, when most men succeed they give themselves credit (and a lot of it). When they fail, they blame someone else—and anyone will do. To combat this negativity, banish put-downs ("I'm such a klutz," "What an idiot I am," "I never do anything right," "The credit belongs to everyone else on the project, not me") from your vocabulary. Instead, replace these esteem bangers with positive statements like "I am making progress," "I'm doing things I never thought I could do," "I am giving it my best shot," "I am competent," "I am valuable." Write these affirmations on index cards and post them in prominent places such as on your bathroom mirror, refrigerator, desk, or car dashboard, and then read them aloud every day.

6. Become a risk taker. Do something you have always feared like skiing, public speaking, or going back to school. Make a contract with yourself to stick with it for at least six months and even if you don't get straight A's or become an expert at whatever it is, at least give yourself credit for having the courage to try. This courage, along with the experience and any new success you gain, can give your self-esteem a tremendous boost.

Now, if you try these strategies and still find it extremely hard to affirm your good qualities or even to find one single good thing about yourself, you might be suffering from depression, but don't let this make you feel worse! Depression, like low self-esteem, is a call to emotional arms. It's a situation you can do something about, and your first action consists of nothing more difficult than turning the page . . .

11

THE ANGER/DEPRESSION
CONNECTION

*If depression is creeping up and must be faced, learn
something about the nature of the beast: You may escape
without a mauling.* **—Dr. R.W. Shepherd**

When you suffer from beastly, no-light-at-the-end-of-the-
tunnel vision, you may be experiencing more than low self-
esteem, you might be depressed. Depression is a paralyzing
and occasionally psychotic mood disorder that strikes fifteen
million Americans each year. Unfortunately, it afflicts twice
as many women as men, and we're not just talking about
"the blues" or "the blahs" that are part of everyday living. No,
depression means you've lost pleasure in things you used to
enjoy, that your sleeping and eating patterns are disrupted,
that you're minus energy, can't concentrate, feel worthless
and sad. You also feel mad.

*I used to be full of energy and wanted to do things . . .
now . . . I don't want to get up in the mornings . . . It's like
I have no interest whatsoever. [It's] not only dealing with
anger in your home but . . . at work when your job's not
going well. So you're getting bombarded from both directions. I've gotten where I just . . . don't care. Sometimes I
eat, sometimes I don't eat. It's kind of like some days I'll
eat everything in sight, but then other days I'm nauseated.*
—Martine

While you might feel nauseated and uninterested in food, your depression works up a voracious appetite and consumes the meat off your mental bones. This can happen regardless of your race, income, education, or occupational level. Indeed, high-achieving women in senior management positions get just as depressed as assembly line workers do. In fact, one fourth of all women have a depressive disorder at some point in their lives. Unfortunately, many of these disorders are never diagnosed or treated. Why? Health care providers often fail to recognize the problem and so do we. When we complain about feeling tired all the time, doctors say we're just "run down" and need more rest. Indeed, doctors say this so often that women's depression is misdiagnosed a whopping 30 to 50 percent of the time—a national disgrace when you consider that we've known the symptoms since the days of Hippocrates.

What we don't know is why more women get depressed than men, but there are theories galore including our alleged "pathologic dependency" (translation: we get sad when relationships fail); our increased risk of sexual, physical, and verbal abuse; our tendency to brood about negative events rather than take action; our status as unhappy wives and overburdened mothers (see Parts Seven and Eight); not to mention the ever-popular chemical changes/raging hormones hypothesis.

As yet, there is no consensus in the scientific community as to which—if any—of these theories are correct, with the exception of the clear proof that chemical changes actually exist and may impact us. But that still leaves us with the chicken-and-egg question about which comes first, the depression or the alterations in brain chemistry. And even if we don't know this answer for sure, there is one answer we are sure about. We now know that the old view of depression as a response to loss is not 100 percent correct because in some cases of depression, there is no loss. Likewise, not everyone who suffers a loss gets depressed. Obviously, researchers still have a long way to go to find some answers. Unfortunately, while they look, we women continue to suffer in large numbers, especially when we wrestle with:

The Anger/Depression Connection

Anger plus depression is a combination that puts women low on the mood chain—really low—and researchers have been trying to figure out the connection for a long time. What's to figure? First, there's the large body of evidence that says denying or suppressing anger leads to depression. Then there's the equally large body of evidence that says expressing anger (especially in harsh, confrontive ways) also leads to depression. Still more studies show that depressed individuals have higher inward and outward hostility. Who's right? Only time will tell, but clearly, the anger/depression connection is far more complicated than the widely held depression-is-just-anger-turned-inward theory suggests.

The Women's Anger Study and several other studies have found that depressed women definitely have greater levels of anger than women who are not depressed. In other words, the more depressed a woman is, the angrier she is, as shown by higher scores on tests of general anger proneness like the one you took in Part Two, and as some women, such as Joyce, have discovered through counseling.

> *Through counseling I've learned that I handle depression through being angry . . . I would lash out at everything and really didn't know why . . . I had all this anger to work through and to understand. I probably developed [it] early in my relationship with my ex-husband and just carried [it] through and it got worse and worse. It . . . [still] hasn't been resolved . . . Twenty-plus years . . . and it turns into depression.* —**Joyce**

Like Joyce, some of us who are depressed and angry tend to lash out. We also use other ineffective anger management techniques including suppression, blaming, attacking, and expressing our anger through physical symptoms like headaches. But as we've discussed, these approaches are double-edged swords that cut deep. In fact, researcher Dana Jack says that in depressed married women these swords cut so deep they actually produce "divided selves." In other words, outwardly, we're sugar and spice, everything nice, and totally focused on pleasing our mates (which eliminates any chance of external anger expression)—but inside, the story's not so sweet.

Inside we may be angry and resentful because we're unfulfilled and our needs for true intimacy are not being met (despite the voluntary self-sacrifices that have us headed for sainthood). This pressure gradually builds up until our emotions go molten and we erupt. After the eruption, guilt and self-blame set in along with a renewed determination to work harder at pleasing our spouses and silencing ourselves.

But we aren't totally silent. In our heads is that constant, nagging negative voice—the voice that's preoccupied with self-critical thoughts, the voice that we use to beat ourselves up over failures and rehash our sadness, fatigue, isolation, and incompetence, not to mention our lack of interest in the world. It's the voice that keeps us up at night:

> *I mill stuff over in my mind all night long . . . "Why didn't I do this?" and "Why did I do that?" and "Why are they doing this?" and "Who do they think they are?" . . . So when you get up the next morning it's like your head's pounding . . . you've got dark circles underneath your eyes and you're going "My God, I'd have been better off just staying up."*
> **—Margo**

When you're mentally exhausted, when your dark circles lasso your chin, and you're depressed big time, your distorted thoughts and perceptions ("No one cares about me," "I've messed up everything," "Life's a bitch") can fuel more anger—at yourself and everyone else. Likewise, if you handle your anger poorly and stoke the fire by brooding, that anger will spawn irrational thoughts and a faulty, potentially dangerous view of reality.

> *I was hospitalized for depression. It made me aware of how much anger was there and it terrified me. I just thought, man, there's no way I'm going to ever deal with all these things and if, if it gets out and out of control it could really hurt somebody, almost to the extent of maybe killing somebody . . . I don't know if that was a logical or illogical fear, but that was a fear . . . I had. Man, I could just do like those people that get up in a bell tower and start taking shots at people. I was in counseling for about five years, dealt with a lot of issues and . . . resolved a lot of anger.*
> **—Violetta**

If you're not sure whether your anger and depression are resolved—if you're feeling down but can't tell if you're out— take the test on the following two pages for an indication of whether you're depressed enough to need professional help.

Add up all the points. If your score is 8 to 9, you are comparable to other "average" women. If your score is 10 to 15, you have some symptoms that indicate mild depression, and even mild depression may affect your ability to function at work or to fulfill your family responsibilities. Researchers have also found that one fourth of all women who have several depressive symptoms will progress to a full-blown depressive episode within a year or two. If this applies to you, you may want to take preventive action now by following the self-help suggestions coming up in this chapter. If your score is 16 or greater, you need to contact your primary health care provider or mental health center. Finally, if you frequently think that you would be better off dead or if you have a suicide plan, you may need to be hospitalized. But don't despair.

EXERCISE

The Depression Test (CES-D Scale of Depression)

Instructions: Following is a list of some ways you might have felt or behaved. Please indicate how often you felt this way during the past week by putting an X in the appropriate box.

During the past week:	Rarely or none of the time (Less than 1 day)	Some or a little of the time (1–2 days)	Occasionally or a moderate amount of the time (3–4 days)	Most or all of the time (5–7 days)
1. I was bothered by things that usually don't bother me.				
2. I did not feel like eating; my appetite was poor.				
3. I felt that I could not shake off the blues even with help from my family and friends.				
4. I felt that I was just as good as other people.				
5. I had trouble keeping my mind on what I was doing.				
6. I felt depressed.				
7. I felt that everything I did was an effort.				
8. I felt hopeful about the future.				
9. I thought my life had been a failure.				
10. I felt fearful.				
11. My sleep was restless.				
12. I was happy.				
13. I talked less than usual.				
14. I felt lonely.				
15. People were unfriendly.				
16. I enjoyed life.				
17. I had crying spells.				
18. I felt sad.				
19. I felt that people disliked me.				
20. I could not "get going."				

Instructions for Scoring: After completing the test, use the following chart to assign points to your answers.

During the past week:	Rarely or none of the time (Less than 1 day)	Some or a little of the time (1–2 days)	Occasionally or a moderate amount of the time (3–4 days)	Most or all of the time (5–7 days)
1. I was bothered by things that usually don't bother me.	0	1	2	3
2. I did not feel like eating; my appetite was poor.	0	1	2	3
3. I felt that I could not shake off the blues even with help from my family and friends.	0	1	2	3
4. I felt that I was just as good as other people.	3	2	1	0
5. I had trouble keeping my mind on what I was doing.	0	1	2	3
6. I felt depressed.	0	1	2	3
7. I felt that everything I did was an effort.	0	1	2	3
8. I felt hopeful about the future.	3	2	1	0
9. I thought my life had been a failure.	0	1	2	3
10. I felt fearful.	0	1	2	3
11. My sleep was restless.	0	1	2	3
12. I was happy.	3	2	1	0
13. I talked less than usual.	0	1	2	3
14. I felt lonely.	0	1	2	3
15. People were unfriendly.	0	1	2	3
16. I enjoyed life.	3	2	1	0
17. I had crying spells.	0	1	2	3
18. I felt sad.	0	1	2	3
19. I felt that people disliked me.	0	1	2	3
20. I could not "get going."	0	1	2	3

There is effective treatment for depression including psychotherapy, antidepressant medication, or a combination of the two—with this caveat. We are concerned about the current trend of relying *solely* on medication—especially when the patient is female. In fact, nearly 70 percent of all antidepressant prescriptions are given to women, forcing us (and others) to ask "what's wrong with this picture?"

> *The whole imposing edifice of modern medicine is . . . like the celebrated Tower of Pisa, slightly off balance. It is frightening how dependent on drugs we are all becoming and how easy it is for doctors to prescribe them as the universal panacea for our ills.* **—Prince Charles**

Obviously, drugs alone are not the answer for everything that ails us. While Prozac and Zoloft are life-saving medications for many women, women who do not receive therapy in addition to these drugs may still be depressed or may relapse into unhealthy symptoms. The problem is compounded if the drugs have side effects or if there are clear contraindications to their use such as for women who are pregnant, trying to become pregnant, or nursing. Most frightening of all, in a society so dependent on medication, these drugs are often the weapon of choice when people try to kill themselves. In fact, antidepressant medications are the most commonly used substances in suicides where the victim overdoses.

Thankfully, there are plenty of positive, non-drug-related things you can do to help yourself out of depression whether or not you're undergoing therapy and/or using medication. Sure, it's hard to imagine the gloom, doom, and mental paralysis lifting, but women we know who try these strategies swear by their effectiveness, and many of the ideas will work for you, too.

Proactive Strategies: Self-help Steps to Take When You're Depressed

1. First, acknowledge that your thinking is distorted and you're being too tough on yourself. You are not inept, unlovable, or a complete failure. If the critical voice inside your head continues to harass you, shut it off. Another way you can counteract it is to keep a "positive-feedback log." Therapist Harriet Braiker describes this as a daily journal in which you record all the positive things you've done and all the complimentary remarks people make to you. You should also list the activities you always do well, the things that require skill and effort but which you take for granted, like cooking a delicious dinner, making your child laugh, or showing kindness to strangers. The log is important because when you're depressed, you develop the aforementioned no-light-at-the-end-of-the-tunnel-vision. You focus only on the negative events in your life and on your own "rotten" personal characteristics. The log can help you alter your perspective and see things in a clearer, more positive light.

2. Put more cherries in the bowl of life, especially if you're "in the pits!" If you're like many depressed people, you give up almost all your enjoyable hobbies and pleasurable activities as you sink deeper into depression. For example, you decline invitations because you don't want to be "bad company." You believe you don't deserve to have any fun or claim you just don't have the energy to get up and go. If this is the case, ask your spouse or a friend to help you select some simple, enjoyable things to do. Ask them to make the plans or arrangements and to go with you the first few times you resume these activities. What should you do? Try a short walk in the park, attend a concert, visit relatives whose company you enjoy, or practice some retail therapy by going on a shopping excursion during which you must buy at least one small luxury item or service for yourself—and it doesn't have to be expensive. Try a massage, manicure, hard cover book, a package of gourmet coffee or tea, a cake of milky, custom-blended soap, or whatever is luxurious to you.

3. Stop chewing your cud! Milk cows and other animals regurgitate food from their first stomachs back into their mouths to be chewed again and again. Does it sound revolting? You bet! Yet some of us engage in a similar activity. Whether you're cruising the interstate or cruising the produce aisle of the supermarket, you might be chewing and chewing your cud of undigested, unresolved emotional issues. You keep bringing up that angry incident at work, that tiff with the kids, or that nasty insult from your neighbor down the street. This can go on ad nauseam as it does for

Margo, who "mills stuff over all night long." The problem is that every time you relive the violation, anger, and hurt feelings, you increase your depression—and women tend to do this more than men.

Research shows that when women are depressed, we cut down on our activities and dwell on our sadness. By contrast, when men are depressed, they distract themselves from their bleak mood by doing something they enjoy or thinking about other things. In addition, men increase their physical activity, and we recommend that you do the same. Exercise (see Chapter 18) is a great way to prevent or eliminate depression—just remember not to chew your cud while jogging around the track because that defeats the purpose! Besides, you could choke!

4. Accept your loss and let it go. If your depression is due to a loss you haven't gotten over—whether it's the loss of a spouse, a job, or even a beloved pet—give yourself the space you need to grieve and work things through. Then, relinquish the idea that you can never be happy again without that lost person, object, or position.

Psychiatrists Silvano Arieti and Jules Bemporad say depressed people often devote their lives to pleasing the "dominant other"—a specific person (husband, mother, sibling, child) whose love is considered vital for happiness. When this indispensable person is lost through death or divorce, you feel helpless and you suffer.

> We are never so . . . helplessly unhappy as when we have lost our loved object or its love.   **—Sigmund Freud**

The lost loved object, or dominant other, can also be a goal that bites the dust; like not becoming a great actor, or some other objective toward which you've devoted your life energy. Although Arieti and Bemporad say depressed women are more likely to have lost the dominant other and depressed men are more likely to have lost the dominant goal, this gender difference may not be so pronounced now that we women have ambitious career goals too. Either way, these losses can cause extreme depression.

However, it's important to remember that mourning your loss and being depressed are not the same thing. After all, "shit happens." We all lose parents, friends, jobs, our youth, our innocence, and more. For each one of these episodes we mourn or do sorrow work, and when we give ourselves permission to cry and rage, we hasten our recoveries. Unfortunately, you can't recover fully unless you go through the guilt, anger, and despair your loss provokes. This rite of passage is the only way you can reach acceptance and internalize the people or goals that've slipped away. When you don't go through the mourning process, you get depressed. Indeed, depression is often the result of incomplete mourning, and it's harder to resolve the mourning if you've had a complicated love-hate relationship with the lost person. In addition, leftover sadness from earlier losses can make things worse. If these sound like the factors in your depression, you will benefit from professional help and we encourage you to seek counseling.

5. Stop blaming yourself for the losses you've suffered. ("It's all my fault. I should have been a better, more perfect wife. He wouldn't have turned to another woman if I had—lost that weight, bought sexier nighties, made eggs Benedict every Sunday," you fill in the blank.) Instead of self-flagellation, try putting your anger where it belongs and mobilize it at the other person. After all, it takes two to tangle, and being angry endows you with a sense of strength and power. In addition, anger feels a lot better than self-punishment, so instead of ragging on yourself, try something like this: "He left me because he's trying to be twenty years old again, not because of anything that's wrong with me—the lousy SOB!" Then make the most of any opportunities to vent your anger in an effective, outward way. Verbalize your emotions and be assertive so you can feel good about yourself and let go of any guilt or self-blame. You can also help your cause along if you review the pointers about assertive speech and body language in Chapter 6.

6. Let your generosity know no bounds, in other words, commit to something bigger than yourself like a project to help others. Martin Seligman believes the increasing rate of depression in the United States—especially among the baby boomers—has something to do with our selfish individualism. He contends that trendy ennui, cynicism, and disillusionment about church, nation, and family have left us relying on

> . . . *a very small and frail unit indeed: the self.*
> **—Martin Seligman, psychologist**

Unfortunately, when we can't depend on anything but ourselves, our personal failures get blown way out of proportion and we feel hopeless and depressed. The best way to alleviate this is to help someone else, then our own problems don't look so bad by comparison. And yes, if you're thinking this advice applies more to men than women, you might be right. As we discussed, most of us are already so busy taking care of others that we barely have time to take care of ourselves! If this is your situation, just remember that balance is the name of the game.

7. Don't look through the glass darkly. When you're depressed, you're wearing sunglasses at night. In other words, you view everything in shades of pessimism and negativity, like this:

> *One woman patient went to a movie and felt very depressed afterward . . . she said, "Oh, it was such a terrible movie . . . I saw myself in it . . . it made me very unhappy." So I suggested to this patient: "Next time . . . see a happy movie." She went to see a very upbeat movie and then . . . came to see me: "Oh, I'm so depressed" . . . she said. "I went to see this . . . very happy movie and I saw how wonderful life could be. It was so different from my life that I left feeling more depressed than ever!"*
> **—Silvano Arieti, psychiatrist**

The moral of Arieti's story? Take off the dark glasses and gradually develop a more optimistic mental outlook—and yes, it will take time. Don't expect to "snap out" of a depression, or blame yourself if you can't recover quickly. One thing you will need to do to get back on your feet is give up your distinguished career as a pessimist. You do this by replacing your negativity with positive, proactive ideas. Dr. Norman Vincent Peale called this the power of positive thinking, and he said if you change your thoughts, you can change anything. To displace destructive fears and emotions, Peale suggested using "thought conditioners," such as

Renew a right spirit within me. **—Psalms 51:10**

Martin Seligman recommends something similar. Seligman says we need to practice "learned optimism," that is, we need to expect good things to happen to us. But no matter what you call it, "learned optimism" and the "power of positive thinking" both take some effort and we have to teach ourselves to employ these skills. To a great extent, our success with these methods depends on:

> *The ability and opportunity to focus our attention, to choose what we will pay attention to . . . Emotions . . . do not, or need not, simply wash over us. We can have a certain control over them by modifying the beliefs we hold. Through selective focusing of attention and shaping the response, we mold our emotional lives.*
>
> **—Robert Nozick, philosopher**

Ironically, you can emerge from the depression mold in better shape than you went in. How so? Psychoanalyst Emmy Gut believes depression can serve an important adaptive purpose because it compels us to clear emotional logjams and leads to new learning and growth. We can actually become more psychologically whole when we've conquered self-defeating thoughts and negativity. In addition, claiming victory over depression allows us to face life with renewed commitment, inspiration, and courage—and it takes courage to be a potato in the cellar.

A Potato in the Cellar

When therapist Carl Rogers was a boy, his family stored potatoes in the cellar. Toward one tiny, high window, the spindly sprouts would strain to reach the light. Rogers saw many of his patients this way—in a dark cellar of fear, sadness, and self-loathing, they were straining to grow and become enlightened. The rest of us are trying to do the same thing and it helps to know we're not alone. Nobody has it easy. As the generous, caring women in our study have demonstrated, everyone experiences loneliness, failure, shame, loss, betrayal, and periods of darkness and confusion. Likewise, every family is "dysfunctional," every person is a bit "neurotic," and we are all eventually broken by life, but because

of this, we have the potential to become enlightened, to gain
wisdom and awareness, and to grow magnificently strong—
like Camille. Camille is now a minister, but she went through
her own personal purgatory and hell when she realized she'd
been sexually abused as a child:

> *I totally suppressed it . . . for years. The way I remem-
> bered . . . was, I was doing a research paper on rape. Al-
> though I hadn't been raped, I'd been feeling a lot of these
> things that these women were feeling and I thought,
> "That sounds like me." After I read what rape was, in the
> same article they talked about abuse of children and sex-
> ual abuse and it was like bing! It opened a floodgate of
> memories . . . and these images started coming back to
> me . . . I just thought, "Oh my God, that happened to me."
> I wouldn't tell anybody for a long time after that, but the
> memories just got so overwhelming that it turned into se-
> vere depression . . . I had to be hospitalized.*
>
> *I was so depressed that I just couldn't hardly think
> logically. I was . . . very, very suicidal. I actually attempted
> taking a lot of pills at one point and played Russian rou-
> lette with a gun at another point—just daring God to let
> that bullet be in the chamber . . . I remember one day
> before I went into the hospital I just cried out, "God, I
> need you . . . I need you because I have no hope in my
> life"—and nothing. I just thought, "Maybe there is no
> God," and it was the most unsettling . . . lost and lonely
> feeling I've ever experienced. I went to bed thinking that
> night, "God doesn't care . . . doesn't even know I exist."
> Shortly after that I went into the hospital and I was real
> angry with God. I just thought, "You did not hear me in
> my deepest heartfelt cry that I could ever give to you. You
> did not hear me."*
>
> *I was in a pottery class—one of the things they do
> when you're in the hospital is keep you busy—and I had
> this vase that I was going to make my mom . . . it was
> greenware still and . . . real fragile. So I'm sitting there
> trying to clean it and get all the rough edges off . . . It had
> a rim on the top and I'm working real carefully around
> that rim and I pressed too hard and it broke. I was so
> angry . . . I just wanted to take it and throw it up against
> the wall . . . I . . . thought, "You know, this is just like my
> life. I can't do my life right, I can't even do this vase right,
> it's all screwed up, it's broken, it's useless, I might as well
> just throw it away." I just sat there and put my head down*

and thought, "Why am I even trying this? I'm not a usable vessel anymore." The thought came into my head then, "Well why don't you break the rest of that rim off and smooth it out and make it into a new vessel?" So I started breaking it off and it was painful . . . I mean it was stress on the vessel just like it would be on my life trying to break the pieces off and make it . . . new—and I broke it off and started smoothing it out. I worked on that and worked on it and worked on it.

By the time I'd finished and smoothed it all out, I made it into a totally different-looking vessel, although the main bulk of it was still the same shape. I painted it and fired it and I went to the chapel right after that and the preacher talked about the potter and the clay. I just thought, "God, here you are again! . . . You just showed me an illustration where I was broken and you made me into a new vessel and I know that vessel's not perfect, I'm not perfect. It still has some cracks in it. I have cracks in me but I'm still usable. It's not hopeless." It was from that point that I began to know God was there and He was working and He could reshape me.

I went to church several months later to share my testimony and brought the vase with some flowers in it. I said, "It's a usable vase and it's beautiful. You wouldn't know what this vase has been through unless you get real close and . . . look at those cracks and scars that are on the rim . . ." After church a little kid came up to me and said, "That's a beautiful vase." I just thought, "Thank you, God, cause you've given me a beautiful life. There's still hope in my life and I still can be used." I was about twenty-one, twenty-two . . . when I went through that ordeal, but it's been a constant healing since then.

—Camille, minister

And a constant learning process—although some of the lessons never make true sense. We often can't comprehend why bad things happen to good people including us and those we love ("Why Mary? Why leukemia?" or "If a random victim could be anyone, why couldn't this happen to someone else?"). But that's when we must remember:

The greatest and most important problems of life are all fundamentally insoluble. They can never be solved but only outgrown. **—Carl Jung**

And with this growth comes peace, resilience, and coherence. Eventually, instead of handicapping our tragedies, we find the native granite in our characters that allows us to manage in the midst of chaos and stress. We learn to take life as it comes, stop blaming others, and forget feeling like we've been screwed. As we get beyond our anger, pain, and blame, we become masters at going with the flow:

> *A rushing stream of water flows around the obstacles that stand in its way. It doesn't stop to dwell on the injuries sustained by a projecting rock or a submerged log. It keeps moving toward its goal, encountering each difficulty as it appears, responding actively, then moving along downstream . . . It washes away its own wounds in its present purposefulness. The water bears no scars.*
>
> **—David Reynolds, *Water Bears No Scars***

And eventually, neither will you.

PART FIVE

ANGER AND YOUR PHYSICAL HEALTH

12

ANGER'S IMPACT ON PHYSICAL HEALTH

In the beginning of my work, I matter-of-factly presumed that emotions were in the head or the brain. Now I would say they are really in the body and are part of the body. I can no longer make a strong distinction between the brain and the body. —**Candace Pert, researcher**

What changed this researcher's mind, as well as the minds of other medical professionals and assorted doubting Thomas physicians? The amazing discoveries of the past two decades that show that the central nervous system (home of all thoughts and emotions), the endocrine system (site of hormone production), and the immune system (source of defense against disease) are all interconnected. In other words, these systems "talk" to each other. And what do they say? That emotions are the response of the whole person and they are expressed throughout the "bodymind."

The same can be said of disease. Disease results from the potent combination of genetic, emotional, and behavioral factors, and their interrelationship with the endocrine, nervous, and immune systems. This interrelationship is the focus of behavioral medicine, a new branch of the medical arts that studies the emotional and behavioral factors contributing to disease and disease prevention. And what has behavioral medicine taught us so far? That anger is a key component of "disease prone personalities"—or maybe we should say "dis-ease."

Those of us who are filled with excessive, unsettled anger may be vulnerable to a wide range of illnesses in which anger is identified as a contributing factor (along with a host of genetic, environmental, and biological causes). The good news is that angry thoughts and behaviors can be changed and, hopefully, this means disease can be modified too, and maybe more than modified. If we learn to handle anger, perhaps we can heal the whole person, the person who is more than the sum of our genes, our spleens, and our self-esteem.

But before we can heal our spleens or any other body part, we have to understand how anger and hostility relate to physical ill health. The first thing to note is this: Highly hostile people have more frequent, extreme anger outbursts and these are accompanied by exaggerated reactions in their cardiovascular, nervous, and endocrine systems. In addition, their anger lasts longer because they tend to dwell on whatever set them off. Eventually, all this hyperreactivity just wears their bodies out and wears their immunity down—or so the theory goes. Other scientists blame the relationship between anger and ill health on the high stress in angry people's lives or on the social support they don't receive—ideas that seem tailor-made for us women.

Unfortunately, while the ideas seem tailor-made for us, much of the research behind the ideas is not. Why? In many of these studies, anger is equated with physiological arousal tracked during straight-from-the-B-movies laboratory experiments, or it's confused with hostility and aggression (see

Chapter 2). But such research fails to consider the meaning and significance of the anger provocation for each individual, particularly if that individual is female—and in the past this wasn't often the case.

Over the years, the majority of anger researchers were men housed in predominantly male medical schools and assorted ivory towers, men who were content to study themselves (or those just like them), and until recently, the National Institutes of Health and other deep-pockets agencies allowed them to do just that. As a result, there are gaps the size of a small planet in our knowledge of anger and women's health. And anger research isn't the only place where women have been ignored. We have been omitted from almost every major study of heart disease, high blood pressure, aging, and even—unbelievably—early studies on breast cancer.

> *I was stunned when I learned that early clinical trials on breast cancer were done on men. That had to be a bad joke.* **—Hillary Rodham Clinton**

It's all quite a scam—especially when you consider that we women spend two of every three health care dollars in the United States while the bulk of all research money goes to study male diseases! Indeed, as late as 1990, the NIH allocated only 13 percent of its $7.7 billion budget to female health issues, and up until a very few years ago had just three gynecologists—and thirty-nine veterinarians—on staff.

And has the situation improved today? Have the NIH and other researchers learned to jog a mile in our aerobic cross-trainers and give women's health its due? Not exactly. Despite the establishment (in 1991) of an Office on Women's Health in the Public Health Service and the growing pressure from the NIH to include females in any studies it funds, every week our professional journals feature research reports based on predominantly or exclusively male samples. But you don't need to read *The New England Journal of Medicine* to see that this is so. Just pick up your morning paper. There you'll find reports on any number of health issues and buried deep in the body copy, usually in the last paragraph, the reporter casually mentions that the study was conducted on men only—even if the subject matter is equally important to women. It's enough to make your blood run cold—and that might not get studied either . . .

For all these reasons, and because the majority of the Women's Anger Study research team are nurses, the link between anger and health was a big impetus behind our work. So were our clients—the women who needed health-wise methods of managing their angry emotions. Through our study results and through current research by other investigators, we discovered methods to meet their needs—and yours—and those methods start with an honest answer to this question: Are your physical reactions to anger so strong that you secretly worry "If I burn out my body, where will I live?"

If the answer is yes, if your lifestyle is filled with bad habits and/or high-risk activities that get worse when you're mad, then your anger is impacting your health in the most heartfelt sense of the term . . .

13

ANGER AND HEART DISEASE

I got so mad at my grandson that I told him he was going to give me a heart attack! Little did I know it was true!
—Annabelle, age seventy

Heart disease is the number one killer of both women and men, but that's where the similarity ends. Why? Women have heart attacks later in life, and afterward, we don't fare as well as men do. In addition, we are twice as likely to die soon after an attack or coronary bypass surgery. The reasons why are unclear—perhaps because the overwhelming majority of heart studies were done on men. Nonetheless, we have learned a few things from research about the link between anger and heart disease.

For starters, doctors noticed that heart patients had certain behaviors in common. First, these patients were so impatient they literally wore out the upholstery on waiting room chairs as they perched on the edges of their seats. They were also overtly hostile, aggressive, ambitious, and competitive. In an attempt to connect the dots between these behaviors (christened Type A) and coronary heart disease, researchers conducted a longitudinal study of healthy people with the same characteristics to see if they developed the condition, and bingo! They did. In fact, the Type A men (all the research subjects were men) were twice as likely to develop heart disease as the Type B's—the men who did not have an angry, competitive style of behavior. The study also found that Type A behavior increased the men's cardiac risk independently of other known risk factors. The bottom line? Out of all the men who died from coronary heart disease during this first landmark study, 88 percent were Type A's—and in the twenty years since this study took place, the *A* has come to stand for aggressive.

Aggressive, hostile behavior remains the most consistent predictor of coronary risk, and you'll recognize these high-risk people when you see them. They're cynical and suspicious; they believe all's-ill-with-the-world and that others are out to get them. To make matters worse, these individuals are convinced of their own superiority and the "rightness" of their judgments against fellow human beings. While there are hostile women, most of these charm school dropouts are men. In fact, national studies consistently show that men outscore women of all ages on hostility tests, but if you were to ask them about it, the majority would respond "Say what!?"

Indeed, many of these men just don't see the extent of their hostility—but their spouses do. In one study, spouses accurately identified their partners' hostility levels, and these assessments were extremely useful for predicting the status of cardiac disease. There was one interesting difference though. Female spouses consistently rated their cardiac patient husbands as more hostile than the male spouses rated their cardiac patient wives.

This may explain why a full-blown heart attack is often the first symptom men with coronary heart disease experience. By contrast, most women suffer chest pain (angina) first and all too often arrive at the emergency room only to be told take-two-aspirin-and-don't-call-in-the-morning. Why? Studies have found that doctors are twice as likely to attribute women's cardiac symptoms to psychiatric causes as men's.

Perhaps the diagnoses of women with chest pain would be more accurate if physicians asked about our anger. Indeed, researchers have found that there is a direct correlation between chest pain and anger in heart patients. This is why: When anger reaches an intense level, the coronary arteries—

already narrowed by atherosclerotic plaque—constrict even more. Blood can't get through and WHAM! Chest pain results. Unfortunately, more women are experiencing this whammy than ever before. A recent study in Oregon showed that the incidence of angina pectoris in women has increased 69 percent over the past fifteen years compared to a 31 percent increase for men.

Maybe the increase is due to women's rising levels of stress and anger—and maybe not. After all, just feeling angry does not seem to zap the cardiovascular system—you have to be hostile too. Psychologist Ed Suarez has discovered that in hostile people, anger actually causes dangerous increases in blood pressure, muscle blood flow, and stress hormones. By comparison, in those with low hostility, anger does not necessarily contribute to an increased risk of heart disease. Suarez made this determination based on experiments with an obnoxious lab assistant. The assistant intentionally harassed research subjects until they became angry, and the highly hostile subjects didn't just get angry, they went ballistic. So did their blood pressure and other physical symptoms, all of which were being monitored. But this was not the case with the less hostile subjects.

The less hostile people interpreted the situation differently. They did not mistrust the lab assistant or expect unfair treatment the way their more hostile counterparts did. Indeed, many of them merely overlooked the assistant's behavior or considered it a trivial irritation—certainly nothing to make a big deal about. The lesson is this: Making a big deal of your anger and expressing it in a highly antagonistic, outward way may strongly increase your odds for cardiovascular hyperresponsivity.

By contrast, it seems a little less chancy to have angry feelings, speak softly and carry a big stick. What's the difference? Current research evidence says it's not your angry feelings but rather your level of hostility and style of anger expression that determine if you have an increased cardiac risk. So if you want to save your heart, the fire and brimstone approach is not the way to go, and you'll hear this advice again. In Chapter 23 we explain why you need to turn down the volume during marital spats so you can be more effective, and in Chapter 28 we suggest that you stop yelling at the kids because it scares them and they tune you out. But now there's an even more potent reason not to vent your angry feelings in a loud, ferocious, man-woman-and-child-eating way—it could destroy your heart.

Consider this: Studies show that women's risk of heart disease directly correlates with high levels of conflict in our personal lives and with a tendency to express our anger outwardly toward people and objects in the environment. The risk is also affected by our volume. To wit, researcher Aron Siegman conducted experiments in which subjects talked about anger-arousing events in one of three ways: "fast and loud," "slow and soft," or "normally." Siegman's team found that speaking about events fast and loud not only caused greater increases in blood pressure and heart rates, but could actually push these stats into the danger zone. In addition, study participants felt even angrier when they spoke in a rapid, earsplitting style compared to a slow and soft or normal tone of voice. To counter this, Siegman trained his subjects to talk "slowly and softly." As a result, their anger dropped dramatically and so did all their cardiovascular elevations. The same thing happens when you make an assertive response to anger because assertiveness (see Chapter 6) significantly decreases diastolic blood pressure.

But what goes up—blood pressure, heart rates, and the risk of coronary disease—will only come down if you talk about your anger calmly and rationally. In fact, your chance of heart disease actually increases if you don't show your anger or if you refuse to discuss it. And this silence can be deadly.

An eighteen-year, Tecumseh, Michigan, study, found that women who suppressed their anger were twice as likely to die of cardiovascular disease, cancer, and all other causes than women who expressed their feelings. Likewise, researchers tracked a group of women who had survived one heart attack to see if they could identify any predictors of subsequent death. The biggest predictor turned out to be the suppression of emotion. Indeed, the women who died were divorced, socially isolated, undereducated, and highly dissatisfied with their lives—but instead of expressing their anger and resentment, they seethed all the way to their graves.

Unfortunately, heart attacks aren't the only consequence of suppressed anger that can have us pushing up daisies. This withheld emotion is also strongly related to high blood pressure (hypertension), which can lead to stroke, kidney damage, and other serious health problems. Of these, the high blood pressure that leads to stroke is a particular concern.

14

ANGER AND HYPERTENSION

When my kids get mad, they say "I'm having a stroke."...
[but] my Mom ... died of a stroke. I never wanted to be
... like her and I ... don't want to die like her, so I handle
my anger differently—I try never to let myself get to the
boiling point. **—Reva**

When some of us get angry, our blood practically boils.
Indeed, as we age, our chances of having high blood pressure
and dying from stroke are higher than men's. In fact, the
prevalence of high blood pressure increases steadily during
women's adult years, and 72 percent of us aged sixty-five to
seventy-four suffer from it. In addition, hypertension is more
common among black women of all ages. Our greatest concern is that almost half the people with hypertension don't
even know they have it.

To be sure you're not part of the unknowing masses, ask
your health care provider for your blood pressure numbers.
He or she will give you two figures like 120/70. The top number is your systolic pressure. Systolic pressure is measured
when your heart contracts to pump blood into your arteries,
and this number should be less than 140. The bottom number is your diastolic pressure. Diastolic pressure is measured
when your heart relaxes between beats, and it should be less
than 90. High blood pressure is diagnosed if you have a series
of elevated readings over a period of time. However, if you

are older, slightly higher blood pressures are permissible—check with your health professional.

Overall, for women, the risk of high blood pressure is increased by obesity, the use of birth control pills, a family history of hypertension, pregnancy, and—according to an impressive body of research—anger. That's right, anger. When you feel burned up, hot under the collar, or steamed, your blood pressure may be headed off the charts. In fact, some participants in the Women's Anger Study claimed they could actually feel it rise. Unfortunately, the medical establishment has been slow to acknowledge anger as a risk factor in hypertension, and publications from the American Heart Association are completely mum on the subject. Studies on the anger/hypertension connection will help you decide for yourself, and they're pretty convincing. They demonstrate that:

- Anger is always accompanied by significant increases in blood pressure. In fact, the increase associated with anger is the largest jump associated with any emotion. Likewise, increases in women's general anger proneness (along with other well-known predictors) can accurately foretell increases in systolic and diastolic blood pressure.
- In women, blood pressure goes up when they do not share their angry feelings with family members, friends, etc.
- Studies of young adults show that suppressed anger plays a role in elevated blood pressure before hypertension ever develops. Anger also accelerates the development of this condition.
- The overall tendency to anger is higher in those with a diagnosis of high blood pressure. In addition, although they become furious when criticized or treated unjustly, hypertensives habitually suppress their intense, angry feelings.
- Blood pressure numbers shoot up when women go to work. While these increases are strongly related to each woman's individual anger style, there is, unfortunately, a logical explanation for the connection between anger and high blood pressure at work. We women are often

in subordinate positions where we're prohibited from directly expressing our angry feelings. As a result, we can literally feel our blood rise. For black women, these constraints may be especially severe:

In four years, I have never gotten a positive job perform-ance evaluation. The supervisor . . . doesn't like black peo-ple. There have been firings. I worry that I might be next. My blood pressure goes up and my hands get shaky. There is no way to vent frustrations. I was counseled at work not to be angry. So I go to the restroom and pray . . . that I can make it through the day.

—As told to researchers P. Stevens, J. Hall, and A. Meleis

If you, too, pray for patience in a work situation that keeps your blood pressure revved, see Chapter 20 for some ideas about changing the situation or changing your reaction to it. Whether you talk it out, walk it out, or just get out, don't let workplace anger—and sky-high hypertension—make you part of the corporate body count. Remember, if hostile thoughts and cynicism are your forte, work toward greater tolerance and compassion for other people and for yourself. This is much easier to do if you learn to relax. In fact, relax-ation is vital to better health and in people with high blood pressure, the regular use of relaxation techniques may actu-ally decrease the need for medication. This is why.

Relaxation interrupts and decreases the activity of the sympathetic nervous system—the adrenaline that causes in-creases in your blood pressure and turns you into a category four storm. Now you can achieve this relaxation in several ways whether through deep breathing (see Chapter 7), medi-tative prayer, yoga, self-hypnosis, napping, one of the many store bought relaxation audiotapes or videotapes, or the fol-lowing easy method, which was developed by Professor Her-bert Benson of the Harvard Medical School, and which is practiced by thousands of people.

Proactive Strategy: Benson's Relaxation Technique

1. Sit quietly in a comfortable position.
2. Close your eyes.

3. Deeply relax all your muscles, beginning at your feet and progressing up to your face. Keep them all relaxed.

4. Breathe through your nose and become aware of your breathing. As you breathe out, say the word *one* silently to yourself. Remember to breath easily and naturally.

5. Continue for ten to twenty minutes. You may open your eyes to check the time, but do not use an alarm. When you finish, sit quietly for several minutes, first with your eyes closed and then with your eyes open. Wait several minutes before you stand up.

6. Don't worry about whether you have been successful in reaching a deep level of relaxation. Maintain a passive attitude and permit relaxation to occur at its own pace. If distracting thoughts arise, don't dwell on them. Instead, try to ignore them and return to repeating "one." Eventually, the relaxation response will come with little or no effort. Just continue to practice the technique once or twice a day, but not within two hours after any meal.

The Benson relaxation technique will help you calm down enough to discuss your angry feelings in a composed, constructive way (see Part Two). This is important, as neither scathing attacks nor silent seething are good for your heart—and you should take heart in the fact that discussing your anger is a healthful alternative to stuffing it or shouting it out.

In fact, sometimes discussion is the only healthful alternative. In the Women's Anger Study, it was the lone anger variable to show a positive correlation to health. The importance of anger discussion to health is even more significant when you consider our new data, which shows that participants who usually discuss their anger not only have lower blood pressure than seething, silent types, but also have a lower body mass index (appropriate weight for height), a higher sense of self-efficacy, and see themselves as having a better overall level of wellness. These individuals also place greater importance on being healthy and are so consistent in their exercise they could practically do aerobics on demand. Maybe you should try their anger workout. All you have to do is talk . . .

Once I started talking . . . I couldn't stop. It was like that discussion just cut the anger right out of me. —**Lauren**

And sometimes talking can do more than cut out anger—it can help cut out disease. Sound hard to believe? It's true. Especially when you consider the connection between anger and cancer.

15

THE ANGER/CANCER CONNECTION

A cancer is not only a physical disease, it is a state of mind. —**Dr. Michael Baden, Chief Medical Examiner, New York City**

And that state of mind may well involve anger. Although there is no single, unifying theory about what causes cancer, there have been centuries of speculation about possible psychological precursors behind the disease, or should we say *diseases*. Because cancer is actually a group of diseases that result from different factors interacting at the biochemical, cellular, tissue, and organ levels. Add to this body stew proven chemical carcinogens and smoking, drinking, and bad dietary habits, and the result is the second leading cause of death in the United States. Unfortunately, this mix gets more potent all the time. In the last fifteen years, there have been substantial increases in cancer in both men and women, especially lung cancer. In fact, lung cancer is now the leading form of cancer death for women, followed by cancer of the breast, colon, ovaries, and other sites. But regardless of where the cancer occurs, some researchers feel suppressed anger may increase our susceptibility to the disease, and study results seem to bear them out:

- One longitudinal study found striking similarities among cancer victims including low scores on closeness to parents, nervous tension, depression, anxiety, and anger. In fact, compared to patients who died from hypertension, heart attack, mental illness, and suicide, cancer patients had the *lowest* scores of all on depression, anxiety, and anger.

- Using this "antiemotionality" (low levels of depression, anxiety, and anger) as a tracking device, researchers achieved a 78 percent success rate in the prediction of cancer incidence during a 10-year Yugoslavian study. Indeed, the incidence of cancer was forty times greater among individuals who believed they should act in a rational, unemotional way.

The irony here is that there's nothing "rational" about antiemotional behavior, especially when it comes to your health. According to contemporary psychologist and researcher Lydia Temoshok, nonexpression of emotion is the key factor in establishing dangerous, cancer-prone patterns. Temoshok calls this "Type C behavior," and it sounds like it's right out of an etiquette book because Type C includes unfailing pleasantness, passive coping, appeasement, and the inability to express emotions—especially anger. Sadly, people who get their lives from this book seem to write volumes on cancer.

This became apparent to Temoshok in tests on patients with melanoma (a potentially fatal form of skin cancer). Doctors had discovered that the patients with the thickest tumors had a "flat" emotionality syndrome. In other words, they were nice. Too nice. After hours of conversation with the patients, Temoshok learned that they were not focused on their own problems but on pleasing their spouses, parents, and others with whom they had relationships. In addition, these patients never expressed anger and only rarely showed any fear or sadness. Also, compared to heart patients or healthy individuals, they were almost unaware of their own physiological arousal during upsetting experimental procedures. The individuals who finally died of melanoma were those whose lifelong, repressive coping style was short-circuited by the cancer diagnosis. Why did this happen? Because for perhaps the first—and last—time in their lives, these people experienced conscious anger, fear, and sadness that they were not equipped to handle.

London-based Dr. Steven Greer found something similar in a study of women who developed breast cancer. Greer and his team discovered that the only distinct difference between women whose breast tumors were malignant and those who were benign was the way they handled their emotions— especially anger. Both "extreme suppressors" (those who had only expressed anger once or twice in their entire lives) and "extreme expressors" (those famous for frequent temper outbursts) had higher rates of diagnosed breast cancer than women with "normal" emotional behavior. But the "expressors" were heavily outnumbered by the "suppressors"—those who tried to maintain control at all costs.

These extreme, ineffective anger expressions were also an important factor in Gayle Garrison's research on women over forty with breast cancer or cardiovascular disease. Garrison conducted in-depth interviews in which each woman was asked to describe two or three times she had been angry. From the outset, the women with breast cancer proved unique because 70 percent had trouble recalling incidents that made them mad—and only 30 percent could think of more than four anger episodes in their entire lives! For these women, anger was a "terrible" feeling of tightness, heaviness, and inner turmoil that they experienced when they were denied something important or felt unsupported. Since expressing their anger didn't bring relief (and was often followed by half-hearted, anxiety-ridden attempts to make amends), the breast cancer patients remained helpless and resigned, resigned to angry feelings that were forever hidden, forgotten, and unclear.

> I don't think clearly when I'm angry . . . I can't talk through things . . . I get distracted by my . . . tears . . . my head gets rattled by the anger . . . We [my husband and I] have these reoccurring arguments . . . I get frustrated because . . . I know there's no [way] to resolve it . . . and it's not going to go away . . . So . . . I'll just let it ride. I'll just forget it. I'll get over it.
>
> **—Kathleen, breast cancer patient**

By contrast, women with cardiovascular disease don't "get over" it. Garrison found that for these women, anger was a much more violent, intense, all-consuming experience. The cardiovascular patients wanted to control others; had negative, "off with their heads" thoughts about anyone who crossed them; and an almost compulsive need to act. Controlling their anger was a tremendous struggle, a struggle they usually lost as they expressed their anger in a combative, high-decibel way. After their outbursts, the cardiac patients usually felt better, but this relief was short-lived because they reexperienced their anger just by talking about it:

> I exploded . . . It was as [though] if I didn't get rid of it [the anger], then it would destroy me . . . I was furious . . . I talked loud and . . . repeated myself at great length. I felt better. I was a little ashamed that I had lost my temper so thoroughly.　　　　　　　　　　　　　　　**—Kate**

Since Garrison studied women who already had cancer or heart disease, her study does not prove that anger caused the breakdown of their body systems. However, the women's descriptions of their anger experiences are right in line with the coronary- and cancer-prone behavior patterns found in the preceding studies. Which leaves us with the big question: If anger does play a part in cancer, can you use effective anger techniques to circumvent this disease, improve your health, and possibly save your life?

Effective Anger Techniques Can Improve Your Health and May Save Your Life

The answer is a resounding yes. If you are cancer prone, you can make the changes that will help you save your own life. How? Research evidence shows that those of us who are cancer prone do not consciously choose to be the way we are. Early in life, we began keeping our emotions under wraps as a defense mechanism against loss, stress, or trauma, or because our families forbade emotional expression. For this reason, cancer patients should never be blamed for bringing the disease on themselves. After all, we had no way of knowing that the anger suppression/repressed coping styles we adopted to survive would ultimately have the opposite effect.

But that effect can be reversed. Therapy can change Type C behavior. Temoshok has found this with her "Type C Transformation" therapy groups. So has psychiatrist David Spiegel of the Stanford University School of Medicine. Over a decade ago, Spiegel began working with advanced breast cancer patients in group therapy. Spiegel had no plans to focus on Type C, but he quickly discovered that most of his group's time was spent discussing strong, negative emotions that needed to be expressed. In addition, group members gave each other support and encouragement to proclaim these angry feelings. The group support empowered the women. It helped them take charge of their medical care and avoid the passivity that puts one foot squarely in the grave. And this is no exaggeration. In a ten-year, follow-up study, Spiegel found that the women in therapy lived almost twice as long as those in a control group receiving routine medical care.

Likewise, Dr. Steven Greer found that there was nothing routine about the cancer patients who fought their way back to health. Greer grouped cancer patients into four categories: helplessness/hopelessness, stoic acceptance, denial, and fighting spirit. At both the five- and ten-year follow-up examinations, the patients with fighting spirit (and interestingly, denial) were more likely to be alive and cancer free than those who gave into stoic acceptance or helplessness/hopelessness. Convinced that fighting spirit is the key to survival, Greer has designed a therapy that mobilizes this true grit into a force for health.

Why does it work? While Greer and other advocates of group counseling for cancer patients haven't identified the precise reason, the answer probably lies in this mix—the group members bond, the therapist instills hope and confidence, and suppressed anger explodes into empowerment. Suddenly, these empowered patients find they're addicted to being alive. By acknowledging their anger and using it assertively, they can get more attention and potentially better medical care than their passive counterparts. What's even more astonishing is that anger seems to mobilize the body's energy to fight off the physical assaults of the disease itself. Witness Lydia Temoshok's discovery that cancer patients who openly expressed anger and other emotions actually had more cancer-killing lymphocytes—immune cells—at their tumor sites! What's the bottom line? Not only do openly angry patients get better, they get an attitude, an attitude that can change—and save—their lives.

This is what happened to Alice Epstein. Epstein was diagnosed with inoperable cancer, but is alive and well. All her life she suppressed her anger and sacrificed her own needs to please everyone else. Once she even got the highest grade possible on a test for the nonexpression of hostility! Then Alice got cancer, and the Big C spun her off on a journey of self-discovery that not only reorganized and revitalized her personality, but hurled her cancer right into remission. Epstein has now written a book on reversing her cancer-prone personality. In it she says that therapy enabled her:

> *. . . to rid myself of feelings that I had experienced over a lifetime in a matter of months and sometimes weeks.*
> **—Alice Epstein, author and cancer survivor**

Many other patients in cancer counseling have the same experience. Glenna found herself expressing emotions openly for the first time in years:

> *I actually found it easier to cope with some tough . . . cancer treatments than to . . . talk about things I had kept locked away inside myself for years. But once I started nothing could stop me. Counseling can be . . . very challenging . . . but it can also be soothing, stimulating, exciting, and comforting.*
> **—Glenna**

Unfortunately, not every angry woman turns to counseling for comfort. Some of us prefer to pickle our anger with alcohol. Others reek of Valium—and neither group may understand that angry feelings can forge iron clad links to substance use and abuse.

16

ANGER'S LINK TO
SUBSTANCE USE
AND ABUSE

I was so mad at my husband that when he ordered a Margarita and offered to drink to my health I thought, "Honey, I'm way ahead of you. I don't drink to my health, I drink for my health"—at least that's what I do when I'm mad.
             —Helen, age fifty-six

When we feel angry, many of us try to buy an over-the-counter "antidote" in the form of alcohol, tobacco, and/or legal drugs. While therapists, support groups, and Alcoholics Anonymous have known about this habit for years, research on the link between female anger and substance use/abuse (another one of those taboo topics) has been practically nil.

Our own studies show that women's drug* and alcohol use is related to physical symptoms of anger like headaches. This suggests that the use/abuse is to squelch intense anger arousal and relieve the tension and bodily discomfort associated with angry feelings. Just consider:

- In our study of midlife women ages thirty-five to fifty-five, those with a greater number of anger symptoms drank more alcohol and downed more prescription and over-the-counter drugs.

---

*The use of illegal drugs was not measured in our study and is not discussed in this chapter.

- Women's Anger Study participants who had higher levels of uncomfortable, physical anger symptoms also consumed more alcohol and drugs. In addition, over-the-counter and prescription drug use was related to anger in women of all ages.

Now, certainly an occasional martini or aspirin-aided limp back from anger to equilibrium is not a problem—but the habitual consumption of alcohol and drugs in megadoses is. Studies show that highly hostile women (and men) consume larger quantities of alcohol and are more likely to drive under the influence, increasing their risk (and everyone else's) of accidental injury or death. In addition, relying on drinks or pills to manage your emotions has other serious consequences. Both are addictive (especially psychoactive drugs like tranquilizers, sedatives, and sleeping medications) and with both, you eventually need more and more of the chemical to achieve the same mood-altering effect. With alcohol we have particular concerns. For starters:

- Women weigh less than men and have a lower volume of body water. As a result, the same amount of alcohol gives us a higher blood alcohol level than our male drinking buddies (like dropping the same size shot in a smaller glass of water). In addition, the enzyme responsible for metabolizing alcohol in the stomach does a less thorough job in us, so we're more vulnerable to the physiological effects of drinking.
- If a man and woman drink the same amount of alcohol, the woman's memory and ability to perform reaction tasks will be more impaired than the man's.
- Compared to men, we progress more rapidly from one and two drinks to too many drinks. That is, we go from the onset of drinking to problem drinking to alcoholism at a much faster rate. A shorter period of drinking also gives us more anemia, ulcers, malnutrition, high blood pressure, fatty livers, and other health problems.
- Younger generations of women are more likely to be heavy drinkers than their mothers or grandmothers were at the same age.
- Women who have more than four drinks per day experience more alcohol-related problems than men.

- When we women use one chemical heavily or frequently, we are more likely than men to use other chemicals simultaneously, such as alcohol with marijuana, tranquilizers, sedatives, or opiates.

As if all this isn't enough, there's a strong social stigma attached to women's drinking. The stigma forces many of us into the closet, where we hide to avoid community disapproval—the same disapproval that makes us too ashamed to get help. And even when we do find the courage to get effective treatment, some sources seem closed to us. Employee assistance programs, which are a major source of referral for men, are far less likely to refer women for treatment and rehab. To make matters worse, our families and friends are not always the pillars of support we hope they will be—and some may actually oppose our efforts. In fact, one study showed that compared to 2 percent of the men entering treatment, 23 percent of the women had to grapple with family opposition. Even when we finally overcome this opposition, it's no easy street because most programs are designed for males and do not accommodate our uniquely female concerns. But we have to start somewhere to address the problem, and we suggest you begin with these signs that your drinking may be problematic.

EXERCISE

The Problem Drinker's Test

Instructions: Answer these questions to see if you have a drinking problem.

	YES	NO
1. Do you ever feel guilty about your drinking?		
2. Does your spouse (or other relative) worry or complain about your drinking?		
3. Are there times you cannot stop drinking when you want to?		

YES   NO

4. Have you ever lost friends because of your drinking?

5. Have you ever had trouble at work or lost a job because of drinking?

6. Have you ever awakened the morning after drinking and found you could not remember part of the night before?

7. Do you have physical problems connected to your drinking?

8. Have you ever been arrested for driving under the influence or while intoxicated?

9. Have you ever gone to anyone for help about your drinking?

10. Do you believe your drinking is out of control?

Scoring: The greater the number of "yes" answers, the greater the likelihood that you need professional help. In fact, even one "yes" may indicate a serious drinking problem.

Check with your physician, minister, family, and friends for personal referrals to counselors or therapists, and/or try Alcoholics Anonymous, which has chapters throughout the United States. You may also need professional help if you suffer from another kind of substance abuse—taking prescription drugs and over-the-counter medications (OTCs).

Over-the-Counter Drugs and Prescriptions for Disaster

Many women who are earth-mother solid won't let so much as a drop of liquor touch their lips. Indeed, according to national surveys, 41 percent of women do not use alcohol at all. But a woman does "have" to follow doctor's orders, doesn't she? And many of us who object to liquor on social or religious grounds find taking medicine quite acceptable. Why? More women than men are willing to take their complaints to physicians, and physicians have been culturally conditioned to expect us to "need" mood-altering medications. Unfortunately, more than moods have been altered—so has the open expression of our anger and other emotions, and this has been going on for quite some time.

In the early twentieth century, prior to the passage of the Harrison Narcotics Act, women eagerly downed Lydia Pinkham's Female Tonic, Mrs. Winslow's Soothing Syrup, and other so-called "female friends"—most of which were liberally laced with opium or morphine. In fact, during this period, twice as many women as men became addicted to opiates, the drugs that induce a state of blissful euphoria. Doubtless, these women felt they needed drugs to get their bliss fix because they sure weren't getting it in everyday life. The early 1900s were difficult and confusing, and of course, women were not permitted to show any anger they might feel. Things weren't much better decades later when the genteel Southern women in Sandra's aunt's Memphis, Tennessee, bridge club proudly announced they were taking Miltowns (tranquilizers), as if Miltowns gave their "nervousness" and suppressed emotions medical legitimacy.

The same thing happens today. Valium, Xanax, and other tranquilizers give us a medical excuse for suppressing our anxiety, hiding our anger, and never losing control. For years, Valium was the most prescribed psychoactive drug in the United States, and although it was found to be addictive, women still use it, often in the interest of "preserving family harmony" and locking legitimate anger away:

> *I take it to protect the family from my irritability . . . I don't think it's fair for me to start yelling at [the kids] because their normal activity is bothering me. My husband says I overreact and . . . so I take Valium to keep me calm. Peace and calm. That's what my husband wants because frankly, the kids get on his nerves, too. But he will not take anything. He blows his top. When I blow my top, I am told to settle down. When he does it, it's perfectly all right, and I have resented this over the years . . . One of these days I'm going to leave the whole kit and caboodle and walk out on him. Then maybe I won't need any more Valium.* **—Leanne, as told to researchers Cooperstock and Lennard**

But it's not like the Valium really helps Leanne cope. She's still smoldering because her anger expression is prohibited and she's been told to settle down. She also wants to run away from home like some of the desperately unhappy participants in the Women's Anger Study (see Chapter 9). And her feelings are not that unusual. In one study of psychotropic drug use among a sample of twelve hundred women, frequent users reported feeling "unhappy" and seeing physicians for "undefined problems." These women are usually married mothers not employed outside the home—the very group that has good reason to crave escape from endless family responsibilities, even if the break is only temporary (see Part Three). On the surface, drugs appear to provide the means, as The Rolling Stones suggested in a hit song that dubbed tranquilizers "Mother's Little Helper." Unfortunately, a lot of medical types agree with Mick and the boys. One social scientist even proposes that Valium:

> . . . has served as a form of social control by containing and deflecting discontent and perhaps even dissent.

This Big Brother attitude is perpetuated by advertisements in medical journals like one that shows a harassed housewife imprisoned behind bars of mops and brooms with the headline, "You can't set her free, but you can make her feel less anxious." In another more insidious spin, physicians are exhorted to "help" the whole family by tranquilizing the mother, all under the banner: "Treat one—six people benefit." And these campaigns have been quite successful, judging from statistics on the number of these prescriptions written for women:

- In a Toronto study, 69 percent of the mood-altering prescriptions written were written for women.
- In a national study of 11,083 U.S. households, nearly twice as many women as men obtained psychotropic drugs.
- Seventy-one percent of the adolescent females who have used a tranquilizer during their lifetimes received it as a prescribed medication.
- Ninety-nine percent of women age thirty-five and up who have used tranquilizers, sedatives, or analgesics during their lifetimes received prescriptions for them.

- In a study of 18,592 adults in Finland, women's tranquilizer use was directly related to conflicts with their spouses.

Although women are receiving drugs for every emotional condition from depression to stress management, the Finnish study suggests a main line to anger. It also suggests a problem, as does the other data listed above. While we do not question the use of psychotropic medications when they are appropriately prescribed, taken as directed, and discontinued in a timely fashion, there are some real dangers. For starters, once we women receive these prescriptions, we continue to use them for an extended period of time. We are also more likely than men to misuse and become addicted to prescription drugs, especially since we mistakenly believe our physicians would never recommend anything that could harm us. Finally, the addictive potential of many psychoactive medications is unknown or underestimated when they first come on the market.

But what is known is that psychiatrists—the medical professionals with the most extensive knowledge of psychopharmacology—write only 10 percent of the prescriptions for these medications. The rest are being prescribed by general practitioners, OB-GYNs, and specialists in everything from ears, noses, and throats to urology. In some instances, they offer drugs without suggesting alternatives or without any assessment of our emotional states. And if we can't get a doctor to do it, many of us are perfectly capable of tranquilizing ourselves into Stepford wives with the help of over-the-counter medications (OTCs).

More than five hundred thousand OTCs are available without a doctor's prescription, and the majority of people using them are white, middle-class women. Women are much more likely to take OTCs than men, particularly when the OTC of choice is a tranquilizer. A random shakedown of women at any office or social gathering would reveal purses and designer suit pockets full of sedatives and analgesics intended to treat headaches, stomach aches, back pain, and a host of physical ailments that may actually be anger related. And it makes perfect sense. After all, when we're angry, we tend to have a more intense physical experience than men. Just think about the women who've described their gut-wrenching, head-splitting, back-breaking anger. And doesn't this apply to you too? Like most of us, when you're mad, you probably have one particular organ or body system that bears the brunt of the attack. For example, maybe you get a headache when you argue with your husband. Indeed, migraine headaches have been linked to situations in which our rage is aroused but unexpressed. Henrietta knows how it feels:

> *It feels like the outside of my body is getting bigger and the inside of my body's getting smaller . . . like my external environment is just getting beyond my ability to cope with it . . . so I . . . try to shrink up and . . . do less and less . . . That's about the only way I can describe the physical sensation. It's like my head just feels like it's going to [makes exploding sound].* **—Henrietta**

Likewise, Jeanette feels the explosion of pain in her stomach and it frequently makes her sick:

> *My stomach gets in knots . . . you have that sick feeling especially when the initial anger occurs, until you have time to deal with that a little bit and calm down.*
> **—Jeanette**

But Rosemary's colon never did calm down, and eventually she realized why: it was her anger.

> *I had so much anger. I really didn't know why . . . or [why I had] the spastic colon . . . it was constant . . . I had wonderful self-destruct modes . . . just keep it all in and . . . destroy your whole body.* **—Rosemary**

Instead of a specific organ, Babs's whole body is being destroyed by her suppressed anger, and she knows it:

> *I've always tried to suppress my anger and not become explosive—because of the fear of rejection from people, you know, they won't like me, or they won't include me, or they won't understand me. It's like everything on the inside is messed up . . .* **—Babs**

Messed up doesn't begin to describe it. For many of us, our anger feels like it's on an internal search-and-destroy mission, just looking for places to wreak havoc. So why shouldn't we enlist medications in our fight against the pain?

After all, our culture gives us permission in thousands of sixty-second TV spots extolling the virtues of pills and potions that offer instant relief for whatever ails us. Besides, this stuff can't be advertised on TV unless it's safe, right? And it can't possibly hurt us if it's taken as directed, right? Otherwise we couldn't get it without a prescription, right? Wrong.

All drugs—even aspirin, Advil, Tylenol, Sominex, and other widely used "minor" pain relievers and sedatives can have potentially dangerous side effects. One of the most dangerous is possible interactions between combinations of over-the-counter drugs or between OTCs and alcohol, or OTCs and prescription drugs, or alcohol and prescription drugs. Any way you cut it, inappropriate OTC and prescription drug use is a disaster waiting to happen—and the problem isn't just interactions. Many women—and men—exceed the recommended dosage. Josie is already gobbling aspirins like M&M's:

> *My anger takes the form of neck aches and they hurt really bad. To the point where I need to take aspirins probably three times a day.* **—Josie**

Eventually, heavy use of over-the-counter-drugs can produce toxic reactions or serious complications such as kidney disease, anemia, ulcers, bleeding from the gastrointestinal tract, and more. Is it worth it? Is it worth sacrificing your body (you only have one) to your suppressed anger? Meg, whom you met on page two, doesn't think so:

> *Drugs are a way of padding the cell, of not meeting it [your anger] head on. And what I mean by padding it, they make you go to sleep and you're not thinking when you're asleep with drugs.* **—Meg**

You're also not solving the problem that keeps giving you the pain in your neck or knot in your stomach. So why not try a productive action like talking it out, exercise, relaxation, or one of the other techniques we've discussed in this book instead of popping a pill—or smoking.

She's Smokin'

When I get ticked off . . . I grab my cigarettes . . . it's a more literal way of handling my anger when I'm so mad I'm, like they say, smokin'. But I am trying to quit . . .

—Shelli, age forty-three, paralegal

If you've tried to quit but can only taper off, you should be aware that research shows a convincing link between anger and smoking. For instance, most people first get hooked on cigarettes during angry, high-conflict situations. Similarly, women's smoking is often associated with marital disagreement and marital dissatisfaction. In young adults ages eighteen to thirty, smoking is one and a half times more common among those who are highly hostile—regardless of race or gender. In addition, quitting cigarettes and then falling off the wagon is directly related to intense emotional states like anger and loneliness. And last but not least, since we women smoke because it tranquilizes our emotions, it's harder for us to quit than men, who usually smoke just for pleasure.

The data from the Women's Anger Study allows us to add some compelling points to this list. We found that smokers and nonsmokers differ in their reactions to criticism and frustration—the smokers react much more angrily. In addition, smoking is more common among those who admit having depressive symptoms. Finally, the number of cigarettes we smoke increases with age—and with the emotional intensity of the situation.

Indeed, in counseling sessions we have often observed clients lighting up just as a strong emotion swells to the surface. As the client puffs away, she creates a smoke screen to hide her angry feelings and "help" her mellow out. Where the rest of us might talk about our anger or use meditation to calm ourselves down, smokers do this with nicotine.

Nicotine [the active ingredient in cigarettes] influences neurotransmitters that are associated with feeling good, so it can lessen the effects of stress and negative moods.

—Dr. Thomas H. Brandon, psychologist

This was reinforced in a recent study in which researchers replaced smokers' cigarettes with either nicotine gum or a placebo. Both the smokers and their spouses were then questioned about the smokers' subsequent emotional states—and it's a wonder the placebo spouses didn't make a run for the hills. Their mates exhibited much higher levels of anger, irritability, and tension than those who chewed the real thing. What's the bottom line? Without nicotine to regulate their moods, the smokers were clearly more angry—and that anger can escalate when they try to quit. Why?

When some smokers try to go on the wagon, their emotions become a runaway stage. One young housewife even told doctors that quitting made her a real "shrew" and her family was begging her to light up again. Comments like this led researchers to conclude that smokers who are angry, tense, and/or depressed might need a special combination treatment to help them break the habit. This special combo usually includes psychotherapy, a nicotine patch or gum, and in some cases, an antidepressant medication. The antidepressant would be prescribed if you're going through intense withdrawal, are severely depressed, or are mournful when you quit:

> *At one of our clinics, a woman was overheard to say that she mourned more when she quit smoking than she did when her husband died!*
>
> **—Drs. A. Christen and K. Cooper**

Sadly, mourning is what a lot of smokers' families eventually must do—and this is especially true since the 1970s. That's when women got liberated and habits that were once considered unattractive and unfeminine—like smoking—became ours to embrace. Ironically, this was just about the time the damaging effects of cigarettes were becoming known and men began quitting in droves. We women haven't quite followed suit, as these alarming, recent statistics show:

- The proportion of women who smoke is almost equal to the proportion of men, and in some age and occupational groups, we outnumber males by a growing margin.
- In the U.S. and other developed countries, female ado-

lescents are more likely to smoke than males of the same age.

- In some educated professional groups, our smoking rate surpasses men's.

While advertisers claim "You've come a long way, baby," about the only thing we've gained from smoking is the "privilege" of more respiratory problems, more lung cancer, and more dates with the Grim Reaper. Just consider these depressing facts:

- Smoking has been implicated in 87 percent of all lung cancer deaths and is associated with cancers of the mouth, esophagus, and other organs.
- Tobacco is responsible for nearly one in five deaths in the United States. In fact, more Americans die from smoking each year than died in World Wars I and II and the Vietnam War combined.
- Nicotine is one of the most toxic, addictive drugs known—and there is some evidence that cigarette smoking may be more addictive for us than it is for men.

But it is possible to quit (nearly forty-four million Americans have) and if you won't quit for your health, how about your vanity? Cigarette smoking causes wrinkles and dry, leathery skin, bad breath, stained teeth, and yellowed nails that no amount of manicuring can hide. In addition, just about anywhere you try to light up, you find yourself in hostile territory, surrounded by indignant nonsmokers and community laws against smoking in restaurants, airports, museums, stores, . . . the list doesn't end—but the habit can, especially if you follow this proactive strategy.

Proactive Strategy: Guidelines for Quitting Smoking

1. There is no "one right way" to quit. Some people succeed cold turkey, others do better with a gradual approach.

2. Don't try to quit when you're in the midst of a tumultuous, emotional event like a divorce. In addition, don't make the attempt until after you learn effective ways of managing your anger and other negative emotions.

3. Keep in mind that physiological withdrawal requires about a week. During the first few days, drink plenty of fluids to flush the nicotine out of your system.

4. Psychological withdrawal can take weeks or years, and it helps if you find a substitute activity like exercise, which is an excellent replacement (see Chapter 18).

5. Throw away all your smoking paraphernalia—anything that reminds you of the habit.

6. Make a public commitment to your friends or spouse and ask for their support.

7. Don't let the fear of being overweight undermine your plans to quit smoking. You would have to gain 125 pounds to incur the same hazard to your health as you get from a pack a day of cigarettes. Alas, we women are more likely than men to report that fear of a weight gain keeps us from quitting.

8. If at first you don't succeed, try again, and again. Remember, very few people succeed the first time out so keep working toward smoke-free health!

You also need to work toward better health if, instead of smoking, drinking, or popping pills, you eat when you get angry. Why? Because anger is linked to obesity and the reason you might be fat is because you're mad . . .

17

HOW ANGER CAN LEAD TO EATING PROBLEMS

When I get mad at my six-year-old, I eat a hot fudge sundae. When I get mad at my ten-year-old it's a pizza. And when I get mad at the thirteen-year-old it's a hot fudge sundae and a pizza. I guess instead of exploding at them I eat—only problem is all that food explodes in me. I've gained twenty pounds in three years and I hate to look in the mirror. **—Sylvia, age thirty-six**

Many of us hold Armageddon on our forks and it shows—especially in the mirror:

- Between 30 and 50 percent of American women are overweight and some sources say the number may be as high as 70 percent.
- Across all age groups, we are more obese than men.
- We continue to gain weight through age sixty-five.
- Being overweight predisposes us to heart disease, diabetes, hypertension, stroke, elevated cholesterol, and more.
- Obesity shortens life. A government panel concluded that the greater the degree of overweight, the higher the mortality ratio or excess death rate.

And it's not bad enough that obesity can kill you, so can being too thin—the very goal most of us strive for. In fact, American women are so obsessed with weight that in one recent survey, a majority of participants said they feared getting fat more than they feared dying—and no wonder. Overweight women practically bear a scarlet F(-a-t) on their chests (hips and thighs) because they do not conform to the lean, leggy look of the ideal woman, but then again who does? The ideal woman slithering down Parisian runways is not the average wife and mother slithering down the supermarket aisle with her toddlers in tow. Indeed, compared to the ideal, the average North American female is 5 feet 3.8 inches tall and weighs 144 pounds. By contrast, Miss Ideal is 5 inches taller and weighs 29 pounds less—a standard that's impossible for mere mortals to attain, even if millions of us are enrolled in weight loss programs (where we outnumber men nine to one) or if we make the average five attempts per year to lose weight. The truth is that sometimes nothing will help because we're fighting Mother Nature. Indeed, science tells us that obesity is partly due to genetics, but there are many other factors that contribute in a big way—including anger and hostility. In other words

You Might Not Be Fat, You Might Just Be Mad—The Proven Link Between Anger and Food

Some feminist experts allege that our subordinate positions to fathers, husbands, and bosses force us to stuff our anger, that is, to literally stuff our mouths full of food rather than express our anger or disagreement. Other experts, whether or not they view fat as a feminist issue, agree that food is a way to deal with feelings:

> Many people literally stuff their anger—they keep it down by putting food on top of it. The process is similar to packing in wadding when loading a cannon—and the results can be just as explosive.
> **—F. Minirth, P. Meier, R. Hemfelt, S. Sneed, and P. Hawkins from _Love Hunger_**

Using food to deal with painful, explosive emotions is not a new idea. There are ancient writings in the Talmud about the effects of good and bad moods on weight, and, in 1893, Miss M. A. Boland, a nursing teacher at Johns Hopkins, advocated "stuffing" as an antidote to melancholia. Boland felt this depressive illness could be cured by giving patients as much food as they could eat and many of us believe the same thing. As a result, we fill our stomachs to capacity whenever we're emotionally distressed, especially when we're angry:

I want to eat . . . there's no question in my mind. Some people's stomachs close up. Mine says "Feed me . . ."
—Jen, on her strong desire to eat when she's mad

And when our stomachs say "feed me," most of us answer "how much?" And that's about as discriminating as our brains get. It doesn't matter whether our anger is due to injustice, discrimination, or rejection, we don't really think about what we're doing. Instead, we just pile our plates high and pull up a ladder:

After the breakup of an affair, isn't it perfectly . . . acceptable to eat an entire bag of Hershey's Kisses in one sitting . . . [and] if it's the end of a long-term relationship, you are then allowed to eat everything in the house that doesn't move or have a given name, since your only secure belief at the moment is that no one will ever love you anyway, pretty much ruling out the idea that you will have to show your naked body to a stranger ever again. When you're facing eternal solitude, what's the harm in ingesting an unfrozen Sara Lee cheesecake?
—Regina Barreca, writer and professor

Whether it's cheesecake, pizza, chocolate chip cookies, ice cream, whatever, many of us first learned about comfort food in the cradle. Indeed, food is the first source of comfort and solace most human beings receive:

Our first discomfort in life is met with food. After the violent passage through the birth canal, we are given milk. And the most frequently repeated comfort given us as infants is food. The bottle is often used to stop crying regardless of the cause. **—Steven Levenkron**

So it's understandable why this tradition continues into adulthood. Regardless of the cause of our emotional distress, many of us—including men—still soothe ourselves with food. While men choose fat–protein or fat–salt mixtures like steak, pizza, and French fries, we women prefer to become high priestesses in the church of chocolate. We seek out fat–

sugar combinations like candy bars, ice cream, and cookies. Cookies and other sweets were the magic potion Gale used to soothe an angry childhood, a childhood that:

> *was limiting and . . . controlling . . . I used food as solace and comfort and nurturance to replace what I wasn't getting. It was a form of escape and rebellion. I can remember specifically that keeping Life Savers in my desk drawer was something I could get away with . . . sneaking cookies out of the cookie jar was something I could get away with. Riding my bike to town and buying a handful of candy bars and stopping at the shade tree to enjoy them before I got home was something I could get away with. And those were about the only things I could get away with.* —**Gale**

But not every woman lets herself "get away" with overeating when she's mad. Some of us go a step further and purge ourselves as a way of cleaning out anger. Suzette has been bulimic since girlhood. She believes bingeing and vomiting help her cope with angry feelings:

> *My coping mechanism is food. I would eat to make myself feel better . . . I've been a compulsive eater since I was about eight or . . . younger . . . Then when I was fifteen, I started throwing up as well, so I was bingeing and throwing up. I think that it is doing something with my anger. I feel helpless when I'm angry because I don't feel like I can effect any change with my anger. If I'm angry with someone I don't feel like I have the right to confront them with my anger. Say if somebody doesn't call me when they're supposed to or if somebody says something hurtful to me at work. So by forcing myself to throw up it's kind of a way of doing something physically, just doing something with my anger purges it away.* —**Suzette**

The unhealthy, self-destructive sport of bingeing and purging is certainly one way the anger/food connection makes itself known. It also makes itself known through a much more common (and visible) problem: obesity. After years of feeding our anger, many of us take up residence in fat city and we pay a high emotional price for living in this state. Why? First we eat because we're angry, then the food takes its toll and we get mad at ourselves for being overweight and out of shape, which sends us back to the fridge for more. Betty Sue knows this vicious circle well, and she shares the guilt and anger expressed by many overweight women in our study:

> *Being overweight—I'm angry at myself for being like this.*
> *I feel like I need to do something about [it] . . . Every*
> *woman thinks she should be skin and bones . . . I'd like to*
> *be skinnier, and . . . have a nice figure again.*
>
> **—Betty Sue**

One way Betty Sue (and the rest of us) can work toward this goal is to start counting anger incidents along with ounces and pounds. Indeed, research provides much support for the anger/obesity connection. For example, regardless of race or sex, one study shows that highly hostile individuals consume significantly more calories each day than people who are not hostile—for black women this is an extra 490 calories per day, for white women it's an extra 295. In addition, stress and covert hostility are strongly related to compulsive eating in college students.

Similarly, the correlation of anger to body mass index (BMI) is shown by several studies. Body mass index is calculated as weight in kilograms divided by height in meters, squared. For instance, if you're five feet four inches tall and weigh 150 pounds, your BMI would be 25.6. For women, obesity is defined as a BMI over 27.3. One study found that undergraduate students who scored high on hostility had higher BMIs and notably outweighed their less hostile counterparts. Likewise, in the Women's Anger Study we found a higher body mass index in women who reported greater use of anger suppression, or greater use of anger ventilation done in an attacking, blaming way—the same two unhealthy extremes of anger expression that are associated with heart disease and cancer.

By contrast, BMI is inversely related to smoking and drinking. In other words, women who eat when they're mad do this instead of drowning their sorrows or lighting up because food is their drug of choice. In fact, in focus group discussions conducted by our research team, women often equated the effects of eating with the effects of alcohol or drugs and were sometimes under the illusion that getting high on food is safer—

*Food is such a wonderful drug. It's so easily accessible.
Nobody's ever gonna bust me for havin' a burger and fries
in the car.*　　　　　　　　　　　　　　　　**—Faith**

but in terms of physical and mental health, it's not.

This is particularly true if you've been yo-yo dieting and
have many diet failures listed in your personal hall of shame.
Indeed, if the anger/food connection has been a factor in
your dismal attempts at weight loss, it might be because
many weight reduction programs don't cover the topic of
emotionally induced eating. They also don't give us ways to
handle our painful feelings (without resorting to food) and
never say a peep about the heavy role anger plays in diet relapse.

Then there's the whole question about whether women
(angry or not) should diet at all. On one side of the scale are
those who enthusiastically assert that all diets are harmful
and doomed to fail, so we should spare ourselves the pain.
On the other side are tables laden with standard criteria according to which every woman on the planet is overweight
and should shed pounds. We don't agree with either extreme.
For starters, it's impossible to determine the exact point at
which poundage becomes a threat to health. A much better
indicator is your waist-to-hip ratio.

The ratio is calculated between the narrowest point of
your waist and the widest point of your hip. When this measurement is more than 0.8 (1.0 for men), your risk of disease
is greater. Likewise, compared to fat in your hips and thighs
(the pear shape most of us curse), abdominal fat (the apple
shape) is more strongly associated with heart disease and
death. So if you're a pear, accept it as a health advantage—
and accept your body for what it is rather than trying to
squeeze into those size 8 jeans that fit you for an hour back
in college.

However, if you do have a reason to be concerned about
your weight, start by talking to your health care provider,
then take a long look at your emotionally motivated eating
patterns. Use your journal to record anger episodes in which
you eat and be sure to list what you consume. Then, develop
healthy alternatives to angry eating like exercise or meditation. And so what if you don't get to a celestial size—even a

modest weight loss of fifteen to thirty pounds has positive, long-term effects on your blood sugar, insulin, triglycerides, and HDL cholesterol. Sound good? So will these strategies for sensible eating.

Proactive Strategies: A Plan for Sensible Eating

If you decide you'd rather be stoned to death with popcorn (lo-cal, air-popped, don't forget the zero-fat fake butter spray) than bon-bons, you're on your way to sensible eating, but where do you get accurate information on food plans, menus, recipes, and exercise? After all, bookstores are brimming with dozens of diets du jour, so how do you choose what's right for you? Our advice is to select your reading material carefully and avoid any "miracle" claims. The programs that work involve long-term changes in eating behavior, increased physical activity (see the suggestions about exercise in the next chapter), and an emphasis on the new Food Guide Pyramid instead of the old "basic four" food groups. The pyramid represents a diet with a broad base of bread, cereal, rice, and pasta; followed by liberal amounts of fruits and vegetables; more limited consumption of animal protein, dairy products, dry beans, eggs, and nuts; and a very sparing use of fats, oils, and sweets. In addition, the pyramid provides hefty amounts of fiber (whole-grain breads, cereals, fruits, vegetables), and because fiber is very filling, you don't have to eat as much food to feel full.

You should also check to see if the plan you're following is in sync with the recommendations of the National Cholesterol Education Program and the National Research Council, to wit: Each day's fat intake should be no more than 30 percent of your total daily calories, and less than 10 percent of these should be from saturated fat; cholesterol intake should be below 300 milligrams per day; and sodium intake at or below 2,400 milligrams per day. But what happens if you're eating sensibly, working out, sticking to your milligram count, and suddenly you get mad? Quick! Before you wolf down a fat–sugar combination and the frosting starts talking, try these:

Alternatives to Angry Eating

Just as we need to find alternatives to smoking and other negative anger behaviors, we also need to find options to replace angry eating. While we each have to decide for ourselves what's most effective, here are some ideas you might try:

1. Sip mineral water or other cool, caffeine-free beverages.

2. Use imagery (see Chapter 20) to zone out and reach a peaceful place where nothing can bother you.

3. If you're in an anger/food crisis, call a friend and arrange to meet for an enjoyable, nonfood activity.

4. Do a household chore you've been avoiding like the plague—something that will give you a sense of accomplishment and distract you from your anger (clean closets, rearrange furniture, paint walls—you get the idea).

5. Indulge in a little retail therapy. Buy something you really want without breaking the bank!

6. Nurture your body by taking a bubble bath, giving yourself a manicure, or getting a massage.

7. Each time your anger gives you a food craving, use that energy on a hobby, craft, or project like your anger quilt, anger cross-stitch, or anger stained glass.

8. Analyze the anger incident that's set you on a collision course with the fridge. Then, make a plan to solve the problem or to react differently in the future (by asserting yourself or removing yourself from the situation, for example).

By using these ideas and the others in this chapter, you can intercept a fast-moving, anger-propelled pizza, sundae, or any random forkful of fat. Plus, by changing your negative anger habits, you can conquer the eating disorders we women face, including overweight, obesity, and bulimia.

Now if you still need convincing that anger impacts wellness—from eating disorders to rheumatoid arthritis to lupus and even the common cold—consider this: One of the strongest pieces of evidence supporting the anger/disease connection doesn't come from the other-shoe-will-drop school but from anger's link to good health—very good health.

18

HEALTHY ANGER—THE HEALTH HABITS ASSESSMENT TEST AND GOOD HEALTH SOLUTIONS

I don't think health is the absence of illness, it's the presence of wellness.

—Dana T., age twenty-nine, personal trainer

Instead of focusing on anger's link to disease, some researchers are investigating anger's connection to wellness and general health via longitudinal studies that last twenty to thirty years. What have they found? The less hostility a woman has, the better her general health is over the years. Of course, the opposite (sadly) is also true.

The Women's Anger Study supports these findings. Although we assessed women at one point in time rather than over several years, we found distinct differences between healthy and less healthy women. These differences were apparent in the women's level of general anger proneness ("trait anger") and in their style of anger management, that is, healthier women are not aroused to anger as frequently; they usually don't suppress their anger or take it out on others; they're less likely to internalize anger and convert it into splitting headaches, churning stomachs, or other physical discomforts; and they are more inclined to discuss their angry feelings rationally with another person.

We suspect that these women are also more inclined to see health as something other than a trivial maintenance duty. That is, because they are less angry, they may put greater effort into positive wellness activities and be less tempted to indulge in the big three—drinking, smoking, and drugs. Unfortunately, angrier women not only have to fight these biggies, but a host of other problems as well . . .

Anger Is Linked to General Health Habits

Anger affects our physical health in several indirect ways. Why? Not only does it promote bad health habits, it puts the kibosh on good ones. Indeed, women who score high on hostility, frequent anger experiences, and overt anger expression, usually get lower scores on tests of good health practices including nutrition, relaxation, safety, substance abuse, and exercise. Which is exactly our point—highly hostile women are not physically fit or active, while less hostile women often are.

In fact, according to the Women's Anger Study, women who engage in at least sixty minutes of moderate to strenuous exercise each week differ radically from "couch potatoes" on almost every anger variable. Indeed, regular exercisers have lower general anger proneness ("trait anger"), are less likely to suppress anger and have physical anger symptoms such as headaches, and are more likely to discuss their anger with a confidant.

By contrast, participants who never bench press anything heavier than a pair of Twinkies or who think a marathon is running from the sofa to the fridge and back before the TV commercial ends have higher levels of trait anger. They are also more likely to hold that anger inside. Unfortunately, a lot of us fall into this camp. Results from a recent, nationwide survey show that 69 percent of women fail to exercise three times a week as health experts recommend.

A lot of us also fail to get enough sleep, and in our study of midlife women, inadequate sleep was directly related to higher levels of anger symptoms. Why? Missing your z's contributes to irritability and anger proneness. It also creates a predisposition to angry outbursts and to physical, internalized forms of anger like headaches. But whether it's lack of sleep, lack of exercise, or improper eating, the bottom line is that when we're hostile and angry, we often direct our unresolved anger (and other negative feelings) at ourselves—sometimes without realizing it. To see if this applies to you, take the following anger/health habits assessment test.

EXERCISE

Anger/Health Habits Assessment Test

Instructions: Answer yes or no to the following questions:

	YES	NO
1. I have frequent headaches (or other recurrent aches and pains).		
2. I have abnormally high blood pressure.		
3. I seldom talk about my anger, even when I feel like it.		
4. I smoke cigarettes.		
5. My use of over-the-counter drugs is high or increasing.		
6. I have trouble letting things that upset me just go by.		
7. I weigh more than the amount that is appropriate for my height and frame.		
8. I have trouble getting enough sleep.		
9. I drink alcoholic beverages to unwind and relax.		
10. My future doesn't look too bright.		
11. I have fewer friends now than a year or so ago.		
12. I don't get enough exercise.		
13. I know my stress level is too high.		

To score: Add up the number of yes answers.

If you have more than three or four yes answers, take a good look at your hidden anger. Could it be the culprit that's dismantling your health? For instance, if you have recurrent headaches, is it really anger hammering away in your brain? Or if you have colitis, is it unexpressed anger eating up your bowels? Is anger responsible for your insomnia, back trouble, or couch-potato inertia? Whatever the case, examine your physical symptoms to see what they're "saying." Symptoms are one way your body gives you clues to decipher what's going on in your life. If we don't mask these clues with drugs, alcohol, smoke, or food, we can learn from them. We can make the connections between anger and what's ailing us, as Fiona did:

> *I very much believe in the mind/body connection . . . I can think of specific examples . . . when something was happening that I just couldn't stand and then that's the way I'd express it—I had lower back pain and I couldn't stand up straight. Then there was another time when I wanted to tell someone something that bothered me and I just couldn't bring myself to do it. I got laryngitis and couldn't talk. Then . . . Dick lived in Louisiana for nearly two years after I'd moved here, so he was in and out. He'd come up here for a week. There was some project he wanted to . . . just bulldoze through . . . I like to do projects, but I'm kind of meticulous. I take my time and do it slowly. Dick just wants to get it done, so he was pushing us through some project . . . and my neck started hurting. It's a "pain in the neck," you know. A couple of years ago I just felt like I needed a break, well, I broke my leg. So then I'm in this cast. It was great. I got to read books, got a lot of attention . . . It was my right leg, I couldn't . . . drive so somebody else had to drive the kids . . . I got a break.* —**Fiona**

How many women have gotten a "break" in similar ways? More than you think. It reminds Sandra of her days as an orthopedic nurse. Among the steady clientele in her hospital unit were twenty- and thirty-year-old wives and mothers with young children. These patients were "down in the back," and doctors usually admitted them for tests and several weeks of physical therapy including massage and hot packs. But mysteriously, the test results were almost always negative. Then Sandra noticed something, the one thing these women had in common: They were all mad at their husbands. Not overtly mad, just mad enough to have a "pain in the back"—perhaps because they each had one at home in the form of an uncooperative spouse.

How did Sandra know? They told her so. As she worked the night shift and made her rounds by flashlight, Sandra often met women who couldn't sleep. So they talked, or rather, the women talked and Sandra listened. In the darkness, these patients could reveal their feelings more comfortably, more anonymously. What did they confess? They were hassled, frazzled, tired of chasing two-year-old terrors and spending their children's nap time mopping floors—and their husbands didn't help. But when these women ended up hospitalized and flat on their backs, who got to take on these "fulfilling" tasks? Hubby—the same hubby each patient was so angry at. Now this doesn't mean that these women deliberately "chose" to hurt their backs to get revenge on their husbands. No, their pain was very real, but it wasn't a ruptured disk and the cure didn't lie in spinal fusions or other procedures. The real solution was to express their anger. Indeed, the symptom communicated this very clearly. If these women (or their doctors) had listened to what the back pain was "saying," they might have found less drastic—and cheaper—ways to express their anger and resentment.

For these same reasons, we owe it to ourselves to figure out what's behind our physical symptoms and to make the necessary adjustments to lead healthier lives.

Use Your Journal to Decipher Symptoms and Identify the Anger That Can Make You a Good Health Care Consumer

Use your journal to track any relationships between your moods and your physical condition, then find a health care provider who will listen to you. Most nurse practitioners are well versed in holistic health concepts and you may find them more willing to discuss the anger/illness connection than some physicians are. In fact, studies show that 60 to 80 percent of the primary and preventive care usually done by doctors can be done as effectively (and for less bucks) by an advanced practice nurse. As another incentive, female doctors and nurse practitioners are more likely to view their relationships with you as a partnership. By contrast, many male doctors have been socialized to listen less and command more—and that can be a problem.

A recent national study showed that 41 percent of women change doctors because they are dissatisfied, and the complaint that tops the list is usually a lack of communication. Fully 25 percent of women (compared to 12 percent of men) have been "talked down to" or treated like a child by their physicians. In addition, 17 percent of women (compared to 7 percent of men) have been told that a medical condition they are concerned about is "all in their heads"—a typical response from doctors educated in the old biomedical model. This is the model that says if there are no germs, ruptures, or broken bones, the patient must be a hypochondriac, medical miscreant, or just playing hooky from work. But most of us don't fall into any of these categories, and those of us suffering from real emotional or spiritual distress deserve the same competent, compassionate care as any patient with a physical ailment. This is what holistic medicine is all about, because from a holistic standpoint, no problem is all in the body or all in the head.

> As you ought not to attempt to cure the eyes without the head, or the head without the body, so neither ought you to attempt to cure the body without the soul; this . . . is the reason why the cure of many diseases is unknown to the physicians . . . because they are ignorant of the whole, for the part can never be well unless the whole is well.
>
> **—Plato, *Charmides***

And for the whole to be well, both body and mind must be healed according to the most exact definition of the term:

> To heal is "to restore to health . . . to cause painful emotions to be no longer grievous."
>
> **—*The New Lexicon Webster's Dictionary* of the English Language**

When we reach this level of healing, we will not only have our health, but will be living the holistic life.

Living the Holistic Life

For too long our shallow, E-mail counterculture has believed that health is the absence of disease or the ability to keep functioning—no matter how poorly—in our assigned roles. You were judged healthy if you somehow made it through the day and were still in one piece when you got home. But not anymore. Now we are in the midst of a health revolution, a revolution gaining steam under the banner of holistic medicine. Holistic medicine recognizes that health is more than a bunch of barely there body systems. Rather, it's an advanced state of vitality, exuberant well-being, self-actualization, and major league wellness, or, as nurse theorist Margaret Newman puts it, true health is ever-expanding consciousness.

And what we become conscious of is that health occurs in context—the context of our lives. In other words, true health is a balance between our physical, emotional, social, spiritual, and intellectual dimensions, with the emotional and physical dimensions getting equal time (for a change). Many forward-looking medical professionals and members of the public have enthusiastically adopted this new way of thinking, and so have we. But if the truth be known, holistic medicine isn't "new" at all. We are simply rediscovering ancient wisdom and wedding Eastern methods of body/mind renewal (yoga, meditation, etc.) to amazing Western innovations like biofeedback (a technique that enables us to consciously control body functions once considered involuntary).

But how do you take advantage of these innovations and make the move to holistic health? First, cop an attitude, an attitude that incorporates stress management, higher self-esteem, a more optimistic outlook, improved relationships with your spouse, children, friends, and co-workers, and everything else you've learned in this book. Once you've got this down, it's time to get physical.

Proactive Strategies: How to Use Physical Fitness for Anger Management

Physical fitness is a key step toward achieving total health, and you don't have to join a spa or Ms. Moneybags exercise club to get in shape. You also don't need to hire a personal trainer, enroll in aerobics boot camp, or equip your family room with enough pricey gizmos to fill an NFL gym. Why? Because fitness doesn't involve any of these things. In fact, "having" to go to the club or get on your Nordictrack can create unseen barriers to exercise because you feel unpleasantly obliged to sweat. No, the truth is that physical fitness really means one thing: making—and keeping—a commitment to your body.

Start with a physical checkup from your health care provider. Then begin a committed, body-wise fitness program that includes:

- Flexibility exercises and stretching.
- Strength-building activities such as sit-ups, push-ups, or, if you have access to them, working with weights.
- Aerobic exercise, which involves rhythmic movement of the large muscle groups for at least twenty to thirty continuous minutes, three times a week. (*Aerobic* means "with oxygen," so don't forget to breathe!) You can jog, bicycle, swim, roller-blade, burst into dance, or (especially if you're a little rusty on the physical stuff) just walk.
- Mini daily workouts like taking the stairs instead of the elevator, hoofing it across town or campus to appointments, doing isometrics in your chair at work (never mind the funny looks from your colleagues), or anything else you can think of to keep your body on the go.

As you work to fit all these components into your very own, self-designed program, remember that each exercise session should consist of a five- to ten-minute warm-up period to prepare your muscles and help prevent injury, and twenty to thirty minutes of aerobic activity in your training heart range. To calculate your range, first determine your maximum heart rate by subtracting your age from 220. Next multiply this number by 0.6 to find the low end of your heart range. Finally, multiply the same number by 0.8 to find the high end. This is the range you should be in for the aerobic portion of your workout. It is also the range where you burn fat. Then, finish off with five to ten minutes of moderate, less-strenuous activity to help your body cool down. Remember, never stop abruptly since this can stress your heart and injure muscles.

No matter how you choose to sweat it out, these are the steps you should follow, and whether your exertion of choice is biking, jogging, or plain old walking, the positive effects are the same. Regular exercise makes your heart, lungs, and digestive system run more efficiently. It also causes the pituitary gland to release endorphins (a natural opiate) into the bloodstream. The endorphins remain in your body up to two hours after a good workout, eliminating the need to tranquilize your anger with food or drugs. Better yet, exercise prolongs your life and reduces your risk of death from every major cause—big payoffs indeed.

But if the payoffs are so great, how come 69 percent of us don't even bother? Because we're so busy caring for others that caring for ourselves brings up the rear in any lineup of our daily duties. Ironically, the only way to take care of our rears, our hearts, and often, our anger, is to take time to exercise. So right now, grab your calendar and make an appointment with yourself to work out. Note the time in ink and consider it as firm a commitment as appointments for your teeth or hair. In addition, remember that "exercise" is not code for "torture." It's supposed to be fun and it can be, especially when you think of it as "time to go out and play." According to exercise physiologist Kathy Alexander, workouts can be even more enjoyable if you acquire a whole wardrobe of great "play clothes" (colorful leotards, warm-up suits, and other cute duds), plus a box of shiny, new toys (in-line skates, doughnut weights, a mountain bike).

You also might want some new playmates. If so, you can find a whole roomful of them at Jazzercise or aerobics classes, and besides any friends you make, you get a lot of other benefits too. These classes can help reduce the anger, irritability, bad tempers, and other negative moods that you feel prior to working out. A solo activity can accomplish the same things if you prefer to exercise alone. Just remember, you don't have to climb Mount Everest or run the length of the Canadian border to get results. Research shows that it's not necessary to engage in a killer regimen or a competitive sport. "Easy does it" can do you just fine. In fact, you may get more psychological benefits from moderate exercise than the rough stuff—just balance out your lower intensity with greater frequency and duration. Try a short, brisk walk, bike ride, or swim to produce significant decreases in your anger, anxiety, tension, and depression.

The whole trick here is finding something that works for you, something you enjoy. If you catch yourself wearing the grim, iron-mask expression of an overprogrammed exercise junkie, make a change. After all, exercise should be empowering and invigorating, not rigid or obsessive. Perhaps you should look beyond Western-style workouts to East Indian power yoga or tai chi chuan, a graceful, slow form of exercise practiced by millions of Chinese. Whatever you choose, make sure it's something you like and can stick with, and you'll be able to stick with it if you overcome the obstacles to exercise.

Proactive Strategy: Guidelines for Overcoming Obstacles to Exercise

If you won't even say the word *exercise* because it's too much work for your jaw, try some of these suggestions:

1. Start small and keep it fun by using music or working out with a friend.

2. Record your progress—your blood pressure, pulse, weight, and measurements. It's easier to keep going when you see encouraging signs of progress.

3. Focus on the rewards of exercise including better sleep, less tension, and tighter buns.

4. Post goals, cartoons, and notes of encouragement for yourself around the house, the office, and on the fridge (read them before you dive into the freezer for that last scoop of cookie dough ice cream!).

5. Use positive visualization to see the new, healthy you.

6. Join a class, get a workout buddy, or if you prefer to exercise alone, make this your sacred downtime and don't let anyone infringe on it!

7. Reward yourself for working toward your goals as well as for reaching them. Remember, success is a process, not just an end result.

8. Use proper equipment and clothing—they make you

feel more professonal about taking care of your body and reinforce how serious you are about getting in shape!

9. Include at least ten minutes of warm-up and cool-down exercises in your program, just to be safe.

10. Stop exercising if you notice any unusual pain or symptoms, and consult your health care provider.

11. After a large meal, wait at least two hours before exercising.

12. Have a good time! Get rowdy and enjoy being alive as you walk that block, jump that rope, or pump that iron.

And if you want, pump up a few belly laughs, robust guffaws, or vigorous giggles too. Amazing as it sounds, laughing is exercise—and this is no joke! In terms of the benefits to your cardiovascular and respiratory systems, laughing three minutes each day is equal to ten minutes of rowing. In addition, laughter has a healing effect. Norman Cousins turned America on to the curative power of laughter in his book, *Anatomy of an Illness as Perceived by the Patient.* In the book, Cousins revealed how he watched comedies throughout his hospitalization for a crippling spinal disease. He discovered that ten minutes of tee-hees, snickers, and hearty roars produced two hours of pain-free sleep. Cousins called this "internal jogging" and he speculated that laughter is a sort of

> *. . . bulletproof vest that can help protect an individual against the ravages of negative emotions.*
>
> **—Norman Cousins**

Psychologist Jerry Deffenbacher agrees. Deffenbacher incorporates humor into his anger reduction groups because it produces an incompatible state. In other words, it's impossible to laugh and lash out at the same time (you'll choke!). In addition, humor puts a different spin on things and gives you a less deadly-serious perspective. It also provides alternative ways to interpret anger-provoking situations. Now Deffenbacher is not suggesting that his clients laugh off the serious, legitimate things that make them mad. Rather, he says that humor is a tool we can use to release our anger and gain control over it until we feel ready to cope with the situation. Here's what he means.

Suppose you're dealing with someone who's full of it, a

BSer who really pushes your hot buttons. Now imagine this person as "totally constipated" in the most literal sense of the term. Think living color, big screen, everyone-can-see-it, and you may be able to manage a chortle instead of an angry curse.

In addition, you may stop cursing the day, the night, your husband, your kids, et al-together if you move to a more spiritual path.

Spirituality, Anger, and Health

Spirituality is the final key to holistic health and for far too long, modern medicine has ignored it. Fortunately, there's a renewed interest in this vital wellness connection. Why? Because your body is the mirror image of your spirit, and all humans reflect their own unique spiritual state.

Now "spiritual" is not the same as "religious." Spirituality means connecting to a universal energy, a greater mystery, or a transcendent being that moves us to enlightened truth, beauty, and love, and which ultimately allows us to fulfill our purpose in life. When we have purpose, value, and hope in our lives we are, according to Sidney Jourard, "inspirited," and we may live longer because of it:

> Assuming that rudimentary "health habits" are observed, it is . . . true that more highly inspirited people become ill less often than less-spirited people. People with much to live for, who love deeply and broadly and draw on their inner resources to solve the mysteries of the universe and to satisfy the needs and wants of mankind, probably live longer than less dedicated people.
>
> **—Sidney Jourard, psychologist**

So if you are dedicated to chronic, festering, unresolved anger, it may be a sign that you are dispirited—unconnected to the energy of life because you are lonely, hopeless, demoralized, or without purpose—and this dispiritation can rob you of your health. Indeed, for centuries, medical professionals have observed that those in spiritual distress are more physically vulnerable and more likely to become sick:

> When a man does not acknowledge to himself who, what, and how he is, he is out of touch with reality, and he will

sicken. The meaning of sickness is protest . . . the protest of a system which has sent warning signals to the "communication center" only to have these ignored. Sickness saves the remnant of the system from total destruction by preventing further operation, until "needs" are taken care of. In fact, "being sick"—going to bed—is behavior undertaken to restore integrity. It is often the only behavior a person has available in our culture to secure some kinds of satisfactions which his "normal" mode of action fails to produce. —**Sidney Jourard, psychologist**

If your normal mode of action is suppressing your anger, if you do not protest your moral indignation in words and actions, your body will do the job for you, and in so doing, will probably make you sick. This suppression, this spiritual sacrifice, may be why we women end up with more health problems than men. In fact, we lose 25 percent more days each year because of illness and we spend 40 percent more time in bed. Women of all ages report more health problems and physician visits than men, and although we live longer, we spend our later years with more disabling conditions—in many cases with three or four chronic illnesses. Is it worth it? Is it worth suppressing our anger and sacrificing our spiritual, emotional, and physical health? We believe the answer is a resounding no! And we hope you agree.

We hope you take stock of yourself and reconnect to the uplifting, life-affirming spiritual energy that is meant to be yours—but be forewarned. If you seize upon this bold step, you are at risk for full-blown happiness and may start to exhibit:

The Twelve Warning Signs of Health

1. The persistent presence of a support network
2. Chronic positive expectations: the tendency to frame events in a constructive light
3. Episodic peak experiences
4. A sense of spiritual involvement
5. Increased sensitivity
6. The tendency to adapt to changing conditions
7. Rapid response and recovery of the adrenaline system due to repeated challenges

8. Increased appetite for physical activity
9. The tendency to identify and communicate feelings
10. Repeated episodes of gratitude, generosity, or related emotions
11. The compulsion to contribute to society
12. A persistent sense of humor

If five or more of these indicators are present, you are on the way to full-blown health—and will discover that you're happy to boot!

PART SIX

ANGER ON THE JOB

19

MEASURING YOUR WORKPLACE ANGER

You'd never know I'm the same person . . . I sing to my kids while they get ready for school, give my family big hugs, pet the dog, wave to the neighbors, feel good, but as I drive to work something happens . . . I clench my teeth and start to feel irritated . . . the closer I get to the office the more upset I become and by the time I hit the front door I'm already mad at the parking lot guy, the guard, the receptionist . . . I find myself chewing out everyone . . . and it's like this every day.

—Kyoko, age thirty-two, manager

When you walk through that office door, do you suddenly become a piranha on a porkchop? Is the intensity of your anger so different at work than at home that you're forced to cultivate two personalities—one for use from nine to five and one that's strictly after hours? To find out, make some measurements using these anger yardsticks.

EXERCISE

Home and Workplace Anger Yardsticks

Instructions: On a scale of 1 to 10, measure the strength and frequency of your anger incidents at work compared to home.

1. How OFTEN do you feel angry AT WORK?

Never	Rarely	On occasion	Often	Very often	Always
0	1	2 3	4 5 6	7 8	9 10

2. How STRONG are your feelings of anger AT WORK?

Never feel angry	Slightly strong	Moderately strong	Very strong	Extremely strong
0	1 2	3 4 5 6	7 8	9 10

3. How OFTEN do you feel angry AT HOME?

Never	Rarely	On occasion	Often	Very often	Always
0	1	2 3	4 5 6	7 8	9 10

4. How STRONG are your feelings of anger AT HOME?

Never feel angry	Slightly strong	Moderately strong	Very strong	Extremely strong
0	1 2	3 4 5 6	7 8	9 10

5. When you feel angry, does your spouse or significant other/best friend know it?

Never	Rarely	On occasion	Often	Very often	Always
0	1	2 3	4 5 6	7 8	9 10

6. Do your co-workers know when you are angry?

Never	Rarely	On occasion	Often	Very often	Always
0	1	2 3	4 5 6	7 8	9 10

7. When you were growing up, did the people in your family show their anger freely?

Never	Rarely	On occasion	Often	Very often	Always
0	1	2 3	4 5 6	7 8	9 10

To score, add up your numbers for anger at work compared to anger at home. Based on the anger yardsticks, where did you get angry most often? If you answered "at work" you're not alone:

> *I stared at the vice president of human resources in utter disbelief. He had just informed me that after coming through a six-year period in which we'd fought off a hostile take over attempt, cut headquarters personnel by almost 40 percent, battled our way back from bankruptcy and had every surviving staff member wear at least two hats, our mostly male senior management team had decided to reward itself with obscene bonuses ranging from 50 percent to 100 percent of their respective salary midpoints.*
>
> *They had also seen fit, the VP noted proudly, to reward the rest of us—the professionals without whom these managers never could have achieved their goal-related bonuses. What was our reward? A free pizza lunch in the cafeteria—a lunch that he wanted the predominantly female committee I chair to serve. My temperature zoomed right to the boiling point and I eyed the marble bookends on his credenza, debating whether I should pound some sense into his brain or maim him just for fun.*
>
> **—Geraldine, age thirty-eight, marketing specialist**

Conflicts with superiors whose brains have moved out, "get them before they get you" infighting among co-workers, pressure cooker deadlines, work overload, and lousy conditions are just some of the reasons why we get mad at work— and much of this anger is related to stress (see Chapter 7). In fact, nearly half of America's workers rate their jobs as stressful or extremely stressful, and in a massive new Department of Labor survey of 250,000 working women, 58 percent of the respondents cited "too much stress" as a serious problem.

The stress and the lack of control it symbolizes make workers angry, especially those employed in dead-end jobs, jobs that offer zip in terms of intellectual stimulation, professional achievement, and personal growth. Who is in these jobs? The majority of fifty million American women that's who, and while there are men stuck in the same career ghetto, it's home to many more females than males. Unfortunately we females are easy to pick out of the occupational landscape because we are the employees routinely assigned to boring tasks, constantly overlooked for promotions, and frequently limited by sex-role stereotypes. Worse yet, we have few constructive outlets for frustration and fury on the job. This is particularly true for those of us who feel we must stay calm at all costs and maintain the perfect public face. Besides, if we "lose it," the repercussions would be too great and our colleagues just wouldn't understand:

> *Recently I was talking to a male colleague about something I considered to be extremely important. I needed his support and I was talking with a good deal of feeling. He minimized what I said and downplayed its importance. I could not agree and I was getting more and more exasperated. He kept saying, "Well, it is really not that important," or "Let's wait and see." Finally, in a kind of apathetic way, I said quietly, "Well, there is this, this, and that . . . ," enumerating the points again, but this time without any feeling. He said, "Oh, why didn't you say that before—instead of coming on like a witch on a broom!" My intense expression of feeling made him too anxious to hear the message, yet I felt that my feelings were just as important to the communication as the words. The point is that women are made to feel they need to curtail such feelings.*
>
> **—Irene Stiver, Director, Psychology Department,**
> **McLean Hospital, Massachusetts**

So we working women keep our anger firmly under wraps. Unfortunately, we have so many good reasons to be angry at work that many of us begin to feel pretty tightly wrapped ourselves . . . (Check out your answer to anger yardstick #6 to see if this applies to you—a score of 0 to 3 means you're suppressing!)

Cutting Ourselves on the Glass Ceiling and Other Reasons We're Angry at Work

Discrimination, sexual harassment, and the "glass ceiling" that prevents career advancement are just a few of the very legitimate reasons we have for anger in the workplace, and that's not all. Throughout the world, we are concentrated in lower-status, lower-paying jobs with salaries that average 30 to 40 percent less than men's. In addition, less than 20 percent of all managers come from the female ranks. This means that most of us are still supervised by men and that men are still the CEOs and policy makers. In fact, only 6.2 percent of all seats on the Fortune 500 corporate boards are held by women. The upshot is that men come first in almost every business environment and women are simply expected to follow behind and enjoy the view. Unfortunately, that view is even more dismal when you consider these depressing statistics about work in the United States:

- Regardless of education or occupation, women earn less than men.
- The average salary of a female, African-American college graduate working full time is less than that of a white male high school dropout.
- Hispanic women earn only 55 percent of the wages of white men.
- Corporate women at the vice-presidential level and above earn 42 percent less than their male peers.
- As of 1994, most women report that they're still in clerical and service occupations.
- Most women return to work within six months after giving birth.
- More than half of the working women with children under age five say that finding affordable child care is a serious problem, in part because only a small percentage of industries provide child benefits and expenses.
- More than one in three women who maintain families and work full-time earn less than a poverty-level income.

No wonder we feel angry and powerless, especially when we know most of our situations should and could be better!

Unfortunately, this lack of power, this low amount of control over a job with typically high-stress demands is characteristic of most "female" occupations. A secretary's position is the perfect example:

*There are pressures and deadlines and angry bosses. And
there is no room for discussion about decisions that affect my work. Nobody appreciates what I do or recognizes my potential. At my age [forty-one], I am a mule. I
have no options. I have to work, but there's no way for
me to get ahead.* —**As reported in the *Western Journal
of Nursing Research***

*"Secretaries are the only ones in the corporate world
whose pay is directly linked to the boss. Instead of a career path of their own, most secretaries have had a hitch-
your-wagon-to-a-star reward system"* . . . *a secretary displaced by her boss's demotion or retirement can be left in
a lurch just as much as a homemaker is displaced by divorce or widowhood . . .*
—**Elizabeth Fried, labor consultant, as reported in *The
New York Times*, March 17, 1994**

Is it any wonder then that "secretary" ranks second of the
twelve highest-stress jobs identified by the National Institute
for Occupational Safety and Health? But secretaries aren't
the only ones who are stressed out. Even those of us with
advanced educations and highly specialized expertise chafe
at our lack of authority, control, and influence on the job. A
recent study of female university faculty members and middle managers in accounting, advertising, banking, and law
bears this out because it shows that despite their titles and
backgrounds, these women too, feel stressed and powerless.

Powerlessness As an Anger Trigger

*I watched helplessly as they forcibly retired my boss . . .
a man of great . . . integrity and in his place put an obnoxious MBA centerfold who expected me to teach him
everything I knew.* —**Monica**

*I had a meeting with the president of the college about
these contracts . . . we have to do. More and more responsibility was being shifted towards [me] . . . I said three
different times "I do not have time to do these." He never
acknowledged it . . . I was so angry I wanted to grab his
face and say "Look at me. Do you hear what I'm telling
you?"* —**Kara**

At a staff meeting several years ago we were discussing a policy change. The person proposing the change was someone who . . . oozed authority and inflexibility which always threatened and cowed me. I agreed to his suggestion even though I really didn't think it was a fair policy. Later at the staff meeting when my boss [whom I respect and admire] was present, we began to discuss the policy change . . . I became more and more uncomfortable and attempted to voice my reservations. The more I tried to talk, the more upset I became. Finally, I burst into tears . . . after the meeting broke . . . My boss suggested that what I was really feeling . . . was anger at myself for agreeing to something that I didn't feel was ethical or fair in the first place. And he was right. I was furious with myself . . . I couldn't articulate or express or even name my fury. All I could do was cry.   **—Laura**

Whether you're a secretary or a supervisor, the lack of power to change frustrating situations on the job is a frequent anger trigger. According to the Women's Anger Study, women say they get mad when: "I'm not offered a choice—as I feel I should be—about something that affects me." "I'm asked to do something I really don't want to do." "Someone tries to boss me and I feel I can do what I need to do without bossing from anyone." "People demand that I help them or take on another task when I already have too much to do." "I have little or no say over what happens to me." "I want to get things done and people poke around and hinder me from doing them." For many of us, this powerlessness goes hand in hand with:

Injustice on the Job

Why are powerlessness and injustice interconnected? Since we're not respected in the powerless positions we hold, we see that others take unfair advantage of us—and it's not a pretty sight. As a result, unjust treatment is a major anger trigger from the office to the factory floor and everywhere in between. Participants in the Women's Anger Study cite these examples: "Being blamed for mistakes I didn't make and things I didn't do," "being talked down to as if I were stupid," "being put down or yelled at in front of a bunch of people," "when someone at work tries to prove me wrong in front of others," "when someone uses me as an excuse to lie or when someone lies to me," "when I'm ignored." But perhaps the most serious miscarriage of workplace justice is the glass ceiling.

The Glass Ceiling

All over corporate America, the cracking sound you hear is not bottles of champagne launching senior-level careers, but middle management women hitting the glass ceiling. The glass ceiling is the artificial barrier organizations set up to prevent certain qualified workers from moving into higher positions. Does it sound familiar? It did to women in Wisconsin, who told Governor Tommy Thompson's task force on glass ceilings that:

> It's just hard to get into the "good old boy network." The good old boys seem to stick around and when one does go, the openings aren't posted because they have someone in mind. There are no postings for higher level jobs.
> There is a boys' club of information that we are not even privy to and are not invited to . . .
> There are older men in high positions with attitudes that women can't do the job as well.
> Because I'm a mother and a wife, it is assumed that . . . I won't be able to devote as much time to my job.
> The guys are used to working together and they are just plain comfortable together.
> —*Report of the Governor's Task Force*, **Wisconsin, November 1993**

Like our Wisconsin counterparts, many of us with competence, talent, and credibility to burn find it almost impossible to progress beyond a certain level. Gender bias stops us, even though we've proven our abilities hundreds of times. The phenomenon is not uncommon. From 58 to 93 percent of the women surveyed in various organizations report glass ceilings in their places of employment. Researcher Eryn O'Brien documents the pervasiveness of this unfair barrier to women's achievement even further.

O'Brien studied nearly eight hundred male and female managers. On all performance ratings including motivation, judgment, leadership, communication and interpersonal skills, women equaled or outdid men, but the women received fewer and lower-quality promotions. In fact, only 8.7 percent of the women's "promotions" were genuine steps up the corporate ladder—and male executives lolling under the money tree still wonder why we're mad. While we, for the most part, crane our necks upward to read the words:

Sex Discrimination

Ten men and I were sitting around a boardroom table discussing some literature I'd designed. The conversation heated up. Suddenly one of them threw his copy at me and said, "Here, Liz, just pass this out at your next Tupperware party to all your little lady friends."
—Liz, age thirty-four, freelance artist

Sex discrimination is a high-octane fuel for working women's anger and all too often, an unwanted cure for working women's dreams. Despite the lip service paid to equality and affirmative action, sexism is still evident in academia, the government, the military, and male-owned and operated businesses. Wherever it's found, it stops the trajectory of female careers. In fact, according to one survey, 55.8 percent of us women—compared to 2.1 percent of men—feel our career progress had been delayed by sex discrimination.

A sobering new study by Deborah Swiss and Judith Walker emphatically reinforces the point—sexism is alive and well in the American workplace. Swiss and Walker surveyed 902 female graduates of Harvard University's law, medical, and business schools, expecting to learn how this elite group of women found innovative solutions to balancing work and family life.

Instead what we found was incredible anger and frustration about the difficulty of being a working mother.
—Deborah Swiss, researcher

Swiss and Walker also found that women receive severe penalties for becoming pregnant, for taking maternity leave, and for cutting back on the number of hours they work. One woman's male mentor told her:

Take my advice. Don't take your whole maternity leave.
Not if you want to keep your job.
—Anonymous male "mentor"

In some cases the pressure was so enormous that women returned to work just three days after giving birth.

Other women have found their careers tied hand and foot to the mommy track too, especially if they opt for flextime. A study of female managers and employees in seventy companies reveals that few organizations support parent-friendly flextime policies, even though flexible hours improve productivity, morale, and the retention of workers. In fact, many women were told point-blank that if they chose flextime, they could hang their careers out to dry. One study participant hit the attitudinal nail right on the head:

I think people feel that when you're part-time you're not as serious about your career, not as dedicated.
—Flextime survey participant

To prove the naysayers wrong, some of the women actually increased their work hours so as not to miss out on opportunities. And what about those who defied convention and chose flextime? Most lost promotions, were removed from supervisory responsibilities, and suffered pay cuts.

Ironically, women aren't the only ones who suffer from this myopic attitude, at least not in the long run. Why? The mommy track gives companies an opportunity to positively impact their own futures because it allows for proper parenting of the next generation of workers—but many male bosses don't seem to get this. Witness one female professional who told the aforementioned U.S. Labor Department Survey:

They [male bosses] act like having children is like having a dog—all you do is feed them and walk them once a day. If someone doesn't become more concerned about how this country's children are raised, our nation is in big trouble. **—U.S. Labor Department survey participant**

Business and industry are in big trouble too, particularly in terms of the talent they lose in the future and right now. In fact, fully 53 percent of the Harvard women changed jobs as a result of their family obligations and many quit the work world entirely. Other women are following suit. And is it any wonder? After all, if these privileged, professional Harvard women with their high incomes and superior education are having such a hard time, imagine what the rest of us face! But there is another side to the story.

Psychologist Faye Crosby points out that sex discrimination is not always intentional and sometimes occurs without any conscious or unconscious desire to keep us down. For example, Sandra serves on a university committee and of the eighteen members, four are women. When a female professor pointed out this gender imbalance to the chairman and suggested the appointment of additional women, the chairman was genuinely baffled by her suggestion. Only as he scrambled to name the female committee members did it dawn on him that there were actually only four—to him the committee had looked balanced!

In this case, the chairman, like many male organizational leaders, was simply insensitive to or unaware of the consequences of his belly-up-to-the-bar-boys style and policies. Other men are savvy enough to know that it's not politically correct to use sexist language or to expect us to make coffee, so for their own sakes, they don't put their biased attitudes on public display. Certainly some males are making a sincere effort to change their behavior, but in many cases it's too little, too late. Sex discrimination continues and for many of us, the consequences are devastating, particularly if those consequences include sexual harassment.

Sexual Harassment

Gary called me into his office and said, "How can you tell if a man got his vasectomy at Sears? When he has an erection, his garage door goes up and down! Hey Rita, wanna play with my door opener?" Then the two men with him laughed.   **—Rita H.**

I've had my fanny patted and my boobs grabbed, you know, the whole nine yards—and the put downs.

—Muriel

My boss offered to drive me home from the dinner meeting . . . Instead, he pulled into a hotel and said, "You're not ready to move up the ladder yet, but a lateral [pro]motion might do you some good, if you know what I mean."

—CeeCee

Inappropriate comments and lewd jokes, unwanted physical touches and brazen advances that rival the Marquis de Sade for their painful consequences are all forms of sexual harassment and all triggers for working women's anger. Unfortunately, these triggers are widespread. According to the New York Public Interest Research Group, 71 percent of all female employees report being sexually harassed at some time in their careers.

For many of us "some time" doesn't mean just one time. Studies show that sexual remarks and the pressure for dates often go on for six months or more. In fact, sexual harassment is usually not an isolated incident, but a pattern of abuse that takes place over time and causes extreme emotional distress:

> *Two female FBI agents recently filed suit . . . reporting unwelcome sexual comments and advances for more than a year by their male supervisor. His behaviors included placing hands on their buttocks or into their skirt pockets as well as comments such as . . . "Maternity has been good to you. Your breasts are really big. Are you breast-feeding? I wish I was your baby." When the women complained, their personnel evaluations were downgraded. Requests for transfer were also refused.*
> —*The Knoxville News-Sentinel,* **March 13, 1994**

Most of us feel we have no choice but to endure this degrading, traumatizing behavior because our livelihood depends on our jobs. Even if the boss does make us so mad our mascara melts in outrage, angrily telling him to go to hell is usually not an option, so what do we do? We tell our co-workers to go instead.

Co-Workers from Hell, or Who Women Are Angry with at Work

One of the surprises of the Women's Anger Study was that more of us are provoked to anger by our *co-workers* than our bosses. Indeed, study participants report that they feel manipulated, dumped on, and taken advantage of by their fellow employees. Furthermore, women claim their colleagues are disloyal, disrespectful, unsupportive, and irresponsible about doing their fair share. Women say they are especially infuriated when: "You've done your job and they put more work on you, while some other people get away with doing nothing all day." "People are irresponsible on their job or don't care." "Individuals have 'bright ideas' for someone else—me—to do rather than doing it themselves." "I have to assume responsibility for a task that a person who has the same capabilities I have has shirked." Or, to put it another way:

> They don't . . . work . . . they just basically sham, get by with things and . . . I resent the fact that upper management would allow that to happen. Not because I couldn't do the same thing, but I wasn't brought up like that . . . I mean when you're supposed to work, you work. —**Jean**

Unfortunately, our anger toward irresponsible co-workers is often directed at fellow females. Why? When we can't vent anger at our male supervisors, we frequently take it out on each other through cattiness, sarcasm, damaging gossip, snide memos, chilly silence, subtle nonverbal signals, and in various passive-aggressive ways (see Chapter 23) that look suspiciously like:

Cat Fights: Horizontal Violence on the Job

Nursing is a perfect example of this phenomenon. The nursing profession, which is comprised primarily of women, has long been dominated by the medical profession, composed primarily of men. In the late 1950s, nurses were taught to stand when physicians entered the room. The nurse walked behind the doctor as he made his rounds, carrying the patient charts, anticipating his questions, jotting down his verbal orders—in sum, dutifully and efficiently enacting the handmaiden role.

Nursing's religious and military origins contributed to women's acceptance of this subservient state. Nurses were also afraid to alienate doctors because they could lose their jobs—an angry doctor could simply march into the supervisor's office and demand that a nurse be fired. The authority of the physician was absolute and unquestioned, and so was the physician's right to have temper tantrums. Indeed, although doctors were permitted to throw surgical instruments, yell at nurses, orderlies, and other underlings, such behavior was unthinkable for nurses. Nurses were allowed to express their anger only to each other through nasty notes taped to locker doors or behind-the-scenes sabotage.

Unfortunately, in many work settings, this behavior continues today. While there have been notable advances in the profession, the majority of nurses are still employed in hospitals or other physician-controlled environments where they continue to be oppressed. For instance, doctors in Tennessee recently lobbied to defeat legislation that would remove restrictions on nurse practitioners. The medical association distributed an extremely nasty brochure entitled "Don't Let Reform Duck Up Health Care" which referred to nurse practitioners and other nonphysician health care providers as "dubious birds" and "daffy ducks." The physicians convinced legislators that the overall quality of patient care would suffer if nurses were allowed to practice independently. Many male legislators agreed, and one made the following blatantly sexist comment during the debate:

> *It's hard not to like the ladies in white dresses with beautiful hats. But if you take the shackles off the nurse practitioners . . . you're taking a gamble.*
> **—A male Tennessee state legislator**

The use of the word *shackles* clearly conjures up images of slavery and bondage. Not surprisingly, some nurses—still shackled—continue to display horizontal violence toward their peers. For example, a woman who had a satisfying birth experience in the care of a nurse-midwife wrote a very positive letter to the local newspaper. Other letter writers joined in the ensuing dialogue, expressing largely favorable opinions. There was one major exception—a belligerent letter from an obstetric nurse. She claimed that a woman would only choose a nurse-midwife if

> *. . . there is no higher skilled person available or because they [women] have been misinformed as to the merits of nurse-midwifery . . . I would like to make a point of saying that over the history of legitimate obstetrical care it has not been the nurse-midwife who has made the advances in prenatal care possible for pregnant women. It has been the physicians and the vast bodies of research and development available to them . . .*
> **—An obstetric nurse, in a letter**
> **to a Tennessee newspaper**

The writer practically foams at the mouth as she uses the word *legitimate* to describe physician care and to imply that nurse care is at the opposite end of the spectrum. Likewise, she suggests that "vast bodies of research," while available to doctors, are marked "hands off" for nurses. But by glorifying physicians and denigrating the work of those in her own profession, what this nurse is actually doing is identifying with her oppressor.

And it isn't just women who fall into this trap. In every minority group there are those who identify with the oppressor rather than with members of their own sex, race, or class. These are usually individuals who feel inadequate or inferior so they take on the qualities of the dominant people around them as a way of "acquiring" strength and "elevating" their own status. While this can happen in any oppressed group whose worth has been devalued, the traditionally female, sexually oppressed occupations (teachers, secretaries, librarians, nurses, human resource personnel) are especially vulnerable; in fact, they're regular minefields. Why?

Although the angry women in these professions are just exhibiting the same attitudes, attributes, limitations, and concerns you'd expect of anyone whose work has been shot down, their femaleness complicates the situation. The professional qualities these women are expected to have are virtually identical to the "job description" of a wife or a mother. They're supposed to be warm, empathetic, supportive, and caring; in short, the ideal traditional woman, a woman who is fulfilled by self-sacrifice and service, who sees taking care of a boss, student, or patient as a natural extension of her maternal role. And of course, like a good mother, a good nurse, teacher, secretary, librarian, or human resource specialist is never, never supposed to get angry, except, perhaps, at other women . . .

Woman Against Woman: The Widening Circle of Damage

When we're busily engaged in guerrilla warfare with each other, we women can't mobilize our resources to tackle what's really important. Sometimes we can't even agree on what the really important issues are. Although we are the majority in many organizations and while there could be great strength in our numbers, these numbers are meaningless unless the infighting stops. Indeed, many noble goals and effective female coalitions have been destroyed by bickering, fault-finding, name-calling, scapegoating, and the mistrust created when we talk behind each other's backs. Unfortunately, this is something with which Sandra has first-hand experience.

While serving on an all-female committee at an educational institution, Sandra grew weary of unproductive debate (she's phrasing this politely) about a certain matter. As the meeting dragged on, there appeared to be no way to resolve the issue, so Sandra suggested that a small task force be appointed to bring recommendations back to the larger group. No one voiced an objection and the meeting adjourned shortly thereafter.

To Sandra's astonishment, the next day she was summoned to the office of the program director (also female). The director informed Sandra that her fellow committee members thought she was "rude" and that Sandra had hurt their feelings. Apparently, they perceived Sandra's action as cutting off debate prematurely, but instead of telling Sandra to her face that a task force wasn't the way to go, they simply went behind her back and complained to the program director. The director warned Sandra to be careful in the future and advised her to keep the situation carefully in hand.

Alas, angry women are not only going at it "hand to hand" in the privacy of boardrooms, back rooms, classrooms, and ladies' restrooms, but in the glaring national arena as well. Many prominent women in the feminist movement are dealing each other devastating blows in their recent books and speeches. These public crucifixions of and by fellow women are the single most disturbing aspect of the widespread counterattack on women's rights known as "the backlash."

And *lash* is the correct word. While right-wing politicians and fundamentalist ministers are almost expected to deplore women's liberation, they're nothing compared to the cat-o'-nine-tails we're using on each other. Indeed, a host of women in the public eye have worked to oppose ERA, child care, maternity leave bills, and other legislation that would benefit us all. Clearly, this is horizontal violence, and just as clearly, we need to give it a rest. After all, we women have enough targets to aim at without firing at each other, and hitting these bull's eyes requires one thing—win/win strategies for managing anger at work.

20

WIN/WIN WORKPLACE STRATEGIES

I've reached very near the top of my profession, and I still have a hard time being assertive in business, because that means you're a ball-buster. It's all right for a man to do it. Do you think a man is warped or sick if he acts aggressively in business? No. But if I do it, I'm just a bitch.
                                    —As told to author Mark Baker

While corporate nabobs see men's tantrums as displays of healthy ambition and aggressiveness, the same culture condemns our displays as bitchiness and forbids us from indulging in such angry behavior. And not only are we not allowed to bitch in the halls of commerce, we're not supposed to cry there either—especially if anger has caused our tears. This is the case with Alice, whose meetings with her Hydra-headed department manager are:

. . . extremely tense. At one of our meetings she began to wave her hands around and raised her voice. It was all I could do not to cry. I was terribly angry with her for treating me so unfairly and with so little respect.

But I was not able to verbalize my feelings at all. I was choked with my anger and the only thing I could do was cry and so I left her office—apologizing for my abrupt departure!

She was left, I am sure, thinking that (a) she had appropriately chastised me and made her point; (b) I was sorry for upsetting her and felt shame over my behavior (which I think she was yelling about at the time); or (c) I was an immature, silly woman to react with tears in a professional situation. What I wanted to do was cut her throat with the letter opener on her desk, but that would have been highly inappropriate behavior.   **—Alice**

So what would have been appropriate behavior for Alice and all the rest of us who've felt angry enough to commit the same crime but want to do it without punishment? How about some win/win strategies like these . . .

Proactive Strategies: Win-Win Techniques for Managing Workplace Anger

We've all heard "don't get mad, get even," but since we do get mad at work, and since much of our anger is highly justified, a better strategy is don't get even, get ahead.

Every one of us, whether we openly express our anger or not, must make decisions about managing this powerful emotion in a way that preserves our dignity, our self-respect, and sometimes, our jobs. There are any number of anger management strategies we can choose from. Your choice will depend on the situation you're in and the people you're dealing with. Whether you simply want to discharge your anger or channel it into productive action, the following techniques can help. Best of all, if you use them, you won't ever have to settle for "even" again.

Proactive Strategy: Channeling Anger into Productive Action by Refusing to Take It to Work

I got up this morning and things have been going wrong ever since. I overslept because the stupid bell doesn't work on my alarm clock and I don't have time to get it fixed. I pulled my suit out of the dry cleaning bag and a button was missing—this is the second outfit those morons have ruined! Then I had to stand next to some jerk on the bus. He hassled me for three blocks before I told him to screw off.

Finally, I get to work and what a treat that was, let me tell you. I have three messages—one's a project emergency, one's a project crisis, and the last project, well it's hemorrhaging. I call my co-coordinator on the job that's hemorrhaging and tell him, in no uncertain terms, to get on the stick.

Then I do the same with the people working on the crisis and the emergency and can you believe it, they pick this morning, of all mornings, to give me a bad time!

But the icing on the cake is when my secretary, Nina, calls. Seems her cat is sick and she's taking him to the vet so she won't be in until noon. Well I'll be waiting for her because Nina and I are gonna have a little shoot out at the kitty corral—she can take her pet to the vet on her own time, not mine!

I suppose Nina'll be all upset, but that's too bad. I'm upset too. And it's not just her, it's everybody! Everybody's on my list today! **—Carol**

. . . and every day! In fact, if I'm not on Carol's daily shit list, I feel left out. **—Emily, Carol's colleague**

So many things piss some people off that they probably need a list to keep track of them all. These women (and men) are automatic anger alarms. Everyone and everything rings their bells, and that's before they even walk through the office door. While the average person occasionally responds angrily to events in the workplace, these individuals wear their anger like a corporate uniform and heaven help you if you don't like the cut of the suit.

Researchers say such people have "high levels of diffuse hostility." They get mad faster and more frequently than their colleagues and even they don't know why. Sometimes they're angry at vague, unacknowledged issues and because they don't understand the true source of their anger, they take it out on others. It's not surprising, then, that these women report greater levels of tension and stress on the job. What is surprising is that it's not the job that's the problem, it's the women themselves. Does this sound like it applies to you?

If so, the best remedy is a careful self-assessment and, perhaps, some professional counseling. To do a self-assessment, take a long, hard look at your personal life. Are you going through a particularly difficult time right now—a marital crisis, divorce, illness, death of a loved one, or problems with your children? If this is the case, you might be more anger prone than usual and you might be unfairly taking it out on the people at work.

By recognizing this tendency, you can begin to focus on regaining control of your temper, on leaving your anger at the office door before it intrudes on your job performance and your professional relationships.

But what if your workplace anger is more than you can handle? What if you're angry to the point of constantly feeling physically ill, seriously thinking of hurting yourself or someone else, mad so much of the time that you're emotionally paralyzed, can't function, and have unintentionally put your job in jeopardy, or just can't take it anymore and feel desperate?

If you have any or all of these symptoms, get professional help at once. Many companies have employee assistance programs that offer counseling. You can also get counseling services through your church, synagogue, or community groups like United Way. And don't be embarrassed about asking for assistance. It is an act of courage to get the help you need, to come to grips with the fact that if you don't control your anger, your anger will control you over and over and over again.

Proactive Strategy: Channeling Anger into Productive Action by Turning Off Your Mental Replay Program

> *All I can talk about is how badly my manager treats me. I think I've become obsessive.*
>
> **—Donna, age forty-five, designer**

> *. . . and just a little bit boring.*
>
> **—Anonymous comment from Donna's female co-worker**

Do you ruminate, regurgitate, and resuscitate your grievances to the point where everyone hides when they see you coming? Although it's natural to brood when you've been treated unfairly or believe that a job situation's unjust, how much good does the constant mental replay do you? How often are you going to repeat to yourself (or anyone else who will listen) "I've put in sixty-five hours this week. Why should I keep it up? No one else comes in on weekends. Why am I the only one getting dumped on?" etc., etc., etc.

The problem is that with each telling of the tale your anger escalates and even if your assessment is right on target, perpetuating an angry mood is a waste of time and energy. You must get past this stage if you are to focus on the cause of your anger and decide on a plan of effective action. Need help? Try one of these "off" switches:

1. Smile. That's right, smile. Even if you don't feel like it, a smile gives you the appearance of being in control. It makes you look one up on whoever angered you, and this is important because your goal is not to get even, it's to get ahead. By smiling, you'll eventually believe you are ahead and when you are, you'll have no need of your instant replay tape.

2. Engage in something totally distracting—read an article, clean your files, or learn that new computer program. Better yet, try helping someone in need and soon you'll see your own problems in a whole new light.

3. Throw yourself into a high-energy, high-priority work project that requires the full attention of your little gray cells.

4. Every time you slip and start brooding over the anger incident, put a dollar in your private penalty jar, then distract yourself by thinking about what to do with all that money.

5. You can also try this imagery exercise. First, find a quiet place, then begin by taking slow, deep, relaxing breaths. If you like soft music, play a soothing—but not stimulating— tape or disc. Instrumental selections are good for this purpose since you won't be distracted by the lyrics and their meanings. Just close your eyes and listen to the notes while you continue to breathe in a relaxed, focused way.

Now let your imagination travel to a place that symbolizes peace, somewhere you've experienced moments of comfort, calmness, and tranquility. Maybe it's a smooth, white beach where you can hear the rhythm of the ocean, a meadow filled with fragrant wildflowers, or perhaps a crisp, clean pine forest next to a mountain lake—anywhere that lulls and assuages you when you're upset.

These images are most effective when you use all your senses, when you smell the aroma of full-bodied pines, feel the light caress of the ocean breeze, hear the faint sounds of children laughing, or taste sweet lemonade cooling your lips. And if, in the midst of all this tranquility an angry thought intrudes, say to yourself, "I can stop this anger. I can let it go." Then return to visualizing your peaceful place.

For most people, twenty minutes of imagery is highly effective, but take more time if you need it. When you finish, move slowly. Stretch your arms and legs then count from one to five as you open your eyes and, refreshed and renewed, return to your daily activities. Once you're relaxed, you may find it easier to come to grips with the source of your angry feelings and to sort out the issues, a proactive strategy we all need to use.

Proactive Strategy: Channeling Anger into Productive Action by Sorting Out the Issues

Understanding the source of your workplace anger can be a real challenge. Sometimes it's a matter of connecting the past with the present, home with work, or simply getting the right and left sides of your brain to talk to each other.

For instance, the way you currently behave with your male boss is strongly influenced by your previous experiences with male authority figures like your father. Walter Toman calls this the duplication theorem. That is, we tend to duplicate our past experience in each new relationship. It's a simple statement, but a profoundly important idea and it begs the question, what part of your past is influencing the anger you presently experience at work?

Ask yourself why this man (your boss, colleague, or employee) provokes such a violent reaction in you. Why do your knees turn to jelly when he reprimands you or when the two of you disagree? Use these questions to do a little PI work, to probe until you get some answers. A good clue that your boss—on some deeper psychological level—represents your father is if he makes you feel more like an intimidated child than an adult. If he does, you need to decide if this is really the kind of work relationship you want. If it isn't, take steps to change it. Try taking a less childlike attitude and instead, constantly reinforce to yourself that you are both professionals and adults, then act like it.

Now what about the women who always set you off? Maybe you have a pattern of anger toward a certain female co-worker, someone whom you find absolutely infuriating. Try to identify which aspects of "her" behavior push your hot buttons and why. Then see how many of these qualities are things you dislike about yourself.

Chances are that this woman who arouses your ire is really a reflection of your own dark side, that she mirrors the negative qualities you don't like about yourself and may even deny. A strong hint is when you pinpoint something like, "She's such a know-it-all! I can't stand her dogmatic statements," and then realize (to your chagrin) that you, too, like to get up on a soapbox. If this is your situation, remember, people who live in glass houses shouldn't throw stones. Before you get mad at someone else's behavior, try getting your own ducks in a row.

Proactive Strategy: Channeling Anger into Productive Action by Getting Your Own Ducks in a Row

I can't always get my ducks in order to do things. I want to be organized, I really do . . . And yet I look around and I think, "You know, I'm really not." So it's frustration with myself . . . I don't mean to take it out on others, but . . . sometimes it just builds up and comes to a head and that's what happens, it comes out.　　　　　**—Lily**

Are your ducks in disarray? Were you born guilty of disorganization, tardiness, procrastination, memory lapses, and poor time management? Can you honestly blame anyone but yourself for whatever makes you go ballistic at work?

If the answer is no, remember that everyone needs some kind of order to function in their professional lives. The trick is finding the acceptable level of chaos for you. The next time you're angry with yourself over that missing memo, vanishing file, or important note on a napkin you now can't read, use the anger to energize yourself and get your ducks in a row.

First, write down everything you do at work for one week. At the end of the week, get a handle on the anger arousers that are self-induced, like the amount of time you waste or the interruptions you allow. Maybe you need to systematically organize your work materials, trash anything that's outdated, learn some time management skills (this is a great anger reducer—you can't enjoy work if you're always hassled and rushed), develop weekly plans, daily goals, and "to do" lists, use the "n" word—say no to outrageous demands on your time, pace yourself according to your own energy level (decide if you're a day person, a night person, or whatever, and then do the most demanding activities when you feel the most productive and energetic), and finally, disallow interruptions like phone calls or schmoozing by co-workers during your peak energy hours.

In other words, get control over any "kick myself" issues at work because control is really the bottom line. It not only helps you stop kicking yourself, but also helps you start kicking butt whenever something's just got to be done . . .

Proactive Strategy: The ABC's of Productive Action

Too many women think *action* is a four-letter word—but it's not. Sometimes we need to take action to attack the root causes of our anger at work. In fact, workplace anger can be a powerful catalyst for positive change, especially when the cause is sex discrimination, harassment, the glass ceiling, or other injustices in need of dramatic redress.

There are three dynamite strategies you can use to mount the attack. You can increase your sense of personal power on the job by applying:

A—Assertiveness, to state positively and boldly, to affirm your rights
B—Bargaining, to negotiate for better terms or conditions
C—Coalition forming, to form an alliance in support of a common cause.

(A fourth strategy, D—Departing an intolerable situation, is also available, but only as a last resort.)

Many of us who believe we are in powerless work situations never use these action strategies, and this is our fatal mistake. We don't realize that accepting the status quo is absolutely the worst thing we can do. Unfortunately, it happens all the time, especially with females.

Researcher Lisa Mainiero talked to men and women about frustrating work situations, situations in which they felt totally powerless. A much higher percentage of women simply accepted their circumstances by acting in a helpless, dependent manner. The men, on the other hand, were more likely to adopt persuasion strategies and persistently discussed their lot with whoever had the power to help them make a change. In other words, the men took action, and in taking action, empowered themselves.

You can do the same thing.

You can take actions that will empower you, but only if you're willing to make the first move. After all, power is never casually handed out—it's earned by women who have the courage to seize it for themselves. How? Acquire the expertise that makes you indispensable to your organization; assertively request well-deserved promotions, transfers, and raises; bargain with supervisors to resolve grievances; form coalitions to decrease horizontal violence; and work collaboratively with other women to achieve major policy changes like flextime, daycare, extended maternity leave, and more.

> *Five years ago a group of prominent women scientists at the National Institutes of Health were so frustrated by their agency's sexism that they formed an outside lobbying group to alert Congress and the public that women were being excluded from medical research on everything from heart disease to alcoholism.*
>
> *By risking their careers, the women . . . helped reform NIH policies . . . Thanks in large part to [the] group's efforts, Congress instructed the NIH to include women as well as men in all major medical studies and set the stage for a $600 million long-term study of older women's health.*
>
> **—As reported in *Elle* magazine, March 1994**

The women at the NIH did it, and you can do it too. You can use your workplace anger as a source of personal empowerment and as a force for positive social change. The time to start is now.

But what if direct action isn't possible? Or if you know the situation is only temporary and you've just got to grit your teeth for the moment and stick it out? Then discharging your anger is the way to go. This is especially true if you're suppressing your angry feelings. To find out if this is the case, check your scores on the anger yardsticks. If you score high on #1 and #2, and low on #6, you're holding your anger in, and you'll want to use the following discharge strategies to evict this nasty feeling from your soul.

Proactive Strategy: Discharging Your Anger by Pounding It Out at the Gym

Ever notice how some weightlifting equipment resembles a guillotine? Picture the head of your favorite anger provocateur right there and *slam* those weights together. Feels great, doesn't it? So does tennis (you can just see "his" face on one of those little balls as you whack it to kingdom come); swimming (drowning's probably too good for "her"); pounding it out on the jogging track (think of "them" underfoot); and any other physical exercise. Exercise is a great way to discharge the angry feelings you've built up all day, and as an extra added bonus, it's good for you too (see Chapter 18).

The kicker, of course, is finding time for a regular exercise regimen. Researchers say that working women tend to exercise less, yet we need it more because of the many anger provocations we experience each day. The trick is to make the time, to realize that part of your responsibility as a professional is to keep yourself mentally and physically healthy. Exercise will help you do both, so make it a high priority in your daily schedule. Remember, even a twenty-minute walk can work wonders, whether you're working out anger or just plain working out.

Proactive Strategy: Discharging Anger with a Zen-Minute Break

But what if you can't leave the office for a quick jog or brisk walk? What if your boss has you so mad you could climb the walls but there's not a StairMaster in sight? Try this.

Find a place where you won't be interrupted. Close your eyes. Breathe deeply. Now concentrate and repeat the word *peace* over and over to yourself. Feel yourself regaining control and calming down as the angry tension leaves your forehead and neck, your shoulders and back. Now unclench your fists and stretch out your fingertips. Let the tension ease right out of your body and when you're ready, calmly go back to work.

If your anger returns full force at the very sight of your desk (or "hers"), simply take another short break and repeat the process again. And again. Most of all, remember to breathe. Exhale your anger and let it go-o-o-o . . .

Proactive Strategy: Discharging Anger by Getting It Off Your Chest

They say that discretion is the better part of valor and at work this is often true. The workplace has formidable penalties for those of us who express our anger in inappropriate ways:

> *In a moment of intense anger, one of my colleagues called our boss a faggot. He was fired on the spot. Yet the women in this department have been called broads, bitches, bimbos, and much worse, and we're supposed to put up and shut up no matter how mad we are.*
>
> **—Larissa, age thirty-three, lawyer**

Sometimes it's not in your best interests to duke it out with your boss, even if he's dead wrong. Likewise, it's not always smart or possible to read your co-workers the riot act. Although you may be expressing your anger in a rational, controlled, low-key manner and sticking to the issue at hand, the other person might become defensive or vindictive—and work is hard enough without someone holding a grudge against you.

But what if you've just got to get it off your chest? Then what should you do? The safest alternative is to share the angry episode later with a close friend or relative, someone you know you can trust. Wait until you're off your employer's property and have some privacy, then go at it! Do whatever it takes to talk it out completely—but don't get steamed up all over again. Remember, your goal is to discharge your anger, not to get psyched up for round 2.

That's why it's so important to choose a trustworthy confidante, someone who listens carefully, but doesn't add fuel to the fire. You don't want to be goaded on with comments like "That dirty SOB! I would be furious!" or "You should get even with him for all the hell he's put you through!" Such incendiary words prolong your anger and if you act on them, they can land you right in the unemployment line. However, by discharging your emotions in an intelligent (and if necessary, loud) discussion with someone you trust, you'll be back in control and may even realize that whatever ticked you off wasn't such a big deal after all. In retrospect, you may even find it amusing . . .

Proactive Strategy: Discharging Anger with Laughter, the Best Medicine

Next week there can't be a crisis, my schedule is already full.   **—Henry Kissinger**

Some days it takes nothing short of a palace coup and a full-scale riot to set you off. Other days it's that run in your pantyhose, the evil eye of the malfunctioning copy machine, the "Customer from the Black Lagoon," the student from hell, or just the guy in the office next door who always wants to chat when you're busy. It's simply a matter of which straw will break the camel's back first.

But some of us carry far too many straws. We seethe silently, offended by every glitch and irritation, piling one little thing on top of another until BOOM! Our colleagues run for cover, our assistants cower in the corner, and every innocent bystander from the snack room to the executive suite checks to see if he or she is wearing a bulletproof vest.

If you recognize yourself in these stories, if you are an aficionado of annoyances, an impresario of irritation, or just plain ornery, lighten up. You're probably taking things far too seriously or are a bit too much of a perfectionist. Remember that minor glitches occur in every occupation and you should learn to overlook the small stuff or to laugh about it. Laughter can release your tension and prevent anger buildup, so try posting cartoons in your workspace or taping them to your locker. Also, be sure to share your jokes with others. After all, as the bumper sticker says, "Shit happens," and some of it is genuinely funny:

> *In the Beginning was the Plan,*
> *And then came the Assumptions,*
> *And the Assumptions were without form,*
> *And the Plan was completely without substance,*
> *And darkness was upon the faces of the workers*
> *who spoke among themselves saying:*
> *"It is a crock and it stinketh."*

*And the workers went unto their Supervisors and
sayeth:
"It is a pail of dung and none may abide the odor
thereof."
And the Supervisors went unto their Managers and
sayeth unto them:
"It is a container of excrement and it is very
strong such that none may abide by it."
And the managers went unto their Directors and
sayeth:
"It is a vessel of fertilizer and none may abide
its strength."
And the Directors spoke amongst themselves saying
one to another:
"It contains that which aids plant growth and it is
very strong."
And the Directors went unto the Vice Presidents
and sayeth unto them:
"It promotes growth and is very powerful."
And the Vice Presidents went unto the President and
sayeth unto him:
"This new plan will actively promote the growth and
efficiency of this Company and in these areas
in particular."
And the President looked upon the Plan and saw that
it was good and the Plan became Policy.
And that is how s—— happens.*

**—Fax received anonymously at companies across the
country, author unknown**

And that is why, whenever you can, you might as well laugh.

PART SEVEN

ANGER AT MEN

21

WHY MEN FEAR WOMEN'S ANGER

Bobbitt—another word for the cut felt round the world. It makes me want to weld my fly shut just in case I piss off some woman.

—Graham, age twenty-six, designer

Bobbitt." Just whisper the word and men from Kansas City to Kalamazoo quake in their wingtips. Why? Because Lorena Bobbitt's actions epitomize many men's greatest fear, their fear of us, angry women. It's the same fear Rush Limbaugh capitalizes on so cleverly in his daily diatribes against "feminazis," the same fear that has stereotyped our anger as a phenomenon so terrifying, so destructive, that it must be stopped at all costs—and usually is. The big question is why. Why, over the centuries, have powerful religious, social, and family forces joined together to ensure that our anger is subdued so it won't cause testosterone meltdown and sweep men away in its path?

Preventing Testosterone Meltdown or, Why Men Fear Women's Anger and How They Do Damage Control

We were at a party and all I could think when my date blew up was that I had to get the situation under control because I was afraid someone might hear her.
—Robert, age fifty-four, contractor

For many men, an angry woman is a blind date with fear, a fear so subconscious that most males don't even recognize it. This fear comes from experiences in infancy that permanently affect the way men respond to women. You see, deep in the male psyche lives this powerful image of the perfect mother—the mother who gives nourishing breast milk to the hungry baby, the mother who hugs the toddler when he falls and provides positive affirmations to the boy struggling to become a man. This perfect mother is inexhaustible. She has an endless supply of love, compassion, and understanding—the only problem is that she doesn't exist.

Unfortunately, many men don't realize this. They expect all us women to continue supplying the breast, the soothing lullaby, and the devoted attention of their "perfect mother" ideal. And of course, their ideal, perfect mother "never" gets mad because if she did, that would make her "bad mother," and "bad mother" is a source of great fear for these men because she doesn't just get mad, she gets "even."

Bad mother gets even because she confers pain instead of pleasure—she doesn't feed the infant on time, she punishes the toddler's impulsive actions, and firmly says no to his selfish, childish demands. Now because mothers are only human, every mother, by this definition, is sometimes bad. As a result, every male's (and female's) first experiences with deprivation, frustration, and punishment are at the hands of mother. What makes the situation worse is that despite the fear, hostility, and resentment he feels, the male can't complain because he depends on his mother to survive. This dependency is terrifying to him because he's convinced that if mother gets mad enough, she might just withdraw the love, milk, nurturance, and other vital supplies he needs to stay alive.

This is why most men are so afraid of women's anger—it takes them back to a time of helpless dependency that they fear and resent.

> *Men go back to their three-year-old selves several times a day—seeing woman as a giantess with enormous power.*
> **—Robert Bly, men's movement spokesman**

Of course, it doesn't matter that in the real world this power is just a myth—in many a male's unconscious mind it exists, and so his primitive fear lives on. Alas, it's a fear that's hard to shake. Why? Because the unconscious mind can't be touched by logic or reason. As a result, some men go to the opposite, unreasonable extreme—they put up their guard and keep women down.

Keeping Women (and Girls) Down

Some men want a pocket Venus, a well-behaved, never-angry woman who will always see to their needs, come when called, and then quietly agree to be put away until the next time her services are required. Feminists say the male taboo against female anger reflects an intense desire to maintain the status quo and help these men remain the dominant members of society. It also "keeps us women in our place" and assures the men that the caretaking services they're so dependent upon will continue. After all, as psychoanalyst Jean Baker Miller points out, most male interactions are competitive or confrontational. Since they don't make commitments to look after each other, they have to get someone else—women—to do it for them. However, to get us to fill this role, some men are convinced our behavior must be subordinated and restrained.

So when the female natives get restless, these men move quickly. Their fear that our anger will disrupt the traditional balance of sexual—that is, male—power compels them to take immediate steps to keep us under control. And what do they do? According to Jean Baker Miller, they act out the following predictable behaviors of a dominant group—a few of which may sound familiar, very familiar . . .

- Acting destructively toward subordinates
- Restricting the subordinates' range of actions
- Discouraging subordinates in the full and free expression of their experience
- Characterizing the subordinates falsely
- Describing the subordinates' situation as normal, ordained by God, biology, or some other ultimate authority

As to this last item, although the deity might forgive any discrepancies between the divine plan and our womanly desires, many mortal men won't. So to stay in control, these guys trace the "correctness" of female subordination all the way back to Eve. Of course, they trace the "correctness" of their own actions back to God. To see how it's done, just compare the stories of Prometheus and Eve as psychologist Miriam Polster did. Polster points out that when Prometheus defied Zeus and stole fire for human use, he was put on a pedestal, declared a brave hero and a manly man. By contrast, when Eve defied God, she was condemned as evil, evicted from the Garden, and has been on the lam ever since.

> In seminary I would get real angry in classes where men would take certain Scriptures and interpret them in a way that I thought was wrong, in a way that was putting women down. I remember going to a church conference where they were talking about women voting. All the lay people could vote and up until recently, the lay people consisted of just men. The women could not have a vote in the business of the church. Certainly I was very angry about that because they certainly would take our tithes and certainly would let us work for hours and hours—but we could not have a say in decisions.
>
> I remember specifically sitting in one of our church conferences where it was proposed that women could start voting. The argument that some of the ministers brought up was that, you know, to have women making decisions when their hormones are always so messed up. Or, to have a woman in ministry doing baptism when she may be having her period. They were saying this on the

floor of a general conference. It was so demeaning of women—the way they were putting us down—it was just so dehumanizing. At that point, I didn't feel the calling for the ministry. But I hurt for the women that I knew did. Women have always been less than men in the church's eyes and I've been very angry about that.

—Zoe, age thirty-one, chaplain

So what does all this say about the divine implications of proper male/female behavior? For us, the word from the bully pulpit is loud and clear—we better acquiesce to the status quo, can our anger, and let the male deity define our world. And it doesn't matter if that deity is named God, Buddha, or Allah, all the major religions have drafted Him for the male team.

It certainly took cunning and political savvy to draft God for the masculine team. His endorsement has sanctioned women's oppression in the name of religious principles; His divine approval has been used by men as a smoke screen to conceal their own defensive psychological machinations. And women, as products of their culture, have believed the lies, have at times accepted the myth of their own evil, and have remained in second place . . .

—Janet Muff

Indeed, many of us have been brainwashed into believing we are weak, unworthy, and have no right or cause to be angry. In fact, from an early age, we females are taught the deeply ingrained cultural and religious ideology that says we're inferior to men and boys. Unfortunately, we've bought into this concept hook, line, and sink-her:

I know what's wrong, I'm not good enough. No girl is good enough for Stan to be her boyfriend.

—April, age thirteen, student

All along the boys had been . . . becoming responsible members of an actual and moral world we . . . girls had never heard of. They had been learning self-control. We had failed to develop any selves worth controlling . . . we were vigilantes of the trivial. The boys must have shared our view that we were . . . in the long run negligible.

—Annie Dillard, *An American Childhood*

Women, as children, receive "dependency training." In one study, small children in playpens tried to reach toys outside their enclosure. Parents of girl babies were much more likely to hand the toys to their children than were parents of boy children. Boys . . . were permitted to take care of themselves. **—Jean Withers**

Boys are also permitted to use controlling behavior and dominant gestures from the moment they climb out of the cradle. Girls are not. Consider: In studies of thirty-three-month-olds, boys physically dominate play whenever they're paired with girls; from ages three and a half to five and a half, boys try to influence playmates by making direct demands while girls use polite—and often ineffectual—suggestions; elementary-school-age boys frequently intrude on girls' games and activities, control larger amounts of space, and treat females as "contaminating." In response girls tighten and tense their bodies so they take up less room, tolerate interruptions of their speech and actions, hesitate, apologize, smile too much, and fall silent on cue.

All these gestures brand girls as the "underclass" and cement their subordinate status. In junior high and high school, this subordinating process continues. During their teenage years, many girls are subjected to humiliating sexual harassment in the halls of higher learning including bra snapping, fondling, taunting, and unflattering catcalls.

This boy started looking at me, giving me weird looks. Soon he was making fun of me, snapping my bra, calling me a fat horse (when I'm not really fat), pinching me (both on my bottom and on the top), trying to go up my skirt, and the list goes on and on.

I've had boys put their hand in my shirt, ask me if I was a virgin, and touch my body. It is humiliating. The teachers act as if there isn't a problem; they try to ignore it, but you wouldn't believe how often it happens.

—Participants in a study of four thousand teenage girls by the Wellesley Center for Research on Women

And how does such controlling, dominating behavior make girls feel? According to a new national study by the American Association of University Women, this widespread, growing problem is not the harmless mischief it seems, at least not when measured by the damage to girls' self-esteem:

I thought that I was dirt . . . I just wanted to die.
—Black female, age fourteen

It made me feel that a woman isn't worth much.
—White female, age sixteen

Which is the whole point. Because these low blows to the female psyche convinced many of us, as girls, that women aren't worth much, we also concluded that women's emotions, ambitions, and abilities aren't worth much either. As a result, we've been seduced into being the weaker sex, the sex that must be taken care of, the sex that can't survive without male guidance and protection—so of course we can't get angry because if we do, we'll be cut loose from the male lifeline we think we need to survive. But sometimes, hanging onto that lifeline means putting our necks in an emotional noose and our feelings under house arrest.

Why We Suppress Our Anger Toward Men

Emotional house arrest happens all the time, and often, it's voluntary. Many of us arrest and suppress our anger toward men not because of some obsolete, fondue-age value system, but out of fear—our fear that female anger can disrupt heterosexual relationships and send the world spinning out of control. Most of us don't want to tip this precarious balance because we "need" men's approval and support to boost our self-esteem and make us feel fulfilled. Besides, getting angry could get us fired from our culturally assigned vocation, the one that comes with the job description that says "we must love and nurture men." But loving and nurturing men is a hazardous occupation and marriage is seldom an equal opportunity employer. Indeed, many of us desperately try to maintain relationships with indifferent, unfaithful, or abusive mates. We stay in these situations because we believe there's no way out—we're economically dependent and don't want our children deprived. That's why we grab at the nearest male shirtsleeve and hang on for dear life.

And even if we aren't hanging on to that shirtsleeve, we may still have to iron it. Frequently, those of us in good affectionate relationships must work our buns off to keep those relationships running smoothly. Like our counterparts in more difficult situations, we must anticipate partners' needs; placate cranky mates; keep children out of the receding male hairline; and provide countless other support services like cooking, cleaning, sewing, and ironing.

> *This appears to be the natural order of things. So it just happens "naturally," that men are spared the drudgery of domestic chores, can have most of the best jobs, and status and wealth that go with them, and can expect women to want to please and service them.*
>
> **—Margaret Marshment, British professor**

But most of us get pretty tired of providing service with a smile and eventually, it drives us straight up the wall.

> *You can get to hate it . . . there isn't a man I have ever met who does not have a natural assumption of his centrality in his life that places me at a peripheral place. After years, that can make you kill.*
>
> **—Leah, in an interview with author Judith Levine**

Psychiatrist Teresa Bernardez-Bonesatti says that when we have this kind of anger toward men, we often redirect it against ourselves, our children, other women, or weaker individuals. We also vent it in futile outbursts that accomplish nothing, or express the anger in ineffective ways like pouting, whining, manipulating, or using sarcasm instead of direct, forthright anger messages. Some of us go a step further and kill off our feelings, our primary relationship, and our family ties, getting an emotional divorce from the world and everyone in it. But it doesn't have to be this way, not if we can overcome our fear of female anger and in so doing, help the men in our lives overcome their fear too.

22

IDENTIFYING YOUR ANGER ISSUES IN INTIMATE RELATIONSHIPS

Sometimes it's a marriage and sometimes it's the Wild West. The only trouble is Steve always hits his target and I just shoot blanks.

—Carrie, age thirty-five, married two years

Do you feel like the target in every showdown at the love corral? If you do, you'll discover that the corral is pretty crowded because anger in intimate relationships, especially anger at your mate, tops the list of all anger provocations ranked by participants in the Women's Anger Study. The reasons why are complex.

Intimate relationships revive the intense love/hate experiences that we women, as children, had in our families. They also bring many unresolved psychological problems to the forefront. In addition, most relationships are rife with poor communication, unrealistic expectations, and a range of self-defense maneuvers Napoleon himself would envy. Put it all together and the one thing this petri dish is sure to spawn is anger.

This anger is even more complicated if you're married, and a lot of us are. Ninety percent of all Americans get married at least once, and some walk down the aisle so often they qualify as track stars. Indeed, the average contemporary woman spends more than forty years of her life married (although not always to the same man) and for many, these decades form a rich collection of errors. Why? Married women consistently report lower levels of marital happiness than men; greater dissatisfaction with marital companionship and emotional interaction than men; more mental health problems than (married) men; and more visits to marriage counselors than men.

Often, mismanaged anger on your part and/or your husband's is a crucial factor in these tummy mint moments of marital unrest, and in many cases, it's the primary cause of divorce. This idea is supported by observational studies of communication between distressed and nondistressed couples. What researchers found is that distressed couples have more intense, frequent, and hostile emotional exchanges than their nondistressed counterparts. In other words, their anger is so strong you can divine it with a toothpick, but that in itself is nothing new.

Indeed, anger in relationships dates back to the Flood and if you want an explanation for it, take your pick. For starters, it's never easy to adjust your personal habits so you can live harmoniously with another human being. You might be a day person while he's a nighthawk. Maybe you're meticulously neat while your mate is messy and proud of it. In addition to these fairly basic issues, you and your partner may disagree on more complex subjects like religion, values, politics, money, and child rearing. You can also be mismatched in terms of birth order, that is, if you and your husband/boyfriend are oldest children, you may both try to be dominant like you were growing up with your siblings. Similarly, if you're both youngest children, each of you may want to be babied and taken care of. However, these problems are all old hat compared to the new, pervasive pessimism about whether relationships, especially marriage, work at all.

Witness a recent national poll in which 84 percent of the respondents said they think it's harder to have a good marriage today than it was in the past. In addition, nearly half the single women surveyed—compared to just one third of the men—claimed they didn't ever want to get married. What does such a dramatic reversal of traditional gender roles mean? Simply this: The fundamental inequity of marriage no longer appeals to women who are high on the economic food chain. Many of these financially self-sufficient females prefer their own independent lifestyles and are frustrated with men who want "old-fashioned women" (translation: women who put men and their jobs first) for wives. Not only do women not want to marry these men—we don't want to date them either:

> I feel like a performing seal when I'm with men, like a cute little toy they pull out of their pocket to display. "Isn't she adorable, she has a great job and she makes lots of money and I'm so proud of her" are the kinds of things I hear them say to their friends. Sooner or later, though, they say very different things to me. My job takes up too much of my time, or I'm not available enough, or interested enough in them. I get called selfish a lot too.
> **—Lisa, age twenty-nine, an unmarried stockbroker, as told to Hilary Cosell, journalist**

> I told Joe I was taking one night a week off to take a class and have some time for myself. He told me I was being selfish and that this was a really irresponsible thing for a mother to do, yet he travels and does business dinners at least once a week plus he golfs on the weekend while I'm home with the kids. You tell me who's selfish and irresponsible.
> **—Becky, age thirty-four, teacher's aid**

Irresponsibility, powerlessness, and injustice are as old as Eve's mother and for at least that long, our anger over these issues has been short-circuited. Why, as late as 1850, the anger-free family was considered ideal and avoiding quarrels was the preferred form of behavior. Generations of women adopted this silent, long-suffering martyr role, but what they didn't always take into account was that martyrs are dead and by withholding their anger, these women killed off an important emotional part of themselves.

Unfortunately, some of us are in the same boat, especially if we're convinced that love and anger cancel each other out; if we think it is incumbent upon us—not our mates—to curb our anger for the sake of domestic harmony; and if we believe

> To keep your marriage brimming,
> With love in the loving cup,

> *Whenever you're wrong, admit it;*
> *Whenever you're right, shut up.*
> **—Ogden Nash**

Fortunately, this attitude toward anger in relationships is beginning to change—albeit at glacial speed. Today, society acknowledges up-front that too much suppressed emotion is harmful and couples now realize that if they are going to be honest with each other and with themselves, they have to admit their anger. They also have to admit that on occasion, an emotional hailstorm may clear the air:

> *I'm glad we talked it out—yelled it out actually.*
> **—Doris, age twenty, student**

> *I was glad I stood my ground, but then I felt guilty and wondered if I should've just kept it to myself.*
> **—Regina, age thirty-one, clerk**

For many of us, standing our angry ground is fine until that ground quakes with guilt. Indeed, when we get angry our guilt scores (which are higher than men's) fly off the emotional Richter scale. This is why we often feel ambivalent about expressing our strong, angry feelings to our partners. Also, we've been exposed to a lot of bad historical press about the expression of anger in relationships—from popular articles that suggested we put the genie back in the bottle, forget our own anger, and concentrate on easing our mates' stressful bread-winning roles

> *Don't ever let irritation show on your face. When you're angry, sit still, be quiet, smile if you possibly can.*
> **—1940s dating tip from *Seventeen* magazine**

to ventilationist, guerrilla marriage manuals of the sixties and seventies that urged us to "get in touch with our feelings" and scream at our mates. Doubtless, this kamikaze approach laid the illusion of an anger-free relationship to rest forever, but it also produced a lot of confusion, so if confused is how you feel, you're not alone.

> *I would say things that he would never acknowledge and so I grew very, very angry . . . I actually became a bitch because I did not know how to deal with my anger.*
> **—Grace**

. . . I don't have to be right. I'm not a person who has to be right in things but I do want him to listen . . . we still can't do that very well without having a huge argument . . .   **—Cora**

Our arguments are always in code, the problem is after seven years, neither of us has cracked the code. **—Char**

Before you can communicate your anger effectively to your mate, you have to be able to decipher it for yourself. This is why it's so important to identify your anger issues in relationships.

Exercise: Identifying Your Anger Issues in Relationships

Start with your journal (see Chapter 3). Record your fights and quarrels as well as any anger you've buried. After a month, look for recurring patterns and themes. These are sure to exist because while the provocations appear to change, most couples really argue about the same things ad nauseam. Your own dog-eared repertoire might include power struggles over money, housework, and disciplining children, as well as anger triggers that are part of a repetitive cycle:

You: I got angry because he drank.
Him: I drank because she was bitching and nagging.

And so it goes, with one person's behavior provoking and maintaining the other person's behavior until your relationship becomes a wary, circular

. . . dance of anger . . .   **—Harriet Lerner**

As you study your journal entries, you may find yourself dancing furious fox-trots, tempestuous tangos, or plain old rock 'n' roll (emphasis on the rock). Whatever's on the dance card, remember that it's not your husband or partner's actual behavior, but the symbolic meaning behind his actions that counts. For instance, when you hit the roof because he forgets to call from Chicago, as promised, does it mean he doesn't care, he can't be trusted, he's too self-absorbed, or just irresponsible? Or does it mean you're afraid of being abandoned? Past experience will dictate your response

> *What is so frequently sought out in a mate—and then*
> *fought out with that mate—is some unresolved (and thus*
> *unconscious) dilemma about a parent.*
> **—Maggie Scarf, *Intimate Partners***

and you should interpret this response very carefully.

In fact, we can't emphasize enough the importance of careful introspection as you search for symbolic meanings in the anger you feel toward your partner. In addition, if it's hard to reconstruct your fights because they rapidly degenerate into a mass of accusations, recriminations, threats, pain, and confusion, you need to write down your conflicts in order to get some clarity and understand what happened. And we're not just talking clarity. Recording your angry conflicts, like recording your dreams, can be surprisingly revealing, especially if you commit yourself to making notes on anger episodes and working toward new insights.

To get these insights, start by asking yourself what you've learned. Do your journal entries show that you handle anger differently with your mate than with colleagues and friends? And what about your anger style? Is it the same as your partner's or totally different? This is important because frequently partners have opposing styles that are hard to reconcile. For instance, venters often marry suppressors. When there's a fight, venters let it all hang out and quickly get the ire out of their systems. Then they expect their partners to do the same. But suppressors can't let go of the bad feelings so fast. They may continue to seethe and feel resentful long after the argument's over and this sets a bad pattern for the future.

Fortunately, bad anger patterns can be broken. It's all a matter of adjustment, an adjustment you can start by taking this relationship adjustment test, which has been used in more than one thousand research studies.

EXERCISE

The Relationship Adjustment Test

Instructions: Most people have disagreements in their relationships. Please indicate the approximate extent of agreement or disagreement between you and your partner for each item on the following list.

	ALWAYS AGREE	ALMOST ALWAYS AGREE	OCCA-SIONALLY DIS-AGREE	FRE-QUENTLY DIS-AGREE	ALMOST ALWAYS DIS-AGREE	ALWAYS DIS-AGREE
1. Handling family finances	5	4	3	2	1	0
2. Matters of recreation	5	4	3	2	1	0
3. Religious matters	5	4	3	2	1	0
4. Demonstrations of affection	5	4	3	2	1	0
5. Friends	5	4	3	2	1	0
6. Sex relations	5	4	3	2	1	0
7. Conventionality (correct or proper behavior)	5	4	3	2	1	0
8. Philosophy of life	5	4	3	2	1	0
9. Ways of dealing with parents or in-laws	5	4	3	2	1	0
10. Aims, goals, and things believed important	5	4	3	2	1	0
11. Amount of time spent together	5	4	3	2	1	0
12. Making major decisions	5	4	3	2	1	0
13. Household tasks	5	4	3	2	1	0

	ALWAYS AGREE	ALMOST ALWAYS AGREE	OCCA-SIONALLY DIS-AGREE	FRE-QUENTLY DIS-AGREE	ALMOST ALWAYS DIS-AGREE	ALWAYS DIS-AGREE
14. Leisure-time interests and activities	5	4	3	2	1	0
15. Career decisions	5	4	3	2	1	0

	ALL THE TIME	MOST OF THE TIME	MORE OFTEN THAN NOT	OCCA-SIONALLY	RARELY	NEVER
16. How often do you discuss or have you considered divorce, separation, or terminating your relationship?	0	1	2	3	4	5
17. How often do you or your mate leave the house after a fight?	0	1	2	3	4	5
18. In general, how often do you think that things between you and your partner are going well?	0	1	2	3	4	5
19. Do you confide in your mate?	0	1	2	3	4	5
20. Do you ever regret that you married? (or lived together)	0	1	2	3	4	5
21. How often do you and your partner quarrel?	0	1	2	3	4	5

	ALL THE TIME	MOST OF THE TIME	MORE OFTEN THAN NOT	OCCA- SIONALLY	RARELY	NEVER
22. How often do you and your mate "get on each other's nerves"?	0	1	2	3	4	5

	EVERY DAY	ALMOST EVERY DAY	OCCA- SIONALLY	RARELY	NEVER
23. Do you kiss your mate?	4	3	2	1	0

	ALL OF THEM	MOST OF THEM	SOME OF THEM	VERY FEW OF THEM	NONE OF THEM
24. Do you and your mate engage in outside interests together?	4	3	2	1	0

How often would you say the following events occur between you and your mate?

	NEVER	LESS THEN ONCE A MONTH	ONCE OR TWICE A MONTH	ONCE OR TWICE A WEEK	ONCE A DAY	MORE OFTEN
25. Have a stimulating exchange of ideas	0	1	2	3	4	5
26. Laugh together	0	1	2	3	4	5
27. Calmly discuss something	0	1	2	3	4	5
28. Work together on a project	0	1	2	3	4	5

These are some things that couples sometimes agree on and sometimes disagree on. Indicate if either item below caused differences of opinions or were problems in your relationship during the past few weeks.

	YES	NO
29. Being too tired for sex	_____	_____
30. Not showing love	_____	_____

31. The dots on the following line represent different degrees of happiness in your relationship. The middle point, "happy," represents the degree of happiness in most relationships. Please circle the dot which best describes the degree of happiness, all things considered, in your relationship.

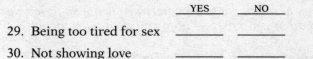

EXTREMELY UNHAPPY	FAIRLY UNHAPPY	A LITTLE UNHAPPY	HAPPY	VERY HAPPY	EXTREMELY HAPPY	PERFECT
•	•	•	•	•	•	•
0	1	2	3	4	5	6

32. Which of the following statements best describes how you feel about the future of your relationship?

   5 I want desperately for my relationship to succeed, and *would go to almost any length* to see that it does.

   4 I want very much for my relationship to succeed, and *will do all I can* to see that it does.

   3 I want very much for my relationship to succeed, and *will do my fair share* to see that it does.

   2 It would be nice if my relationship succeeded, but *I can't do much more than I am doing now* to help it succeed.

   1 It would be nice if it succeeded, but *I refuse to do any more than I am doing now* to keep the relationship going.

   0 My relationship can never succeed, and *there is no more that I can do* to keep the relationship going.

To compute your score, add up the numbers that you circled. The highest possible score is 151. (The average score, in a study by Graham Spanier, developer of the test, was 115.)

This test gives you some idea of the levels of compatibility and incompatibility in your relationship. Ironically, it's the incompatibility that determines whether or not your partnership is a success:

> *What counts in making a happy marriage is not so much how compatible you are, but how you deal with incompatibility.*
> **—George Levinger, quoted in *The New York Times*, April 16, 1985**

And dealing with incompatibility means understanding why you and your mate can feel so hot and bothered when bed is the furthest thing from your minds.

23

IRRATIONAL RELATIONSHIP ANGER AND HOW TO RESOLVE IT

Some of our worst arguments are over stupid things like whether . . . new rolls of toilet paper should be put on the holder face up or face down. First, Mr. Know-It-All does them his way, then I undo whatever he did. Then we fight. This happens every day. Only trouble is, it takes a lot of energy and I'm not sure it's worth it.

—Nance, married one year

When your anger, indignation, and resentment are fresh, you feel perfectly justified in sending Mr. Know-It-All back to the lab to have his bolts tightened. But later, when you've cooled down, you may realize that not all your anger is rational and you probably need to rethink it.

To find out if this applies to you, sort through the data you've collected in your journal. Zero in on any incidents in which your anger was unproductive or irrational and then consider whether you need to revise unrealistic expectations, stop scapegoating your partner, banish tantrums from your emotional repertoire, quit sulking, or all of the above. Now if any—or all—of these items catch in your throat sprockets or cause a nasty twinge of recognition, you have some work to do, beginning with:

Revising Unrealistic Expectations

In many relationships, what you see is what you get. Unfortunately, you may not see very clearly if you're busy looking through rose-colored glasses. In other words, you might expect your partner to be exactly like (or unlike) your father. Or maybe you don't anticipate that your mate's once-charming personality quirks will mutate into something selfish, unreasonable, or downright weird. Then there's the "happily ever after" that never seems to happen, or the glass slipper filled with shards, or the popular lyrics that claim "all you need is love" but which forget to mention that mutual respect, professional opportunities, and personal fulfillment are also necessities of life. The upshot is that if love is blind, marriage and cohabitation quickly restore your sight. To put it another way, the realities of living together sometimes clash so strongly with your romantic expectations that anger is inevitable, especially if those expectations include:

Unrealistic Expectation #1—Love should be unconditional: "I should be accepted just as I am." "I should be cherished, admired, adored, nurtured, prized, etc." "When I find the right man, this is the way his love for me will be." "If my marriage isn't like this, I'm with the wrong man." "If my marriage isn't like this, I have a grievous fault or flaw that prevents my partner from loving me in this unconditional way."

Reality #1—Only infants receive unconditional love. As psychologist Jane Goldberg points out, love between adults can't possibly fulfill all the impossible expectations placed upon it, especially this one.

> *Of all the myths about love, the myth of unconditional love is the most pernicious and will create the darkest, most destructive moments in love relationships.*
>
> **—Jane Goldberg**

Unrealistic Expectation #2—My partner should understand me: "He should know who I really am." "He should know what I value." "He should know what I dream of for the future." "He should know what I want from him right now." "He should do what I want without being asked."

Reality #2—Whether you ask them or not, most men don't have a clue as to what we women want. (You've heard the joke about the world's shortest book—*What Men Know About Women.*) They are genuinely mystified, bewildered, and baffled by females, not to mention totally flummoxed when asked how to please the opposite sex! So if this is one of your unrealistic expectations, your life will be much happier if give it up—like Jan.

Jan telephoned a radio call-in show Sandra was on in response to Sandra's statement that men don't understand women. She agreed and talked about how angry she used to get because her husband didn't understand her. But Jan eliminated this source of anger when she stopped expecting her spouse to read her mind. Now she feels much better because she simply tells him "this is what I want." Telling your partner what you want up front can work for you too.

Unrealistic Expectation #3—My mate should share my interests: "I want him to do everything with me because that's what couples do." "When he's not working, I expect him to spend all his free time with me." "We're a couple. That means we do things together. It keeps us close."

Reality #3—Closeness and sameness are not the same thing but you, like many women, may be whipsawed by confusion when it comes to this issue. As a result, when your mate dances to a different recreational drummer or pursues his own social interests, you get mad:

> *I was racing around all weekend doing things by myself, things that are important. We both had done our assigned chores, but he just stayed on the couch reading his stupid magazines. By myself I put in a new flower bed in the front yard, and I got sixteen signatures on a petition for recycling and he just lay there the whole time. I was so mad I could have exploded. I wished I could have blown him up.* **—Marnie, to her therapist**

You, like many women, can spare yourself the stress of this bombs-away attitude if you accept that your partner often has little interest in—or commitment to—the things you (and your fellow females) consider top priority. But you shouldn't take this attitude as a personal affront, as Marnie eventually learned.

With the help of her therapist, Marnie came to see that even if her husband didn't share her activities, that didn't make those activities less worthwhile. Nor was his couch-potato behavior an automatic indication that he lacked commitment to her or their marriage. Once she understood this, Marnie also understood that neither she nor her husband needed to change in this area.

Unrealistic Expectation #4—My partner must change or we'll never be happy: "You must be more considerate!" "I expect you to work harder at this relationship." "Get a better job!" "Stop drinking—do it for me." "I demand that you change from the night shift—or else!"

Reality #4—Demanding that your mate change produces angry confrontations and not much else. In fact, research shows that this tactic regularly backfires because when six out of ten spouses are confronted with an angry accusation, they don't change one iota to accommodate their irate partners. So what's the irate partner—you—to do? First realize that

> *The stronger person is not the one making the most noise, but the one who can quietly direct the conversation toward defining and solving problems.*
> **—Aaron Beck, founder, cognitive therapy**

The stronger person is also the one who realizes she must

> *Stop "musturbating!*
> **—Albert Ellis, founder, rational-emotive therapy**

In other words, eliminate the absolute, Hitlerian demands that your mate must behave a certain way and replace these ultimatums with realistic wishes and preferences. Most of all, remember that too many "musturbatory thoughts" make you go blind to your partner's good points!

Unrealistic Expectation #5—My partner will change when . . . : "Things will improve when we're out of debt." "I know things will be good again when you finally finish law school [med school, vet school, flight school, your MBA, your CPA, the PTA]" "We'll stop fighting when _____" (Fill in the blank with anything, anything at all!)

Reality #5—This is basically a future-oriented version of unrealistic expectation #4: "He'll change when . . ." And the answer is "when hell freezes over." Women often delude themselves into thinking that their mates are surly, demanding, remote, or inconsiderate because of specific situational pressures and stresses. You tell yourself, "When the pressure lifts, he'll change and all will be well," or "I'll just hang in there and give him love and support." Unfortunately, "hang" is the operative word. Many women are left hanging as they wait and wait for their men to evolve. Eventually, you tire of this waiting game. Your patience wears thin, your anger flares up, and you renew your strident demands for change, but honey, don't hold your breath! And don't waste time and energy angrily confronting him or trying to coax, cajole, or convince him through logic to change. Instead, work on changing yourself. You should also ask yourself what you would do if he did change as you requested, because then you would have to consider that old adage, "Be careful what you ask for—you might get it!"

In fact, sometimes you get a lot more than you bargained for when you ask your partner to change. Why? He changes all right, but not in a way that pleases you, his mate.

I suggested he get his bachelor's degree and he did. Then he got a master's. Now he wants a second master's. I feel like I've created a monster . . . All this education would be great, but I'm the one supporting him and I want him to be something besides an eternal student! In a lot of ways, I liked him better before—the way he was when we first got married. **—Arliss, age thirty-one, journalist**

When you angrily claim "he's not the man I married" (or moved in with), you're right. Your mate has changed and so have you. Indeed, it's normal for partners to grow and develop over time, particularly as you take on the challenges of living with children, with each other, and with assorted family members who join your household.

In fact, the relationship between you and your partner is profoundly altered each time someone joins or leaves the family nest. Social scientists call these changes stages of development and they begin with the arrival of your first child. A couple has usually been married twenty-four months when this blessed event occurs. You then spend the next twenty years up to your eyebrows in child-rearing responsibilities followed by an eight-year "launch" period (the average amount of time between your oldest child's departure and when your last child finally leaves home). When the launch is complete (and sometimes it never is), you spend twenty-five years or more in the postparental stage. But often, what you each find waiting in the wings is a very different person than the one you married. Why? You were both unique people to begin with, people who then developed individually over the years while meeting the demands of your respective professional and parental roles. It's unrealistic for you to expect each other to grow and change at the same rate and in the same way! But a committed relationship gives you a chance to succeed despite your differences:

> *One advantage of marriage . . . is that when you fall out of love with him, or he falls out of love with you, it keeps you together until you maybe fall in again.*
> **—Judith Viorst, *Redbook*, February 1975**

> *A successful marriage requires falling in love many times, always with the same person.*
> **—Mignon McLaughlin, *Atlantic*, 1965**

And if you are truly in love, you don't make your mate the fall guy when things go wrong with your life . . .

Proactive Strategy: Find Another Fall Guy, or Stop Scapegoating Your Partner

Sometimes you lay the blame so fast you leave skid marks—usually across your mate. Your monologue may vary "Don't blame me because (we got lost, the checkbook didn't balance, the party flopped, the kids were bad in church—fill in the blank with your favorite disaster), it's *his fault!*" But that heated closing line is always the same.

Psychiatrist Willard Gaylin calls this the "hot potato

game" and the object is to pass the hot potato, otherwise known as guilt, on to someone else. The most convenient person for this purpose is usually your partner, but when you pass him the spud it's often in the form of anger. Why? Women (and men) frequently convert their guilt into anger toward their mates because anger is the less painful of the two emotions. But this technique usually fails because most men get steamed. They refuse to passively accept the blame for things they didn't do (and even for some things they did do), and a fault-finding free-for-all erupts. These fault fests don't solve a thing. In most cases, it will serve your relationship better if you admit (to your chagrin), that perhaps you could have been the one who forgot to mail the house payment or walk the dog! It will also help if you are more tolerant of your partner's flaws, the way you are with lapses by co-workers, friends, and strangers. When you're tolerant and forgiving—and quit holding your mate to perfectionist standards—you can stop playing the blame game. Besides, many of life's frustrating glitches are really nobody's fault, so give it a rest and stop scapegoating your partner! You may also need to temper your tantrums.

Proactive Strategy: Temper Your Tantrums!

Some women—possibly you—hold in their anger day after day until they become so hot their bones fuse together and they erupt, spewing bile and cutting a wide path of destruction. Although these tantrums may temporarily relieve your anger, they don't do much for anyone around you, and they certainly don't promote the kind of change you're seeking. In fact, it's just the opposite.

Therapist Harriet Lerner says that ineffective fighting, blaming, and coming across as a hysterical bitch can actually perpetuate the status quo in your relationship—the very thing that made you mad in the first place. Why does this happen? Because your partner has been through the grind so many times that he no longer takes your irrational explosions seriously. He simply figures "there she goes again," which makes you even angrier. At this point, no one is in the mood to do any problem solving so nothing changes and the situation becomes an uneasy standoff.

But sometimes an uneasy standoff can escalate to a dangerous skirmish, especially if you're married and you threaten your husband with divorce. This is a risky tactic, because once the "D-word" passes your lips, one or both of you may actually consider calling it quits. The moral of the story here is that even friendly fire can be deadly, and unless you're willing to take this chance, you should keep your tantrums under control. The big question is how.

Proactive Strategy: How to Banish Banshee Behavior

Start by putting a volume control on your jawbox, that is, repeat the phrase "I don't need to scream and yell to get my point across" two or three thousand times a day. This is what marriage counselor Doris Wild Helmering instructs her clients to do, and many of them are a tad skeptical of the procedure:

> *People look at me like I'm a little nuts; how can anyone say something two or three thousand times a day?*
> **—Doris Wild Helmering**

But she's never had anyone who couldn't control his or her temper after doing it.

Another temper control technique is to take a "time-out." Use it whenever you feel your fury building and know you're about to explode at your partner. Hendrie Weisinger, a psychologist who conducts anger management workshops, recommends these steps:

Time-out Steps

1. Say aloud to your mate, "I'm beginning to feel angry and I want to take a time-out."

2. Leave the situation for one hour. Tell your partner when you will return.

3. Do not drink or take drugs.

4. Do something physical like walking or biking.

5. If you find yourself thinking about the situation that made you angry, repeat to yourself, "I'm beginning to feel angry, I want a time-out."

6. After one hour, return to the situation and speak with your partner—if both of you are ready to do so. If your partner is not ready to talk, be sure to respect his wishes. Once you start talking, if you find yourself getting angry all over again, stop and take another time-out.

Using a time-out tells your partner that even though you're angry, you respect the relationship and don't want to damage it by going ballistic. In addition, by returning to the situation in a cooler, calmer state and proposing a rational discussion (more on this in a minute), you convey your commitment to the partnership.

Now, some women don't need a time-out to calm down because they've cooled off already. In fact, anger makes their emotional temperatures downright frigid.

Sighing, Sulking, and Sex Avoidance, or When a Woman Feels Frosted

Some women don't have temper tantrums and would never even consider turning the heat on their mates. Instead, they maintain a cold silence, sigh heavily, sulk, pout, and refuse to be good company. In short, they're about as much fun as a pleasure trip to the poles—otherwise known as being passive-aggressive.

You are passive-aggressive when you act sincerely underwhelmed; when you drag your feet, stonewall, are intentionally forgetful and inefficient; or when you do a job so badly that it would be better if you hadn't done it at all. And of course this is accompanied by much wailing and gnashing of teeth as you complain bitterly of your misfortune, are unreasonably critical, express envy or resentment, or substitute the silent treatment for clear, direct anger messages, and we all do this occasionally:

I'm really good at pouting. And the quiet treatment, I'm good at that . . .   **—Karen**

When I get mad at him, I just clam up. Sometimes I'm so angry that I enjoy watching him squirm as he tries to figure out what's wrong.   **—Christine**

Sometimes your partner may be so mystified by what's wrong that he couldn't squirm out of it if he tried—but at least he knows he should be squirming. At this point, if he's like most men, he'll start running through all the possible causes in his mind from "Is it her birthday?" and "Did I forget our anniversary?" to "Is she upset because I have to work this weekend?" and:

> *I don't know what I did, but I do know I'm supposed to feel like shit about it. That's what it means when she sulks.* —**Brad, age forty-eight, married fifteen years**

If you're a sulker, you're pleased when your mate feels shitty and is in obvious discomfort. After all, the whole point of this passive-aggressive behavior is to make your partner suffer because "With the way he behaved, he deserves it!" You want him groveling, apologizing, and kissing the hem of your skirt—and even when he does make overtures to set things right, you, as a world-class sulker, don't want to give in too soon. As a result, you might draw your anger out in thinly disguised ways such as "forgetting" to run an important errand, misplacing something your husband needs to take on his business trip, burning dinner, or turning your back on him in bed. In fact, avoiding or refusing sex has been a female anger strategy since Lysistrata:

> *I was so %^&*% I wouldn't help him get it up with a block and tackle!*
> —**Carolee, age twenty-four, married four years**

> *When my husband refused to say he was sorry, I told him flat out—if you don't give me a pleasant apology, I won't give you any pleasure either.*
> —**Darla, age thirty-nine, married nine years**

In many ways this is the ultimate boomerang strategy because when the pleasures of the flesh are rigorously denied, you suffer as much as your mate by denying yourself the joy and intimacy of lovemaking.

But sex avoidance and other passive tactics aren't just confined to women. Even five-star husbands and boyfriends have their favorite passive-avoidance ways of dealing with anger.

> *We were having the neighbors over for dinner . . . but I was @#$%@ because I get so little free time as it is and I didn't want to spend it with these boring people. So . . . I got home after they left. [My wife] was furious and I told her that by being late, I was just proving how strongly I*

*felt about the situation, but she said I was just getting
even.* **—Peter, age thirty-six, married thirteen years**

You usually know when you're being manipulated and
dumped on, or when your mate is just getting even for some
ambiguous, unnamed transgression. You and your partner
also know that such tactics are unsatisfying, self-defeating,
and ultimately, detrimental to your relationship. So how do
you stop leapfrogging over each other's egos and get beyond
these childish, ineffective anger expressions?

Psychologist Richard Driscoll says that first the sulker
(otherwise known as Mr. or Ms. Passive-Aggressive) must acknowledge what he or she is doing and then openly state the
grievance. For instance, Samuel was unhappy because his
wife left him to baby-sit while she went to her evening church
group. When she returned, he acted distant and uninvolved
to show her how neglected she "made" him feel. But when
Samuel recognized that he had to make himself miserable
to convey this message, he changed his behavior because he
finally realized there were better ways to get his point across.
The same thing is true for your partner and you, especially
when your anger is rational, your grievances are legitimate,
and Prince Charming isn't.

24

WHEN PRINCE CHARMING ISN'T

E [my husband] has continued having friendships with women he has dated in the past and he has remained very close with one of them. And even though I have expressed my feelings and my hesitancy and my insecurity about that, he has said that I'm the one with the problem. That makes me very angry. I don't like being told that. E said I shouldn't feel this way, that I shouldn't have those feelings. Well, they're my feelings, and no matter how illogical or whether they're rational or not doesn't matter.

—Amy

When your feelings are so strong that nothing else matters, your anger is sending you a message. It's calling on you to defend your own true, magnetic north of decency because you have a legitimate grievance, a situation in which your anger is justified and should be disclosed. Most of these legitimate grievances occur in intimate relationships when we confront the three major anger themes of **irresponsibility,**

We live on a street that borders a seriously dangerous neighborhood and he always forgets to lock the front door . . . It makes me crazy because with that kind of irresponsible behavior, we'll all be history fast.

—Jeannette

injustice,

> *We had a fight over his drinking and I told him that I just couldn't stand it when he got knee-walking drunk. [I asked him] couldn't he go someplace and just have one or two drinks? Did he have to get knee-walking drunk? And he told me no, he couldn't . . .*   **—Patsy**

and **powerlessness.**

> *. . . I weigh pros and cons . . . but he just jumps in and decides . . . and that's it . . . his mind's made up, don't confuse him with the facts, which makes me really mad. I think he sees it as a power struggle and I just generally want to work it out. He knows he's right because—well, he never even thought about why, he just knows he's right . . . That's why it's right. I'm sure he grew up where the head of the family's the man and he makes all the major decisions.*   **—Susan**

The big three anger themes are particularly strong triggers in marriage. In fact, they trigger marital bouts so frequently that many of us believe our relationships are really stops on the pro-wrestling circuit. This is especially true with powerlessness—a situation in which we feel we just can't win.

> *At first I do not win these fights, because of love. Or so I say to myself. If I were to win them, the order of the world would be changed, and I am not ready for that. So instead I lose the fights, and master different arts. I shrug, tighten my mouth in silent rebuke, turn my back in bed, leave questions unanswered. I say, "Do it however you like . . ."*
> **—Elaine, in *Cat's Eye*, by Margaret Atwood**

But most of us don't like being on the losing end of things, especially if the only reason we "put a lid on it" is to preserve the "proper" balance of relational power. The same is true if we squelch our anger out of "love" because deep in our hearts we're usually asking ourselves:

> *What's love got to do with it?*
> **—Tina Turner, singer/actress**

The answer is "not much." Many women who withhold legitimate anger don't do it out of love, they do it because they're afraid of being dumped. They think back to those girlhood lessons on catching and keeping a man and remember the most important dictum of Relationships 101: A man doesn't stay with an angry woman. The situation is even worse if you depend on a man for your identity or your economic survival. You may very well hold your anger in check if your mate holds the checkbook. (After all, he who holds the checkbook holds the power.) Likewise, you may hold your tongue if you feel emotionally vulnerable and want affection or attention, and fear cutting off your supplier. In fact, some women in this position will go to any lengths to avoid anger and get what they need:

> . . . that willingness to hang on a meathook and call it love, that need for loving like a screaming hollow in the soul. —**Marge Piercy**, *Circles on the Water*

That same love judge in your psyche condemns anger because it causes separateness, aloneness, and a feeling of disconnection from the partner of your dreams. It also causes an imbalance in power because if you care more than your man does about preserving the relationship, you are automatically operating from a weaker position. In other words, you're suffering from Waller's principle of least interest, which says the one who cares the least controls the relationship because the one who cares more defers to the first person's wishes. The bottom line here is that the more powerful partner has the stronger say in the amount and quality of time spent together, as well as in matters of recreation, conversation, socialization, and sex.

> I get mad at him over sex. He could be almost dead and want sex. He wants it every night and there are some times I don't want to. And it's not I don't love you anymore, it's, I'm tired. I want to come home, take a shower and relax. But then he gets pouting and gets mad. And it's like he won't talk to me the whole night.
>
> It makes me feel like shit. I mean it's like this one night's not going to kill you. I'm tired and I have a right to be tired. This thing about sex makes me feel belittled . . . I feel like two people who have been married for nine years like us, if there is a night when we don't want to have sex we ought to have that night, be able to say no.
> —**Margie**

But the less powerful partner—the one who cares more about preserving the relationship—usually doesn't say no. She will usually not take the risk of expressing legitimate anger, even if she (or he) feels used or upset.

> *My primary reason for going back to school is because my husband wants me to . . . He's putting a lot of pressure on me—if I make a B, he gets disappointed. And sometimes it gets to me that I have to do so much (sighs) . . . I can tell you right now I don't feel like I express my anger in an appropriate way.* —**Brenda**

But unless Brenda and the rest of us learn to express our anger in an appropriate way, we will forever remain in the powerless position, victims of relationship inequality.

Relationship Inequality

If it hasn't happened already, there will come a moment when you realize that the dictionary definition of equality is just pulp fiction. Indeed, while 90 percent of American women say equality is important to them, 68 percent claim they lack equality in some part of their lives and 49 percent state that they have no equality at all. This includes social inequality (see Part Ten) and relationship inequality, and we can use our anger to do something about both, especially relationships.

Like most women, you probably give more than you receive in many of your intimate relationships, but the imbalance is worst when you're coupled with a man—and this can make even wholesome cheerleader types feel like a nouveau bitch. A poll by the Roper Organization bears this out. The poll found that women are "fed up" and "even angrier at men than they were twenty years ago." In addition, according to Roper, nineties women are far less likely to consider men paragons of virtue and far more likely to see them as vigorously inattentive to relationship responsibilities.

This same description of relational irresponsibility, of he-who-looks-out-for-number-one, shrieks at us in the data of the Women's Anger Study, and "discontent" doesn't begin to describe the way it makes us feel. But "angry" does. Fortunately, we can use our anger to correct the situation, to benefit ourselves and ask for a fairer shake, but only if we express our feelings, like Mandy needs to do.

Mandy, a nervous, stressed out, forty-year-old secretary and mother of three, told the Women's Anger Study that her anger is triggered

> *When everyone seems to expect me to handle everything: job, kids, housework, yardwork, etc.*   **—Mandy**

But instead of telling "everyone" (translation: her husband and kids) how unfair she thinks the situation is, Mandy gets frustrated, broods in silence, and in so doing, makes herself the number one target of her own anger. Although she's so mad she feels "like hitting someone," Mandy is operating under the false assumption that conflict should be avoided at all costs. In addition, by holding her anger in, she inhibits her own personal growth, makes herself miserable, and denies her husband the chance to learn that

> *Helping . . . is a small price to pay if it means I'm going to be married to a human being instead of a hell queen.*
> **—James, age thirty-nine, married ten years**

The only way you will get help—and eventually relationship equality—is if you identify and communicate your legitimate grievances (see Part Two) including these identified by participants in the Women's Anger Study: "I feel angry when my husband 'forgets' something I feel is important." "I feel angry when my husband spends a lot of money without telling me." "When my husband tells me 'there you go again' or compares me to my mother!" "Husband staying out late." "My husband refuses to go to socials with me." "Husband does not show love and care." "Husband not doing his share in our home."

This last grievance is especially common among working women because many of us have discovered that the career–relationship roller coaster is a very bumpy ride:

> *I'm just interested in growing as a person and a professional. You'd think that would make me more attractive to my husband, but it doesn't. He told me dealing with me as a wife and an employed woman is like being on a roller coaster, then he mentioned that he always gets sick on roller coasters.*
> **—Terese, age forty-one, marketing manager**

The Career–Relationship Roller Coaster, or What Goes Up Might Bring You Down

The rapid social movement of the past three decades has severely strained relationships in the United States and made more than a few males motion sick. Whether actively or passively, many of these men have resisted our growth and forward progress, leaving us women hopping mad. Part of the problem is that the roles of men and women have changed. There are few, if any, models to follow and currently, the rules of "proper" behavior are about as clear as mud. To make matters worse, some men resign their happy-camper status the minute we take paying jobs. Why? Jobs decrease the amount of time we're available to provide wife-type services.

> *A girl becomes a wife with her eyes wide open. She knows that those sweetest words, "I take thee to be my wedded husband," really mean, "I promise thee to cook three meals a day for sixty years; thee will I clean up after; thee will I talk to even when thou art not listening; thee will I worry about, cry over and take all manner of hurts from.*
>
> **—Alan Beck, "What Is a Wife?"**
> ***Good Housekeeping*, July 1957**

And these are the services to which many of our mates have grown accustomed:

> *I remember saying to [my wife] Jane ten years into the marriage that I felt like the game rules had been changed on me. I hadn't changed, but society had. And now I was being asked, or rather told, that I needed to be different. I married with an expectation that I would come home and find dinner on the table and that I would provide the money. My wife's end of the bargain was to take care of the house and kids. So it's been hard. I felt like the rug was swept out from under me.*
>
> **—A professional man interviewed by Lisa Silberstein, psychologist**

Many men are shaken to the roots of their Y chromosomes by women's professional success and earning power—a supreme irony given the salary inequities between the sexes and the fact that most of our paychecks will never equal—let alone surpass—our partners' (see Chapter 19). And should you or any other woman begin to muscle in on the primary bread-winner's role, some men predict genital sparks will fly . . .

> *But . . . if she can make real money, she is co-opting the man's passport to masculinity and he is effectively castrated.* **—Robert Gould, psychiatrist**

> *My husband's way of congratulating me on my promotion was to tell me I "had balls," then he proceeded to whine to our friends about how I'd abandoned him for my job, which couldn't be further from the truth—I took the promotion because it meant I'd be home more and out of town less, but he never gave me a chance to explain that!* **—Joanne, age thirty-eight, account executive**

While many men are complaining that their wives and girlfriends are AWOL, many women are complaining about the men's lack of support for female careers. This is reinforced by Sandra's study of working couples, which shows that women are not only angry and disappointed, but genuinely distressed and resentful when it comes to their mates' unenthusiastic response:

> *I resent Bill in that he doesn't make me feel like it would be okay if I quit and took a job that I enjoyed more. He doesn't seem to encourage me to do what I enjoy. I don't feel that he would support my doing something different, so I don't do it. Then I get mad at myself.* **—Georgeann**

Of course, men might be a little more enthusiastic if they realized that two-career households are here to stay. In fact, currently, 75 percent of all families (compared to just 34 percent in 1970) have two wage earners. But most women aren't simply punching a time clock and chasing the almighty buck, they're having careers in the most seductive sense of the term:

> *Business is like sex. When it's good, it's very, very good, when it's not so good, it's still good.*
> **—George Katona, Director, University of Michigan Business Research Bureau**

> *It is work, work that one delights in, that is the surest guarantor of happiness.* **—Ashley Montagu**

But that guarantee will run out fast unless you and your mate seriously consider the career issues that might become a source of legitimate conflict in your relationship including whose career takes top priority, what factors will weigh most heavily when one of you is offered a promotion that requires relocation, who will take time off for child and elder care, and how the two paychecks will be spent.

The bottom line here is that you should approach these issues with a sense of equity. In other words, both you and your partner should be fair about sharing resources and responsibilities. Now, this doesn't mean everything will always be fifty-fifty, but it does mean that the two of you should feel you've achieved a sense of balance over the years. For instance, if your mate's career gets priority for a specified period of time, there should be a firm agreement that you will have a similar opportunity later on. The same thing goes for education, watching the kids, etc.,—you get the drill.

Unfortunately, the rest of the world doesn't. Although the idea of equity looks great on paper and receives tremendous lip service from word-smitten young couples, it's difficult to achieve in real life. In fact, equity is so remote from the reality of most contemporary women's lives that the very word provokes peals of skeptical feminine laughter. Instead, most of us identify with Hilary Cosell's seesaw syndrome—when our careers are up, our personal lives are down and when our personal lives are up, our careers are down. Dizzying can't begin to describe it.

> It's a merry-go-round. When things are going well at work, things fall apart at home. When everything's together at home, work goes to hell in a hand basket. It's not equity, it's real life.
>
> **—Fran, age fifty-three, office manager**

One study of men and women in the same profession put equity to a very real-life experimental test. Researcher Dianne Wimberley used a questionnaire we developed to survey more than two hundred married veterinarians who had all graduated from the same institution. Compared to the men, the women reported that marital and family stress had a significantly greater impact on their career progress. They also reported considerably less spousal support for their work. Unfortunately, this scenario has become a bad national habit. Why? Traditionally, even when the wife is a well-educated professional, her husband's career is given top priority—often by the woman herself.

> *As a young woman, I never questioned the assumption that when I married what I could do would take second place to what my husband could do. Twenty-five years later, I have slighted my own value so often that it is hard to learn to take it seriously. These attitudes show up again and again in the texture of everyday life. For at least twenty years, whenever I interrupted my husband when he was busy, he finished what he was doing before he responded. When he interrupted me, I would drop what I was doing to respond to him, automatically giving his concerns priority.*
>
> **—Mary Catherine Bateson, anthropologist and author**

In a study we conducted, women who followed this traditional path were categorized as "accommodators." In other words, their own professions followed a circuitous and erratic path because their first order of business was to accommodate their partners' careers. These women either dropped out of the work force (in some cases for as long as eight years), worked part-time, turned down promotions, postponed graduate study, or accepted the limitations of being place-bound.

Predictably, more than half the women whose careers were compromised reported significant relationship dissatisfaction to our research team. This is not surprising because other longitudinal research has shown that when one partner's valued plans and strivings are repeatedly disrupted, not only is there chronic anger and conflict, but there is also the very real possibility that the relationship will dissolve.

That possibility is even stronger if you're forced to take sides in:

The Late Bloomers vs. the Career Burnouts

If your career blossoms in midlife, you may cop an attitude that's so genuinely energetic and enthusiastic your partner can't stand it. Why? Often "late bloomers" postpone their own professional lives until their mates and/or children are successfully launched. When they finally get themselves on track, these women become Niagaras of excited details, pouring out stories of job-related ideas, events, and successes. Unfortunately, their men don't want to hear it and maybe yours doesn't either.

The reason is that many men's careers are burning out just as women's careers are heating up. While you are pushing the envelope, raising the bar, and running in quality circles, your mate feels pushed to the brink, barred from the future, and caught in a vicious circle after twenty or more years on the job. The bottom line is that it's hard for him to adjust to your career ascent when his own career has plateaued or is in a decline. Unfortunately, this happens all the time.

One late bloomer in our study spoke excitedly about entering private counseling practice after graduate school, but she described her husband as "bored with his job." Another woman reported that her husband was not only jealous because she was "super-charged" about her new career, but he was also insecure because she was working closely with a male store manager and male colleagues. Although the effect of such asymmetric career development and coordination on relationships has not been adequately researched, the potential for tension and conflict is obvious. Fortunately, some of this tension and conflict can be avoided if you and your partner both come to understand what women in dual-career relationships want.

What Women in Dual-Career Relationships Want

Time and again, studies show that women in dual-career relationships are more highly stressed than their partners. This is true regardless of the woman's age, education, or occupation. It is also true that these women all want the same thing—more emotional support from their mates. However, getting this support might be a real trick because most men seriously underestimate the amount of stress women are experiencing and they overestimate the amount of emotional intimacy in their relationships. That is, the women say this intimacy is not as great as the men report. In many cases, it would relieve some of the women's stress—and perhaps some of yours—if men did something as simple as help around the house.

I think housework is the reason most women go to the office. **—Heloise Cruse**

Housework, if it is done right, can kill you.

—Erma Bombeck

Cobwebs, stained toilets, and dust bunnies measured in the double digits are just some of the reasons why housekeeping is a killer job. Unfortunately, whether you, as a working woman, are married, divorced, or single, you are considered the "keeper" of your house even if it's a job you'd just as soon give away.

I wish they'd take this job and shove it . . . it's labor intensive and it isn't exactly intellectually stimulating. I work full-time and to me, housecleaning is like putting all my energy and precious free hours into a blender and pressing the "obliterate" button. Worse yet, it's never done.

—Delila, age twenty-five, musician

For many of us, "a woman's work is never done" is more than a cliché, it's the truth. Plus, an unkempt yard, messy house, or even a dirty sink are very visible, chronic stressors because they remind you (and everyone else within eyeshot) that you're just not cutting it—at least not according to society's standards. One reason for all the pressure and stress is this: Regardless of the type of household (men alone, men living with children, women alone, women living with children, couples alone, or couples living with children), studies show that the person who does the most housework is the woman who lives with a man. This is the case whether there are children present or not. In fact, some adult males create even more housework than a child under ten:

It was midnight and I was scrubbing the floor because my husband's family was visiting the next day . . . I'd just finished . . . when I heard Frank come in from the garage. I went . . . to meet him and found big, greasy footprints all over my clean floor . . . I just wanted to drown him in my scrub bucket!

—Maureen, age thirty-six, married eight years

I get really mad at him when I feel like I have to tell him everything to do at the house. Do this, do that . . . If I didn't tell him what to do, it wouldn't get done . . .

—Dotti

To some men, doing household chores sounds about as reasonable as adding a Nobel prize to their résumés. This in itself is nothing new. What is new is that we contemporary women expect our partners to share much more of the work, and if this sharing doesn't happen, we get mad. Why? Even when we have full-time jobs outside the home, we women still have a disproportionate amount of responsibility for virtually all the cleaning, cooking, and errands. Although the number of employed wives has risen greatly over the last few years (along with tremendous demands on our time), the amount of hours our husbands spend on household tasks has increased only 6 percent over the last two decades. Study after study bears this out with similar, discouraging findings—especially when it comes to the weekends:

I felt like my weekends were spent cleaning the house while his weekends were spent playing, and I resented that. I think he thinks that he helps a lot, and he does help more than a lot of men I know. On the other hand, like I told him when I was angry, "You don't want to compare what you do and what I do because you'll lose, trust me." . . . *He knows I do most of it and he likes it that way and he wants to keep it that way.* **—Kay**

Given all this, what are you to think when your mate claims he's a hausfrau in the making? Or when he firmly states that he's doing a greater proportion of the household chores than he really is? In some cases, he might be trying to convince you that it's really true. In other cases, he's trying to convince himself and avoid any guilty feelings. Either way, the reality gap is great when it comes to domestic bondage, as shown by Sandra's study of dual-career couples.

The study revealed fascinating discrepancies between husbands' and wives' perceptions of household responsibilities. For instance, one husband, a sales manager, reported that he and the children shared home management tasks and that this sharing produced a "positive outcome." His wife, a real estate broker, reported that she had "tried to convince [her] spouse to help at home more." In her viewpoint, the outcome was negative.

Likewise, another couple made a list of the jobs and divided up the labor. The husband stated that the strategy "seems to work" while his wife stated that the "outcome [was] negative, [her] husband did not follow through."

Many of us are driven witless by our partners' apparent apathy toward household chores. Yet, psychologist Faye Crosby proposes that some men's lack of cooperation and follow-through is really due to insensitivity, not malice. A case in point is one recently divorced individual who thought of himself as "a good family man" doing his "fair share" around the house. His wife didn't agree, and unfortunately the man didn't notice her dissatisfaction until it was too late:

> *For several years I was ignorant but content and she was furious but silent.*
>
> **—A recently divorced man interviewed by Faye Crosby**

> *I just couldn't keep quiet about it anymore. For years, whenever my husband thought he was helping . . . he was making a mess. I'd always wait until he went to work and then redo it [his housecleaning], but now that I'm working myself, I just don't have the time.*
>
> *I finally told him and he seemed to take it okay, but now he's trying to fix my car instead. Joe's no mechanic which is . . . why my car is in pieces all over the garage. When I asked him how I was supposed to get to work, he suggested I research a van pool or take a bus, neither of which are convenient. Sometimes I wonder if he's trying to tell me something.*
>
> **—Beverly, age fifty-two, store manager**

He probably is. A man who fails to help or helps so incompetently that you end up redoing the job may be subtly sabotaging your career. This sabotage is a passive-aggressive form of anger. In addition, because it is irresponsible behavior that makes you feel cheated and powerless, sabotage incorporates all three of the major anger themes discovered by the Women's Anger Study.

Obviously, with sabotage and similar situations, you have

a legitimate beef, and when you have a legitimate beef, you should express your anger by talking things out and applying conflict resolution. Why? Talking things out strengthens relationships and mastering conflict resolution not only helps you achieve peace in your relationship, but peace in your world.

25

TECHNIQUES FOR EFFECTIVE CONFLICT RESOLUTION

We argue about the same thing over and over again—it's just at different volumes, in different locations, on different days.
                                                            —Jody

Despite different times and settings, most relationship conflicts are cut from identical cloths. This is especially true when the same anger-provoking problem keeps resurfacing to pummel away at the love that's supposed to exist between you and your mate. To keep these persistent problems from eroding your partnership, try to express your anger by talking it out because talking things out strengthens relationships—besides, you have the right to express your anger in this positive, proactive way.

Proactive Strategy: Talking Things Out Strengthens Relationships

We believe women should be empowered to voice their legitimate anger to their mates. After all, for a relationship to be satisfying, both partners must feel they can be themselves (warts and all) and still be loved. Unless you disclose your anger, you—and your husband or boyfriend—are not revealing all of yourselves. Plus, squashing your anger down will not make it go away. In fact, this will ultimately cause more damage to your relationship than open fighting because your partner may be totally unaware that there's a problem.

Suppressing relationship anger can also damage your physical health. Researchers have found that if a person is aware of his or her anger but chooses not to express it, this suppressed anger can play a major role in the elevation of blood pressure (see Chapter 14). Another group of investigators found that partners who hold their anger in during unjustified attacks by their spouses were twice as likely to die over the twelve-year follow-up period of the study than those who openly expressed their anger to their mates—all good reasons for you to start talking it out.

Now talking it out means just that. Both you and your partner have to cap your thundermouths and have a rational discussion—and research shows women actually prefer to handle anger this way.

> If we're having a period when our marriage seems troubled, I can't sleep until we talk it out. Or at least I try to talk it out. **—Terri**

Studies of distressed couples reveal that wives in bad marriages often try to air out complaints and negative emotions, but just as often, their partners minimize the issues, deflect responsibility, and withdraw from the conversation. Why does this happen? Why is talking it out—even though it's the preferred mode of anger expression—usually such a bust?

Part of the problem is that even if you're as eloquent as Shakespeare's sister, it won't help because men and women don't speak the same language. Witness the many marriage counselors who, day after day, hear "we can't communicate." Or better yet, try eavesdropping on practically any intimate discussion. What you'll overhear is women who want less controlling conversations and more sharing of feelings.

> I tell you mine, you can tell me yours . . . or at least just tell me if you still have feelings! You can share that much can't you? **—Rosemary, age fifty, to her husband, at a family wedding**

For most women, sharing feelings comes naturally. We find it easy to discuss what's happening in our lives and in the lives of loved ones. We also find it difficult to understand why men can't or won't respond in kind. Indeed, many men seem distant and uninterested in what their wives have to say.

> *What's made me angry is I talk a lot and he talks very little. And we definitely don't talk about our relationship with each other when things are wrong, that's the hardest part. We can talk about the house . . . the children . . . the dogs. We can talk about everything else except our relationship. It hurts. It makes me feel lonely. It makes me feel empty.*
>
> *The day before yesterday was a sad day for me, I don't know why, I was just depressed . . . all I could see was all this [stuff] to do. I just started crying. He came in here and said, "What are you crying about?" And I said, "I'm just depressed." And he turned around and walked out and shut the door and went back to work on his little project.* —**Vera**

It can be quite a project for you to get your mate to talk, especially if he's unwilling to give of himself and edits his conversation lest he broadcast any real emotion:

> *You've heard of talk radio, at our house it's talk marriage—especially when things are going down the tubes. Unfortunately, Bruce is on a whole different wavelength.*
>
> **—Cecelia, age twenty-seven, married four years**

> *It seems to me that women come cable-ready, but men need a converter box.* **—A friend of Sandra's**

According to linguistics professor Deborah Tannen, it isn't just that men and women are wired differently, it's that we belong to virtually incompatible verbal species. Our vastly different communication styles originate in childhood when, as youngsters, we're first exposed to the "genderlects" of our respective worlds. Take the man in your life. As one of the boys he was taught through competitive, aggressive games that life is a contest in which males have to stay one-up. Meanwhile, you, as one of the girls, learned through cooperative activities with good friends that life is a community where being close to other people is the primary goal. As adults, these dissimilar approaches to life are frequently seen in verbal interactions.

For instance, in Sandra's session at a recent symposium at a scientific conference there were three female presenters and two males. When the symposium was over, the three women enthusiastically discussed each other's research, making positive comments and agreeing to stay in touch. But as Sandra and her colleagues exited the conference hotel, a very different conversation was taking place between the two male researchers walking behind them. One man had claimed during his speech that his study was the first to demonstrate a particular phenomenon. The second man negated this assertion, pointing out that the study had not been the first. The one-upmanship continued. As long as the two men were within earshot, the women heard more of the same. It made Sandra reflect on men's drive to be on top and she came to this conclusion: Whether they're in the scientific arena, in corporations, in sports, or whatever, for some men, life's a pissing contest just the same.

And this contest often carries over into other communications arenas. As Deborah Tannen points out: We listen, many men lecture and explain. We seek agreement, more men challenge and confront. We are more comfortable with small talk and sharing confidences in private, most men are more comfortable with impersonal public speaking. We notice and enjoy discussing details, some men find this irritating. We like to share our worries and troubles, but don't want men to "fix" things (often men offer "brilliant" solutions then are puzzled when we don't accept their advice). We are also more willing to ask for and accept help from other people while many men are stubbornly independent. Or to put it another way, "Why does it take millions of sperm to fertilize one little egg? Because most males won't stop and ask for directions."

They also won't stop arguing until they win. This is no surprise given the best-all-comers way many men are raised. It also explains why some husbands and boyfriends think they must win every altercation—and win, they do.

I'm a win man myself. I don't go for place or show.
                                        —Bear Bryant, football coach

Research shows that men triumph in significantly more arguments than their mates. How do they do it? By employing a whole linguistic armada of techniques including persuasion, manipulation, and factual information, all designed to help them seize control of the decision-making process—a position they're used to. And most men have been used to it since they were knee-high to a playpen.

Indeed, a series of experiments with children shows that from an early age, boys paired with girls expect to dominate the decision-making process. In fact, in every age group, the decision-control scores of the boys were higher than those of the girls, and adolescent girls almost always relinquished control of the decision to their male counterparts. Unfortunately, these findings reinforce the impact of the intensified, sex role socialization that occurs in adolescence (see Chapter 5). They also explain why, by the time we women marry, relational powerlessness is imprinted on our brains.

But certainly men don't want women with the word *loser* stamped on their foreheads. Indeed, today's media hype portrays the "new male" as a different breed—a kinder, gentler man who's shucked his macho attitudes, eschewed the dominant role, and freed himself to admit his doubts, insecurity, and pain. And what has happened as a result?

CATHY © Cathy Guisewite. Reprinted with permission of UNIVERSAL PRESS SYNDICATE. All rights reserved.

So what can we say? Only this: It's a time of transition. Perhaps male–female communication will improve as the members of each sex refuse to conform to old, stereotyped expectations, continue to work toward egalitarian decision making, talk to each other, and master conflict resolution.

Proactive Strategy: Conflict Resolution

Conflict resolution is a rational, nonemotional way of working out issues between partners—a kind of relational Marquess of Queensberry rules. But they're probably not the rules your parents played by and probably not the rules you play by either. Indeed, most couples handle disagreements just like their parents—with just about the same results:

Not only did we inherit his parents' house, we inherited all their arguments about the house too.
—Marti, age thirty-two, retailer

He told me I was just like my mother—and it wasn't a compliment! **—Dawn, age thirty-five, nurse**

No wonder most women want to chop down the family tree and get a fresh start—and with conflict resolution they can. So can you, especially if you remember that conflict resolution is a skill that can be learned. Now, like any new skill, this one takes time to perfect, so be patient with yourself (and with your mate). And speaking of time, make sure the timing is right to begin the conflict resolution process. Don't undertake any major discussions when you or your partner is highly stressed, hungry, or tired, or when either of you is hopping mad. You also might want to avoid the predinner hour since researchers have found that this is the most difficult time of day for people to have a civilized conversation. In addition, before you talk, make sure you've considered the problem very carefully and have a clear idea of your own position. As you practice this technique, you'll learn additional timing tricks that will increase your confidence and allow you to use conflict resolution more effectively, like Sylvia:

I have learned to step back when it's in the heat of the situation and say, "Let's think about it a little while." I used to bring things up at bedtime. We'd be lying there and I'd be going off and he would fall asleep. I would be either crying or upset and he would be snoring. So I have stopped that. I thought, "What am I doing? I'm staying up and he's over there snoring." He had the pattern of falling right to sleep and then there I was left holding the bag, you know, until two or three o'clock . . . **—Sylvia**

But no one has to get stuck holding the bag, and when the following conflict resolution principles are applied in good faith, no one does:

The Principles of Conflict Resolution

1. State the problem in specific terms. For instance, say "The problem is that although we have been talking a lot more lately, you still don't tell me about your feelings. I feel distant from you." Also, avoid derogatory name-calling, put-downs, or labeling like "you're just stubborn" or "you're so lazy."

2. Only discuss one problem at a time. It can be overwhelming to your mate if you dump a whole load of grievances on him at once.

3. Listen carefully—without interrupting—to your partner's responses, then restate them aloud to make sure you've heard all the issues and understood everything correctly. ("It sounds like you had reservations all along about my returning to work. But you didn't want to rain on my parade.") Try looking at the situation through his eyes and see if it gives you a new perspective.

4. Avoid psychoanalyzing or making inferences about the hidden meaning behind your partner's behavior. For example, don't say, "The way you dealt with that situation shows you're insecure."

5. Accept responsibility for your own role in the problem—after all, problems in relationships are a two-way street and never belong to just one partner.

6. Brainstorm to come up with as many alternative solutions as you can, and even if some of the ideas seem Looney Tunes, put them on the table anyway. (If they don't work, at least you'll get a good laugh!)

7. Work out a compromise. To do this, both you and your partner should state what you want, then each of you should make some accommodations. For instance, agree to spend one Sunday with the in-laws, then to relax at home the following weekend; or agree that if one of you cooks, the other will clean up, and so on. Whatever you decide, remember that resolving conflicts does not mean one partner wins and the other partner loses. Nor should either partner feel resentful. This is important. After all, you shouldn't feel compromised, just because you choose to compromise.

Now learning to compromise and resolve conflicts takes practice. In fact, just learning to think of a situation as a "problem to be solved" rather than as something that's "his fault" is a major accomplishment. So is listening to your spouse. Really listening. However, as you listen, you may find your partner ducking the issue, as in this example from marriage counselor Doris Wild Helmering:

Ann: I think we need to sit down and go over our budget. With the bank note coming due on the house and Peter going to college next year, I think we're going to have to start saving more money.

Bob: If we could just get our charges paid off . . . (Bob ignores what Ann said and switches to his own issue.)

When this happens, the challenge is to stick to the topic even though your spouse is trying to switch subjects. There are other challenges to conflict resolution too. For instance:

- Resist the urge to read your partner's mind because you never really know what someone else is thinking.
- Stop overgeneralizing ("you never listen to me").
- Give up all-or-nothing, ultimatum-type thinking, as well as any distorted, erroneous points of view.
- Remember that *no one* should be pushed to his/her knees and forced to navel gaze.

Instead, show respect and empathy for each other's feelings. Use assertive statements (see Chapter 6) and demonstrate your willingness to work together toward mutually agreeable solutions. In other words, both of you should move from "me" thinking to "we" thinking:

We're in this together—otherwise we wouldn't have gotten married.
> **—Ina, age twenty-eight, married three years**

What you get out of a marriage is in direct proportion to what you put into it.
> **—Beth, age forty-six, married twenty-six years**

If you put in the time and effort conflict resolution requires, what you'll get out of it is a new sense of confidence—the confidence that you and your mate can weather arguments and solve problems. As a bonus, your relationship will grow incredibly strong and may even evolve into a peer marriage.

Peer Marriage

> *I told my fiancee that she would be queen of our castle and she said she would only take the job if she and the king were peers.*
>
> **—Norman, age fifty-six, married six months**

There's not much point in being queen if you and the king aren't peers, and peerage—equality—can be the key to a great marriage. Although the idea might strike you as more of a Fractured Fairy Tale than something that happens in real life, researchers know such relationships exist—they're just hard to find.

> *When I talk about peer marriages, and I talk about what they are, people kind of glaze over and they say, "Well, which three did you find?" or "Did you find three in the world?"* **—Pepper Schwartz, sociologist**

The peer marriages that Schwartz does find have four things in common: Both partners wield equal decision-making power, both control discretionary funds, both participate in household chores, and both share child-rearing activities. In addition, peer marriages are characterized by deep intimacy, generosity, and respect. Partners negotiate and talk more than other couples and, ultimately, find their relationships very satisfying.

But lest you think it's all gingerpeachy, remember that peer marriage has disadvantages too. For example, since the relationship is given higher priority than either person's career, peer couples tend to make less money than their traditional, "near-peer" counterparts. This is why "material girls" (and boys) find peer marriage unappealing, but we suspect that many women would be willing to forget the money and forgo pricey status symbols if it meant their marriages would be more equal. And this isn't just a suspicion. Participants in the Women's Anger Study seldom said they were angry because they wanted a bigger cash flow. Instead, they desire things money can't buy—their husbands' emotional support, companionship, an equal division of labor, and as much joy as they can handle. Now if that three-letter word sounds like we're speaking in tongues, then maybe it's time for you to

Put the Joy Back in Your Relationship, or Are We Having Fun Yet?

Sometimes relationships are about as entertaining as watching a car rust. Not only do you not have time for fun, but with careers, child rearing, domestic duties and all, you don't even remember what fun is. Often, you reach a point where your mate is assigned a very low priority, and suddenly it seems like all the good times have slipped away. At this stage, you usually become angry or disillusioned, but instead of accusing your partner of petrification, try taking the initiative and do something with all your angry energy:

> *It was the middle of a frantic work day and I was totally frazzled. Then I called Steve and suggested we sneak off for a romantic lunch. When we were single, we used to do this all the time. It doesn't happen very much now, but at least today I had a meal I'll remember fondly.*
> **—Veronica, age forty-four, married fifteen years**

Fond memories help when life gets tough. It also helps to remember that even when they seem to be on hiatus, the good times usually do come round again. But what if they don't? What if, after all your efforts, the anger in your relationship is still intense, or abusive and out of control? If it's the latter, see the next chapter and take action immediately to protect yourself and your children from any verbal, physical, and/or sexual abuse. If you are not in an abusive situation, but find yourself making mental roadkill of your mate or giving your marriage extreme unction, then consider calling in the pros.

Calling in the Pros

If the strategies you've learned in this chapter do not produce positive results and if your relationship seems hopelessly mired in anger and resentment, you may want to consider getting professional help. The American Association for Marriage and Family Therapy has an 800 number (1-800-374-AMFT), and most local telephone directories list a variety of professionals who specialize in marriage and relationship counseling including ministers, social workers, psychologists, and psychiatric nurses. You should also ask your family and friends for referrals.

The objectivity and support of a third party can be invaluable when you feel hopelessly discouraged or confused. A skilled counselor can also help you explore complicated issues from the past that may be influencing your behavior with your partner in ways you don't understand. If your mate does not want to participate in counseling, go without him. After all, you are the one who is interested in doing something—so do it—like Diana, who found herself in just this situation.

> *I remember . . . saying "I'm going to a counselor tomorrow and I'm not doing it for you . . . I'm not doing it to embarrass you . . . I'm going for me . . . to take care of my mental health." He . . . said, "Oh, don't, I know this counselor, I don't want you to do that." I said, "I don't really care . . . I'm going to do it for me . . . if you want to come later, then fine, but if you don't, I really don't care . . . I'm worthy of this, I have a right to this as a person."*
>
> **—Diana**

You also have the right to express your anger in an honest, comfortable way, and a marriage or committed relationship represents the best opportunity most women will ever have to do this. It's one of the major benefits of being in a loving partnership, a partnership where you can be yourself, cry, tease, complain, let your hair down, or occasionally go ballistic. Indeed, many participants in the Women's Anger Study say they share their angry feelings with their partners, but this only works if you and your mate are committed to each other and are willing to let your relationship be an incubator for personal growth and revelation.

> *Love provides a continuous environment for the revelations of one's self, so that one can yield to life without fear and embarrassment.* **—Mary Caroline Richards**

This is why many women—including the authors— believe in committed relationships, for not only do these relationships provide love, affection, laughter, and invaluable support, they are:

. . . our last, best chance to grow up.
—Joseph Barth, *Ladies' Home Journal,* **April 1961**

26

WHEN RELATIONSHIP ANGER BECOMES RELATIONSHIP ABUSE

I married very young. He was an alcoholic and he began beating me. Well, I thought it was supposed to be like that because that was how I was raised. When I was pregnant with my first child, my ex-husband would beat me. Just before delivery he kicked me in the stomach and I thought I had lost it [the baby]. But I didn't. And I grew real angry then. I hated him but I continued to live with him because I didn't have anyplace to go. After my second child was born I came home from the hospital and he raped me, busted all my stitches after delivery. And he packed me with cotton. Of course I passed out. **—Meg**

Many women pass their lives as coolies, toiling away in harsh relationships where they smother their anger because they fear violent retaliation from abusive mates—and it's easy to understand their fear. From girlhood on, we females are acutely aware of males' greater physical size and strength. First we experience it in roughhousing on the playground, and later in sexually charged tussles in the backseats of cars. We have been overpowered by male siblings, cousins, playmates, and boyfriends, and we quickly learn that physical strength not only determines who has the power, but who can abuse it. Indeed, we stand a much greater chance of being assaulted, beaten, or killed by a man we know than by a stranger. Just consider the following grim statistics:

- A woman is battered every fifteen seconds.
- As many as one in three women will be assaulted by a domestic partner in her lifetime—that's four million women in any given year!
- 14 to 25 percent of all adult women have been raped, and over half of all rapes to women over thirty are partner rapes.
- Spouse abuse is more common than automobile accidents, muggings, and cancer deaths combined!
- Domestic violence is the leading cause of injuries to women aged fifteen to forty-four, and the most typical of these injuries are broken bones, bruises, lacerations, burns, black eyes, and miscarriages.
- Of every 1,000 pregnant women, 154 are assaulted by their partners during the first four months of pregnancy, and 170 per 1,000 are assaulted during the final months.
- Half the women murdered in 1991 were killed by their husbands or other men with whom they had an intimate relationship.

Contrary to popular opinion, battering, assault, rape, and even murder are not due to a man's loss of control. Rather, they are how he achieves control and maintains power in the relationship.

The very first essential for success is a perpetually constant and regular employment of violence.
						—**Adolf Hitler,** *Mein Kampf*

Men use this violence against women of all classes, races, and income levels—it is just more successfully disguised in middle- and upper-class communities, where homes are on larger lots and neighbors can't hear the screams. The situation gets worse if drugs or alcohol are involved, but whether substance abuse is present or not, the end result is always the same: After the assault, the husband or boyfriend "gets religion," says "I'm sorry, I love you, I'll never hit you again," and things get better—until the next time. And there is always a next time, even children know that:

Let's move back in with Dad. Let's just go home, let him break your arm, and then you'll be all right.

—A six-year-old boy, tired of life in a spouse abuse shelter, advising his mother

But it takes a long time before abuse victims are "all right." Indeed, the consequences of physical and sexual abuse are similar to the lingering post-traumatic stress syndrome suffered by combat soldiers and survivors of natural disasters. The symptoms these groups share include shock, denial, confusion, fear, nightmares, flashbacks, and psychological numbing, but that's where the similarity ends.

Neither the disaster victims nor the soldiers were harmed by individuals they loved and trusted, and unlike wives or girlfriends, they do not blame themselves for the attacks, convinced they could have prevented the abuse "if only . . ." In addition, even if women know they don't deserve such treatment, many feel trapped and helpless. They hold their tongues because they truly believe they can't survive economically or emotionally outside of the relationship.

The common characteristics of a battered wife include her inability to leave despite such constant beatings; her "learned helplessness"; her lack of anywhere to go; her feeling that if she tried to leave she would be subjected to even more merciless treatment; her belief in the omnipotence of her battering husband; and sometimes, her hope that her husband will change his ways.

—Robert N. Wilentz, Chief Justice, New Jersey Supreme Court

But he usually doesn't and the epidemic goes on until women are so badly beaten they land in hospital emergency rooms. There, doctors identify abuse only in one out of every thirty-five cases—even though one in every four female hospital admissions is for injuries from battering.

Besides the bodily injuries, women's spirits are battered too. Abused women are at high risk for depression, substance abuse, and worse. Many of these individuals commit or attempt to commit suicide, sadly choosing a permanent solution for a temporary problem. Their children also suffer—they are much more likely to have emotional problems, including high levels of fear and anger, and these feelings are totally justified. At least one half of all abusive husbands batter their children as well, never taking into account that:

> Child abuse casts a shadow that lasts a lifetime.
> **—Herbert Ward, Episcopal priest**

Fortunately, some women do realize this, and when the circle of abuse widens to include their children, they eclipse the shadow and move into the light, like Joyce. When Joyce's husband Frank began physically and verbally abusing her son and sexually abusing her daughter, Joyce was furious. She "made the steps and got out of the marriage," but until that time, she kept silent about her own abuse. Why? Because Frank had successfully brainwashed her into believing she deserved it and Joyce was ashamed and confused.

> *I didn't realize I was being abused in the marriage. . . . I'm the type that is just totally giving and . . . "your needs come before me" and that's really not healthy so I didn't realize how he was manipulating me and how unhappy I was. He was real good at manipulating: "It's just all your fault, Joyce, I'm not the one that needs counseling." You get told these things often enough you believe them . . . like people say, the bad stuff is easier to believe than the good stuff.*
>
> *I didn't want to go to my parents and say, "I'm having this problem with Frank." I didn't have any close friends and didn't want to admit that I was having problems. I wanted everyone to think that I had the perfect marriage—'cause I wanted to think I had the perfect marriage . . . when we separated everybody just said, "Oh Joyce, you were the perfect couple." [I thought] you just don't know what it's been like. That's 'cause I covered up. I was ashamed, you know, of being a "battered woman." I wasn't battered but twice. The first time I thoroughly denied it. It was all my fault. [I thought,] "what have I done?" And then the second time I was scared. This was when we had separated and my husband was coming back to get some things. Sure enough, he grabbed ahold of me, swung me across the den, started beating on me. I had my mother there and she was able to stop him.*
>
> *I don't remember having a lot of anger until I saw how he neglected and abused the children. Of course, I made the steps and got out of the marriage, but only when it*

*began to affect my children. I wasn't willing to take those
steps for myself . . . It took me months before I could tell
anybody what my life had been like.*   **—Joyce**

The reluctance of Joyce and other battered women to
communicate is not surprising. After all, how many of us
would admit we were living under a confidence-cracking
reign of terror? Particularly since the world is often unsym-
pathetic toward abused women and judges them harshly. Indeed, according to psychologist Sharon Herzberger, our
society tolerates—and in so doing, promotes—abuse and
family violence by making excuses, blaming the victims, and
looking the other way. This is borne out in a study Herzberger conducted in which more than 40 percent of the men
and the women surveyed said they understood "why someone would hit a partner who lied." In addition, one fifth of
the respondents thought that people who stay in abusive relationships "deserve the treatment they get." What's more disturbing, some of these same attitudes are shared by
individuals in positions of authority—individuals who can
impact us all:

*There are only twenty murders a year in London, and not
all are serious. Some are just husbands killing their wives.*
   —G. H. Hatherill, former commander, Scotland Yard

Getting serious is exactly what we need to do if conditions
are to improve. We, with the support of enlightened men,
must fight for a complete overhaul of social attitudes, for the
enactment of tougher laws, for educational intervention, and
for the establishment of more legal aid centers and shelters
for abused women and children. We also need to take individual action.

Proactive Strategy: What One Woman—You—Can Do to Save Your Life or the Life of Someone You Love

If you—or someone you know—is being abused, these steps
could save your life or the life of someone you love:

1. Talk about the situation with someone who can help
like the police, your doctor, lawyer, minister, social worker,
nurse, or therapist. If the person you go to minimizes your
problem—an all-too-frequent travesty—then take action and

tell someone else. You can also call the twenty-four-hour, toll-free women's crisis hotline available in most cities. Remember, wherever you are in the United States, abuse is a crime and is punishable under local criminal laws. Your safety—and the safety of your children—is the number one priority, and the law is on your side. Best of all, the law works, so don't be afraid to use it. Consider: A recent survey by the Bureau of Justice Statistics found that 41 percent of the women assaulted by their husbands who did *not* report the first attack to police were assaulted *again* during the next six months. By contrast, only 15 percent of the wives who reported their abuse were assaulted a second time. With this in mind, ask yourself the following questions.

- Do you need immediate police protection or a safe shelter?
- Do you have a plan in case the danger escalates and you decide to leave your husband or boyfriend?
- Is he extremely jealous of you and are you spending most of your time trying not to make him mad?
- Does your partner keep a gun or other weapons in your home?
- Is he abusing alcohol or drugs?
- Is he threatening your children or other family members?
- Did he grow up in a violent family?
- Do you believe he's capable of killing you?

If your answer is yes to the questions about weapons, alcohol, a family history of violence, or his capability of killing you, you may be in grave danger and you should *get help now!*

2. Be crystal clear on this fact—the abuse is not your fault. You do not deserve to be treated this way. You are not a lousy wife or mother and nothing you have ever done justifies the physical or sexual abuse you've been forced to endure. In addition, no one, not even a married woman, should be forced to have sex against her will.

A marriage license [is] not a license for a husband to forcibly rape his wife . . . A married woman has the same right to control her body as an unmarried woman.
—Judge Sol Wachtler, New York State Court of Appeals

In addition, no one should be slapped, hit, or kicked, and if you have any doubts about this, remember: Battering does not get better over time—it gets worse, much worse.

3. Consider the serious consequences for your children if you remain in this relationship. Each year in the United States 2,000 children die from violence in the home and 140,000 are seriously injured. Most of the deaths are caused by a father, stepfather, or boyfriend lashing out in rage. So even if your husband or boyfriend is not beating the kids, it is terrifying for them to see him beat you and the memories of these horrifying episodes will be burned into their brains for the rest of their lives. In addition, boys who watch their fathers physically abuse their mothers are more likely to abuse their girlfriends or wives when they grow up. Likewise, girls who witness violence between their parents are at increased risk for becoming battered women themselves.

4. You have a choice—and the choice can be to end your relationship. Other women have left abusive partners and you can too.

> *I decided to take my life or take control of my life and detach myself from my ex-husband . . . I had enough anger to kill. I can see where a woman would just totally go bananas and shoot her spouse. But there are better ways you can deal with your anger. Talk to people. I have a psychologist that I talk with. I still have anger but I'm dealing with it.*
>
> **—Meg, survivor of two abusive marriages**

Eventually 60 to 75 percent of the women who seek safety in shelters leave the violent man, but extremely careful planning is necessary before you make your move:

- Pack an extra set of clothes for yourself and your children, as well as extra car and house keys, then store the suitcase with a friend.
- Store money, your social security card, voter registration card, medical records, and your children's birth certificates with a friend or hide them in a safe place.
- Take financial records, rent receipts, the car title, etc.
- Know exactly where you will go and how to get there. Also, be aware that some shelters have waiting lists, so

you might need to stay with a friend or relative until there's an opening.

- Do not tell your children about the plan in advance because they may tell their father or someone else. Remember, you are in the most danger when you terminate the abusive relationship, especially if you begin another relationship with a different man. Why? Often the abuser is enraged when he's served with a restraining order or divorce decree, and this rage could make him mad enough to kill. For these reasons:

- Do not confront your mate or take any action that will put you or your children in jeopardy. Be sure you have taken every possible precaution to protect yourself and your kids. You might also need to protect yourself and your kids against verbal abuse.

Proactive Strategy: Verbal Abuse—How to Fight Back When Rapier "Wit" Cuts Too Deep

Many men are so verbally cruel and abusive that conversations with them are the equivalent of a body slam to the soul. Although verbal abuse leaves no black eyes or visible bruises, it can scar your spirit and seriously disfigure your self-image. Sadly, there are more verbal victims around than you think. Indeed, one in every four women admits to being verbally or emotionally abused. This abuse takes several forms including ridicule, criticism, accusations, threats, name-calling, sarcastic "jokes" that aren't funny, and the icy silence that means rejection and is intended to bring you down.

One of the most devastating effects of living in this linguistic quicksand is the insidious change in your self-esteem. As you begin to internalize the criticism and believe it's valid, your self-image sinks lower and lower. After all, your spouse/ boyfriend knows you better than anyone else and if he thinks you're unlovable, dumb, unattractive, clumsy, incompetent— you fill in the blank—then it "must be true." To make matters worse, because you're ashamed of the way he talks to you, you keep the derogatory comments to yourself— circumventing a "reality check" from friends or relatives who could dispute your mate's raging words and cruel judgments.

And if you do summon the courage to challenge the rage

master, he'll probably say, "What's wrong with you, making a big deal out of nothing." This answer can create even more confusion and self-doubt as you think, "Maybe it is me, maybe I am supersensitive and he's only kidding." But maybe he isn't and maybe he's counting on the fact that you won't identify his vocal barrages as abuse. He's not counting on anyone else to identify it either, which is why many verbally abusive men exude charm in public and only display their cruelty in private to an audience of one—their brainwashed wives or girlfriends.

> *I was truly brainwashed by my husband's verbal abuse. Nothing I did pleased him. He criticized my cooking, my driving, you name it. But there was a tiny shred of self that he never completely destroyed because I once had been loved and praised as a small child . . . so every now and then I summoned the courage to challenge his cruel remarks. "If I'm so horrible then why do my friends love me? My students? Our minister and the people at church?" His venomous answer always silenced me: "Because they don't really know you." And so I would return to my former state of self-doubt, helplessness and hopelessness. The years I spent in that marriage were the worst years of my life.* **—Cassandra**

Acknowledging verbal abuse is not an easy thing to do. You may need the assistance of a counselor, a compassionate friend, or a support group to break the fever dream of self-doubt, helplessness, and hopelessness that has taken over your life. But once you acknowledge the situation, it is possible to put a stop to it. First, decide not to tolerate your partner's poison tongue anymore. Then, set limits on his behavior by saying "I will not accept what you're saying," or "Stop that. Don't talk to me that way!"

Next, make plans to create a more nurturing environment for yourself—with or without your mate. Finally, remember that recovering from abuse takes time whether you terminate the relationship or not. There are two excellent books that can aid you in this process, *Stopping Wife Abuse*, by Jennifer Baker Fleming, and *The Verbally Abusive Relationship*, by Patricia Evans. Both provide in-depth information and guidelines for healing. They help you recognize when you're being "dissed" and explain that respect is another word for love.

PART EIGHT

ANGER AND CHILDREN

27

EVEN GOOD MOMS GET MAD

My two-year-old is so infuriating that as I was reading her "Hansel and Gretel," I fantasized that the witch ate her for dinner. —**Gina**

At times you get so mad you could practically eat your young alive. It's not just that children are selfish, noisy, messy, belligerent, and uncivilized, it's that motherhood is the toughest job going. Why? It demands outstanding performance and unquestioned devotion in the face of long hours, rigorous on-site training, drop-dead fatigue, and lousy

271

pay. There's no retirement plan either. Worse yet, if your off-spring don't "turn out all right," society brands you a failure and scholarly psychiatric literature says you're not a "good-enough mother"—and that's enough to make even mega-moms occasionally wish they'd never taken on the job:

> *Sometimes, when I look at all my children, I say to myself, "Lillian, you should have stayed a virgin."*
> **—Lillian Carter, mother of President Jimmy Carter**

> *Of course I don't always enjoy being a mother. At these times my husband and I hole up somewhere in the wine country, eat, drink, make mad love, and pretend we were born sterile and raise poodles.*
> **—Dorothy DeBolt, biological mother of six and adoptive mother of fourteen**

Whether we're raising toddlers in diapers, helping junior high schoolers with homework, or running a taxi service for the postpubescent set, our real occupation is worrying about our children's happiness. For instance, you might worry because your son's an overachiever while your neighbor down the street worries about the exact opposite problem. Another mother frets because her oldest girl is way too popular and her youngest isn't popular at all. Then there are the mothers who sweat over being a professional woman versus a stay-at-home mom, who agonize whether to leave young Sharon in softball or yank her out, make Johnnie practice the violin or give him the day off . . . and finally, every mother alive worries that she's not worried enough.

On top of all this, we're anxious about the outside stresses that buffet our children, and even though there's not much we can do about them, we mothers take on these problems just the same (see Chapter 7). We also feel guilty and blame ourselves when stressful situations don't work out. Why? We can't help it, we're moms:

> *I'm a mother. I worry. That's my job description.*
> **—Isabel, mother of three**

> *I had a baby, but it was really like having quadruplets, because I also gave birth to anxiety, worry, and stress.*
> **—Rose, mother of a newborn**

It's pretty obvious why "mother" is the most stressful of all female roles, and researchers (not to mention you and millions of other moms) confirm it with these new findings:

- Women with young children experience high levels of stress, whether they're homemakers or employed outside the home.
- Mothers with children under five who don't have a supportive partner are more apt to become clinically depressed than any other group of adults.
- Mothers experience higher levels of role overload and conflict than childless women, whether or not those mothers work outside the home.
- Women's risk of depression and demoralization is higher if they are the mothers of young children. This risk increases with the number of children living at home.
- Women retain primary responsibility for child care (twenty-eight hours per week versus hubby's nine hours per week) even when they work outside the home.
- Women are twice as likely as men to experience daily conflicts with children.

Besides daily conflicts, there are other stresses of mothering that shake us by the psyche including our youngsters' incessant needs and demands; the awesome responsibility for kids' safety, health, and well-being; discipline problems; children fighting among themselves; anxiety over their education, peer relationships, moral development, and teenage acting-out behaviors (like precocious sex, smoking, drinking, and drugs); and later, concern over their vocational choice, mate selection, and all the assorted trials and tribulations of adulthood. And then there's the biggest psyche-shaker of all, the one identified by 61 percent of the mothers responding to researchers' questions about stresses of the maternal role, it's:

Worrying about the present and future of my children and whether I have done everything I can just never ends.

—One mother interviewed by researchers
P. Stevens and A. Meleis

While this nagging, never-ending worry is true to every mother's demographic profile, something new has been added to the mix—more moms are working now than ever before. In fact, the percentage of working, married mothers with children age three or younger actually doubled (from 25.8 to 51 percent) between 1970 and 1986. Unfortunately, the stress doubled too.

Paul Cleary, a Harvard researcher, found that the combination of being a parent and an employed worker is so stressful it contributes to women's depression. Cleary also found that the parent/worker role is not as stressful for men. In addition, another team of investigators discovered that employed mothers who have sole responsibility for child care or who have difficulty arranging for this service have high depression levels—and companies exacerbate the situation.

Corporate pooh-bahs have been slow to offer Mommy Track options if we want to work fewer hours while our children are small (see Chapter 19). In addition, there is a hefty shortage of day-care facilities throughout the United States. Even in the best of circumstances—when good child care options are available and affordable, and when your husband is supportive—all of us working mothers are stretched too thin. When our reserves are this shallow, it doesn't take much to make us doubt the amount of "quality time" we're giving our kids. This is especially true if the little darlings have saved up all their rotten feelings from a rough day at preschool to "share" with their tired mom.

And "tired" doesn't just apply to mothers who are professionally employed. Even stay-at-home moms find the care of wee tykes emotionally and physically exhausting, as evidenced by one study of Army wives. The wives were asked questions about their level of emotional distress and the average score of women with babies was only one point away from "severe." This is not surprising since the arrival of the first baby is among the most stressful events in a family's entire life cycle. Why? In the past, we had a week to rest in the hospital after giving birth, a week that allowed us to gear up emotionally and physically for everything the stork brought including feeding problems, sleepless nights, disrupted household routines, marital adjustments, and other challenges too numerous to mention. With today's abbreviated hospital stays, we have to hit the ground running, whether we're ready or not—and most new mothers are not.

It's even worse if you hit the ground and your spouse isn't there to break the fall. Despite the widely publicized participation of fathers in Lamaze classes, labor, and delivery, most males get uninvolved as soon as their infants leave the hospital. This is a great source of anger and disappointment for new mothers, as shown in a study by the husband and wife research team of Philip and Carolyn Cowan. The Cowans studied more than a hundred couples and found:

> *The less involved a father becomes with the baby's care, the more likely it is that he and his wife will become disenchanted with their relationship as a couple over the next year.*   **—Philip and Carolyn Cowan**

For some couples, "disenchanted" doesn't begin to describe it. In fact, 12.5 percent of the marriages in the Cowans' study ended by the time the baby was a year and a half old, making a tough situation even tougher. Why?

Without a partner, many of us fear our parenting efforts are just a bad imitation of a much-loved classic, so being a mother becomes an even greater source of stress. And more of us are experiencing this stress than ever before:

- In the fifteen- to forty-four-year-old age group alone, a fourth of all mothers are single.
- By 1990, 25 percent of America's children lived alone with their mothers, compared to 5 percent in 1960.
- More children are being raised in fatherless homes now than at any other time in U.S. history.
- The single-parent family is the fastest-growing family type in America today.

Most of these single-parent families are headed by women— women who are the primary influence on their children's emotional health and development, women who bear 100 percent of the parenting stress, the stress that can lead us to anger.

> *I hate being mad at my kids because it makes me feel like such a bad mother. The problem is that sometimes you just have to yell to keep them from getting hurt or stop them from doing something wrong. When you do that*

stuff, you're showing that you care—being a good mother. What I don't understand is why being a good mother sometimes has to feel so bad.

—Joan, mother of two

Even if we're "good" mothers, we get mad—usually at ourselves for not handling our anger toward children more effectively. After all, how often have we tried badgering, scolding, griping, nagging, lecturing, or haranguing with no effect? Or been quick-tempered and shouted at our kids, only to discover:

Parents were invented to make children happy by giving them something to ignore.   **—Ogden Nash**

And children aren't the only ones who employ this technique. Many of us ignore our own anger and hold it back to preserve "family harmony." Why? Perhaps we mistakenly believe that this is what real women are supposed to do:

I really do feel like the woman sets the pace. If you're in a bad mood the whole family's in a bad mood . . . The mama more than anybody else is the keystone. If she's got a good attitude I think the children have a better attitude. And if she's in a bad mood, everybody's in a bad mood.

—Clara

But constantly being the pacesetter is no easy job and despite heroic attempts to always be the perfect mother, all of us eventually erupt. In fact, in one survey of parents, 50 percent admitted that they'd lost their tempers and hit their children "really hard" while another 40 percent were afraid of doing the same thing. Moira, a divorced mother of two, discovered that parents aren't the only ones with fears:

I just rant and rave and my kids cringe in the corner and then it's all gone and I'm okay. I've had that blowup and I'm all right. But I didn't realize how those blowups affected the children. They were afraid of me, they were afraid of making mom angry. And no one should be afraid.   **—Moira, who is in counseling to help her control anger**

When we get angry at our children (and especially if we make our children afraid), we may feel like the situation calls for an automatic guilt binge. This is true even for mothers with nerves of steel, the patience of Job, and industrial-strength, Dr. Spock-approved child management techniques. These moms, too, get mad at their kids and when the slugfest is over, they slink away, feeling like dog meat because "after all, they're only children!"

> *My five-year-old gets spankings occasionally and I don't really believe in that but I've done it. And then I feel bad, you know.* —**Carla**

Once we get over our anger, we feel bad about losing control, so we give our kids an extra hug or kiss, and vow to be better mothers tomorrow. But being better mothers tomorrow means knowing what sets us off today.

What Sets Moms Off

The Women's Anger Study found that children's disrespect, carelessness, and irresponsibility trigger motherloads of anger. (Check your journal to see what sets you off.) Moms in the study said they got mad when:

- "My children consistently disobey—particularly away from home or in front of other people."
- "Primarily with teen-aged children being rude, inconsiderate, messy, etc.—especially when they fight, belch in public, and other crude things adolescent males do."
- "Son telling lies."
- "It's a struggle from the time they're born to teach them responsibility and to get them to do things. They're always going to tell you 'No' or that they don't want to right then: 'I will in a minute.'"
- "I can't control them, it ticks me off."

Most of us are especially ticked when our children mouth off in a disrespectful way:

> *You just want to grab them up and shake them, since they are kids and when they mouth off it's a lot worse than I think an adult would [act] . . . with adults you're on a more even footing I suppose.* —**Gladys**

But no matter how sure we are of our footing with adults, kids can make us feel like we're losing ground, particularly when they make demands that trigger anger:

*You walk in, they want you to take them to the store . . .
to buy this . . . to buy that. And yet, you ask them to do a
few things for you and it's like pulling teeth to get anything done. Sometimes I just get so mad that I would like
to jerk them around a little bit but I don't.* **—Georgia**

We women not only secretly think about jerking our kids
around, but from time to time, we get very angry because we
secretly think our kids are acting like jerks. Usually this applies when our children have behaved in a thoughtless way,
haven't considered the consequence of their actions, or don't
give a flying fig about what happens to others:

*I became angry with my daughter for not thinking before
doing something and it involved injury to me. I really
chewed my daughter out and felt awful about it.*

*I was petting the cat and asked her to bring me a comb
so I could comb the cat . . . my daughter reluctantly went
after the comb, stood fifteen feet from me and flipped the
comb at me and the cat . . . the cat proceeded to climb
up my face. My lip split wide open. Blood . . . spewed
everywhere. But my anger was that she did not think,
knowing how skittish the cat is and I was going to have
to go to the emergency room and get antibiotics and a
tetanus booster. But then what . . . gave me more anger
than anything is when I got home at midnight, the
kitchen was still a wreck, the wok was still on, the food
was crusted to the wok.* **—Anna**

In Anna's situation, the anger was intense because her
daughter's thoughtlessness was compounded by irresponsibility. And Anna's not alone in her feelings. Irresponsibility
with belongings and household chores is another common
anger trigger identified by participants in the Women's Anger
Study. It makes us even angrier when the irresponsible offenders are adult children who should know better:

*Right now my biggest anger is with adult children living
at home that expect you to do their laundry, do the cooking, you work all day, you go home tired, you cook supper
for these adult children and then you sit down at the table
to eat, then they get up and leave and . . . you're left with
all the mess . . .*

*I tell them this is ridiculous. They'll help a little bit for
a while, then back to the same old thing. I feel used and*

abused by these children, I feel like they take advantage of a good situation. I guess they think you owe them for life . . . I get to the point [where] I think, "Hey, this is getting to be too much . . . I'll just sell this house and . . . sit them out in the street and move on." But you can't do that with your own kids.

—Ella, mother of four, including two males, ages twenty and twenty-six, who still live at home

However, sometimes you wish you could. Maybe you even dream of evicting all the small (and large) fry, or at least the one who makes you maddest because you feel like you're being bucked:

He bucks me in the morning and then he bucks me in the afternoon, and he bucks me again. Like he'll say, "I'll feed the dogs," and he never has time to feed the dogs. He's always got a reason that he can't do it. Or I'll say, "Your dad wants the lawn mowed." And my fifteen-year-old son replies, "Well I can't, I'm not going to mow it today." . . . and then he's got a very disrespectful mouth. In the end it turns into a big blowup. **—Tonya**

Indeed, blowups are a fact of life with kids, but not every blowup happens because our kids have disrespected us, some of them occur when other people have dissed our kids. Participants in the Women's Anger Study said they get angry when their children are treated unjustly, or when there are threats to children's safety, particularly "when a child takes advantage of my child or hurts her in some way," "when my ex-husband mistreats my children," or "my children [are] treated with insensitivity," as in the case of Faye's daughter:

It was at a gathering of my husband's very chauvinistic family . . . we were all finished [with dinner] and the grandfather said "Get up" to one of my daughters [to get up and go help grandmom in the kitchen]. But there were three boys sitting there her same age . . . I looked at him and said to my daughter, "Don't you dare get up. When you see the boys getting up to go help Grandmommy in the kitchen, then you can go. Or if you choose to go because you want to help her, but not because you're a woman and you're supposed to be in the kitchen." And I was angry. I could've bitten nails in two. **—Faye**

Our anger not only explodes over family issues and personal values, it also is detonated by outside circumstances, like when a mother and her children are just trying to survive but get nailed by life:

> *I feel angry over not having enough money. Not being able to buy my kids a new pair of shoes. Not being able to buy them one thing they want. 'Cause my kids know we're poor and they don't ask for very much but when they ask for something they really want it . . . to have to tell them no really bothers me. And not having enough food . . . which affects our health . . . that bothers me too. We cannot afford any health insurance and my little boy's had pneumonia three times this last year . . . I had to go to my mother—at [age] thirty and ask for money to take my kid to the doctor. It was humiliating . . . it made me angry at circumstances and that is a daily anger . . .*
>
> *In a grocery store if there are things I need but can't afford . . . I feel anger, it's searing. To deal with it, it seems like . . . I see red or black . . . it's almost like I become unconscious . . . for a minute. It's . . . like all time stands still . . . I'm just there and I'm feeling this raw emotion and I'm mad as hell. I want to take all those cans in the grocery store and . . . start flinging them. Or better yet, when I walk through the store, put all this food in my cart and just walk out with it and smile . . .*
>
> *I picture doing this when I'm angry. Then I get all sad and I want to cry. The anger makes me cry because I feel it so. It's just into the depth of my soul . . . I grit my teeth or hold my jaw really, really tight and I just hold back all the tears that I can. I wake up sore all over my body from holding myself so rigid. The next day I feel like I've been hit by a Mack truck. I feel bruised.*
>
> **—Patti, age thirty, mother, student, part-time waitress**

In a similar way, when our children are endangered, anger makes us want to bruise someone else. At moments like these, the mother in us will put on moral blinders and focus the full force of our emotions to keep our children safe:

> *My children's psychological and physical safety was blatantly threatened by an aggressive woman who was sociopathic. Never in my life have I experienced anything close to the rage this elicited in me. It is the one time in my life when I thought I could physically harm someone. Yet, I*

was in a situation where, if she was provoked, she might act on her threats. It is indeed terrible to experience such rage yet be unable to act on it in any way.

At the same time, I was terrified. I felt like a caged animal being tortured by a sadistic trainer. She has been kept at bay only by creating a situation in which the implications of her acting on her threats involve very real consequences for her legally. The situation is not yet resolved to the point where I feel she is satisfactorily contained. But in the face of the most intense rage I have ever experienced, the safety of my children kept me from acting in ways that could put them in danger.

—Kristin, on the "mama justice" coursing through her veins

When you act on your child-related anger, it's usually easy to understand the provoking incident, but occasionally you may feel mad for reasons that aren't entirely clear. When this happens, you need to do an emotional exhumation to uncover the hidden reasons for what you feel.

The Hidden Reasons for Mothers' Anger

Ferreting out the hidden reasons for anger toward our children is akin to uncovering the portrait of Dorian Gray. However, once we understand our own concealed anger issues, we will have a much clearer picture of why we get mad at our kids. Some reasons you might discover are:

- Your child reminds you of someone you intensely dislike or had conflicts with in your own childhood.
- Your child is too much like you and has qualities you don't like in yourself.
- Your child is too shy, too lazy about schoolwork, too unlike other family members, etc., and so does not conform to your beliefs about the way children should be.
- Your child has become the scapegoat for marital tensions or other stresses within the family system.
- Child care itself is honestly distasteful to you. You feel resentful and trapped by the responsibilities of parenthood. In short, it drives you crazy.

Insanity is hereditary—you get it from your children.

—Sam Levenson

If one particular child drives you nuts or if you experience unusually intense anger toward this child, family counseling is in order. There are many resources you can turn to in this situation including local child and family service agencies, mental health centers, employee assistance counselors, a minister, priest, rabbi, or private therapists who specialize in working with families. You can locate these people through personal referrals from friends and relatives, your family doctor, or school principal. Now, whether you feel you need professional help or not, there are a number of things you can do to start handling your parental anger like a pro . . .

28

EFFECTIVE WAYS TO DEAL WITH ANGER TOWARD CHILDREN

The real menace in dealing with a five-year-old is that in no time at all you begin to sound like a five-year-old.
—Jean Kerr

Often, children are awesome in their defiance of conventional wisdom and their mothers, and although we erupt, explode, throw fits, use guilt and intimidation, or stoop to their level, the results of these angry encounters are far from satisfying. To move these interactions into a better place, the first thing we need to do is stop fighting tantrums with tantrums.

Proactive Strategy: Stop Fighting Tantrums with Tantrums

Youngsters often react to frustration with their own private and very loud version of primal scream therapy—otherwise known as tantrums. Kids have tantrums because they don't have much self-control, but we, as parents, do. However, when we choose to lose this control and scream ("Shut up! Stop that right now!") back at our children in an attempt to contain their anger, what we're really doing is adding fuel to the fire. We're also undermining our own credibility as adults:

Do as I say, not as I do!
—Popular cliché every child ignores

This is why it's so important for you to maintain control, to stay calm and do the following when your normally adorable sons and daughters are temporarily possessed by demons:

Step 1: Remember that because you are an adult, you are in charge of your own emotional reactions. Your years of life experience and wisdom do not disintegrate just because you are being challenged by a child younger than dawn.

Step 2: Realize that your children's anger is not a personal affront or a deliberate defiance of your maternal authority. Usually, it's simply a misguided attempt to get something like your attention or a sibling's new computer toy. Sometimes your child just wants to check out her id, that is, the infantile part of the personality that says, "I want it, and I want it right now!" That's what a temper tantrum really is. Remember, when you diffuse your child's tantrum, what you're really doing is helping your child mature. After all, it's important for youngsters to learn that life isn't always a bowl of ice cream—especially when they fling themselves on the supermarket floor and scream at the top of their little lungs. The moral of this story is that temper tantrums must not be rewarded by giving in to a child's demands.

Step 3: To control demands and tantrums, distract very young children with a substitute toy or activity (this is fairly easy since tiny tots change demands faster than diapers), or remove your child from the situation by using a time-out. The third option is to ignore the tantrum completely.

But what if it's behavior that can't be ignored? What if Junior does something so off the wall, so out of line, or such a long way from normal that you have to grit your teeth and sit on your hands to keep from wringing his neck? The answer is: Don't discipline your child when you're mad.

Proactive Strategy: Don't Discipline Your Children When You're Mad

Much of the mother-guilt over anger happens when we get mad, have a nuclear reaction, and unthinkingly discipline our kids in the fallout:

> *I grounded Vic for a month when he got in three hours after curfew . . . Unfortunately, the grounding took place during his high school's homecoming and he missed the dance, the parade, everything. I feel bad that I overdid it, but I didn't think I should go back on my word. Besides, when he walked in the door that night all cocky after I'd been awake worrying, I was so mad I could barely see straight. Still, I felt a little guilty that I was so harsh.*
>
> **—Diana, mother of three**

Sometimes you might feel guilty because your anger causes a blind spot and, as a result, you discipline your children in an inappropriate way. But since it's so hard for you or any of us to see straight when we're mad, how do we know if we're being appropriate or not? Since every child is different and since different misdeeds call for different kinds of reactions, there is no single, all-purpose form of discipline every mom should use. However, one general guideline applies to all parents: Don't discipline your children while you're angry.

Now this rule doesn't mean that you should be soft on your misbehaving offspring. What it does mean is that you should send your errant child to the solitary confinement of his brain cells—in other words, discipline the child in a way that makes him think about what he's done and in a manner that helps him grow and develop self-control. And remember, your child won't develop self-control if he sees you losing yours.

When you get mad and "lose it," your first impulse is probably to give in to the powerful physical arousal of your angry feelings (see Part One). You may want to strike little Bobby or Betsy with your hands, a belt, or a brush, but this is one of the most harmful things you can do. Not only is harsh physical punishment ineffective, it also leaves deep emotional scars:

> *Where does discipline end? Where does cruelty begin?*
> *Somewhere between these, thousands of children inhabit*
> *a voiceless hell.* **—François Mauriac**

Indeed, studies show that children who receive corporal punishment are more likely to be depressed and have low self-esteem. They are also more likely to engage in acting-out behaviors like stealing, lying, and truancy. In addition, there is evidence that children who are punished physically may fail to develop any internal self-control. Why? These kids only alter their behavior when they're threatened by a feared external authority figure. As a result, they don't develop self-discipline, an omission that could eventually end in the worst-case scenario.

> *His father used to spank him but it didn't seem to do any*
> *good. Maybe we should've tried something else, maybe I*
> *should've yelled at Rob more.*
> **—Dee, on her son Rob's arrest for shoplifting**

And maybe not. Yelling and name-calling ("You idiot! How could you possibly do such a thing?") aren't any more effective than corporal punishment. In fact, if you scream and shout you will terrify your children, and in their terror, these small fry will shut out your angry voice. The result? Instead of altering kids' behavior with your vocal gymnastics, you simply create a sense of fear, fear of your formidable mother-power and your lack of emotional control. Think about it.

When you yell, you are the least effective. Why? You're yelling because *you* are angry and it gives you some relief to vent your anger. Instead, try discharging your anger in a healthy way that will serve as an example for your children. After your anger is discharged, decide on disciplinary measures that accomplish what you want: cooperative, considerate, well-mannered children. And disciplinary measures are most effective when you follow these steps:

Step 1. Talk to your youngsters about their behavior before you reach the boiling point. (If your teen is trashing the rec room, don't wait until you go ballistic to put a stop to the devastation.

Step 2. Explain exactly what you want your child to do differently. ("I want this room cleaned up by five P.M.")

Step 3. State the consequences and explain what will happen if the children don't comply with your request. ("There will be no television tonight if you do not finish your chores.")

Step 4. Consistently apply those consequences without giving in to pleading, whining, or manipulating (strategies children readily perfect once you show any signs of waffling).

Step 5. Connect the consequences to the offense. (If your child carelessly breaks something, she must earn the money to replace it.)

Step 6. If all else fails and you're too angry to discipline your child this way, tell him: "I am really angry with you. I need you to go to your room until I calm down, then we are going to talk about this."

When you finally do talk about it, remember to keep your talk short because long lectures are futile. In fact, psychologist Thomas Phelan says you can confuse children with all your words; instead, he recommends "the wild-animal trainer approach." No, not whips and chains. What he means is the quiet, gentle method good trainers use. For example, when your child misbehaves, simply raise one finger and say "That's one." If your little wild animal ignores this, warn him "That's two." When the child reaches three, he goes straight to his room for five minutes. No logical reasoning, no prolonged discussion, no anger, just firmness in applying the consequences of misbehavior, and you and your husband must each apply these consequences in a consistent, uniform way.

> *We both have learned how to discipline our children. Instead of me just being the disciplinarian and him not . . . He just didn't want to hear my loud voice and my anger. It gets on his nerves. So he would sit and roll his eyes when I would discipline the children and then it would just get into a vicious cycle. I'd be filled with hate when I'd see him do that. I'd be like "Just help me out here. Don't do that to me."*
> —**Peggy Sue**

When parents help each other out, when no one always has to be the bad cop, it's easier to discipline your kids, and when you discipline them, this is what your guideline should be:

Parents must always get across the idea that "I love you always, but sometimes I do not love your behavior."
— **Amy Vanderbilt**

You also might realize that you don't love the way you yourself were disciplined as a child, and you may not want to pass this "heritage" along. As a consequence, you might turn 180 degrees to be as different as possible from your own parents. Unfortunately, "different" does not necessarily mean "better," especially if your mother wore combat boots . . .

Should You Follow in Mother's Footsteps If Mom Wore Combat Boots?

Many of us swear we'll be better parents than our mothers and grandmothers were. While this seems like a step toward progress, it's actually more of a stumble. Why? Often, we're still licking our own childhood wounds and even if we've studied all the family dynamics and gained some important insights, it's dangerous to claim "I'm raising my children exactly the opposite of how I was raised." The danger is that by going to the flip side, we'll end up with kids who are the mirror image of the parents we're trying to divest, which is exactly what happened to Mary.

Mary, whose mother excelled in stubbornness and domination, went overboard to avoid bossing her daughter, Sophia. Mary encouraged Sophia to speak freely and make most of her own decisions, but what Mary failed to see was that without appropriate parental limits, Sophia was becoming an overbearing little hell-on-wheels. Eventually, Mary found herself having the same kind of fights with her daughter that she once had with her dictatorial mother. How did this happen?

When you adopt an opposite-from-my-parents approach, I can almost guarantee that your child will come to act like the parent you're implicitly criticizing. It's a natural law of family physics. — **Ron Taffel, parenting expert**

Or to put it another way:

CATHY © Cathy Guisewite. Reprinted with permission of UNIVERSAL PRESS SYNDICATE.
All rights reserved.

You also shouldn't pick on your kids when you really want to vent at someone else.

Proactive Strategy: Open the Right Vent, or Don't Come Down on the Kids 'Cause You're Mad at Someone Else

At last! Half an hour to yourself before you start dinner. The children are playing quietly for the first time all day . . . You fall into your favorite chair, retrieve the biography you're reading and . . . the phone rings.

Your husband didn't realize how late he had worked at the office and needs his blue suit from the cleaners: it closes in fifteen minutes, and he can't get there in time. Will you pick it up? You grit your teeth, remembering that he promised to do this chore himself. But you'll do it. Of course, you'll do it. You always do it! You interrupt the kids, get them into raincoats and haul them out to the car. When Janet protests she wants to see all of Sesame Street, you explode at her. She bursts into tears, and, dejected and ashamed, you watch the rain drip down the windshield and long for your peaceful half hour.

—Jean Withers

This woman not only lost her half hour, she lost her sense of control. How so? She's really mad at her husband because he won't take care of himself and she's "always" bailing him out. But who gets the brunt of her anger? The children.

In fact, it's often the children who catch your wrath in this version of the old "kick the dog" game, especially when your anger is displaced from the real provocateur—your husband—to a less powerful target—your kids. Does it sound familiar? It should, since it's a game we've all played, but surely our youngsters are the losers because they just happen to be in the wrong place at the wrong time. What's really needed in these situations is for adults to work out their anger issues with each other. The other thing that's needed is to ask for help when you're feeling stressed.

Proactive Strategy: Ask for Help When You're Feeling Stressed

When you hit stress overload, cut right to the chase and ask for help before you dump on your children. The first step is admitting that fatigue and vulnerability have tapped you out. Then you should:

- Institute the stress management techniques in Chapter 8.
- Ask your friends, neighbors, older children, and/or your spouse for assistance. Remember, in many families fathers could give up their couch-potato status and help a lot more than they do. After all, child care is Dad's business too, and there's a large body of research showing how important good fathering is to children's emotional development and well-being. In addition, kids want this interaction! In one survey of children's feelings about their fathers, half the youngsters said they wished "Daddy" would spend more time with them!
- Develop creative approaches for dealing with the predinner hour—before you eat each other alive. Why? The hour before dinner is a very high-stress time in most households. Everyone is hungry, tired, out-of-sorts, and recovering from a long day. Kids bicker, parents yell for the bickering to stop, and from there things go straight down the tubes. It's even worse if you've invested a lot of energy in fixing a great meal and then that meal is ruined by squabbling or consumed in stony silence. But supper can be salvaged if you delegate tasks to your husband and older children, enlist a teenage neighbor to read or play with youngsters while the meal is being prepared, or make the predinner hour official family

downtime. This same creative thinking applies to breakfast, bedtime, or any other period that officially qualifies as your family's "arsenic hour."

For example:

. . . when it gets to be eight at night things have deteriorated. I spend a lot of my time . . . just trying to split up fights between my two daughters . . . I've tried sitting down and saying, "What can we do about this when your sister makes you mad and you're really mad?" What sort of strategies are we going to have that will work besides hitting, which is what they do, then yelling and crying . . . I do find myself just snapping at them and I've yelled at them recently. I don't like to yell . . . but sometimes it gets results . . . I can sit around and be Miss Nice Mom and say, "Okay, I need some cooperation" until the cows come home. Every evening around bedtime is a very difficult time—I do end up getting mad. It goes a lot more smoothly when he comes and helps. He's really good during those situations . . . kind of distracting them, making a little joke and lightening the situation.

**—Madge, mother of two girls, two
and a half years apart**

Madge learned that getting her husband to help not only lightened her daughters' outlook, it lightened her own load as well. Something else that takes a load off is:

Proactive Strategy: Prepraising Your Children

Even if you spout prose so sweet it would be rejected for a greeting card, you should prepraise your children. "Prepraising" is a healthy alternative to angry scoldings, as well as a tried and true method for motivating good behavior, because it focuses on the positive, not on flaws and mistakes. There are three steps to the prepraising process.

Step 1. Set the stage. Establish standards and expectations and tell your child what they are. ("I know you will be good in this restaurant," or "I know I can count on you to act nicely.") This really translates into praising your child in advance for good behavior. In addition, you should be very specific about what "good behavior" really means. ("I know you will finish eating all of your hamburger before you ask to go out on the playground.") Also, your expectations should be realistic for the child's age and developmental level. (As a litmus test, just ask yourself if your youngster is old enough to sit still through a symphony or a lecture that would bore the most disciplined adult, then you'll have your answer.)

Step 2. Prove the point. Point out examples of good behavior that meet your expectations, such as when your child remembers to do chores, to return things he's borrowed, to honestly admit a mistake. When you show your appreciation by rewarding your child with praise, it increases the likelihood that the child will repeat the good behavior again, and again, and again.

> *Praise them for important things, even if you have to stretch them a bit. They live on it like bread and butter and they need it more than bread and butter.*
> **—Lavina C. Fugal, Mother of the Year, 1955**

Step 3. Find solutions. Sometimes, despite even the most consistent, specific prepraising, your child does something unexpected and makes a mistake. But a mistake is not a failure because it provides an opportunity for you to teach your child new solutions. For example, take Tommy, who's been busted by his mom for a misdemeanor. Her first impulse is to say, "You've been in my wallet. Why did you do that? What's the matter with you?" But this typical, angry confrontation undermines Tommy's self-esteem and he's left thinking, "I am a really bad boy." In addition, by responding in a temperamental way, Tommy's mother misses the opportunity to teach her son appropriate behavior—like earning his own money by doing a household chore. Parenting expert Linda Lewis Griffith suggests handling the situation this way:

> *In these instances, you still prepraise them for the behavior you expect, then help them discover alternative solutions. Here's what I mean: You have been prepraising nine-year-old Tommy for being honest. Then you realize he has taken money from your wallet without asking. Rather than berating him for being a dishonest crook, you still tell him that he is honest. However, you explore with him other, more appropriate ways to handle his desire to buy something. You might say, "Tommy, I know that you're an honest guy. How else do you think you*

*could have gotten that money you wanted for those base-
ball cards?"* **—Linda Lewis Griffith**

One way Tommy could have gotten that money is if he and
his family used a job jar.

Proactive Strategy: A Job Jar

Parents and children duke it out over chores more than any
other topic, but there will be fewer fights if, instead of giving
our kids a verbal jab, we give them a jar—a Job Jar. Pediatric
psychologist Tom Bluett, the father of five, devised this ter-
rific Job Jar system for eliminating squabbles and getting the
work done. First, basic household chores (defined by Bluett
as bed-making, laundry, and getting meals on and off the
table) are shared by every family member and no one gets
paid for doing them. All other household tasks are written on
slips of paper complete with detailed instructions ("Vacuum
until no paper, crumbs, or dog hair can be seen") and placed
in the Job Jar. A fair wage is attached to each chore. To earn
spending money, youngsters must take on some of the tasks
from the Jar. If they don't, they learn a basic law of economics: No work = no pay!

A Job Jar can have a big payoff for you and other mothers,
both in terms of getting work done and in terms of easing
stress. Something else that can ease stress is learning to think
like your kids.

Proactive Strategy: Think Like a Kid, or Become a Child Development Expert

*All the time a person is a child she is both a child and
learning to be a parent. After she becomes a parent, she
becomes predominantly a parent reliving childhood.*

—Dr. Benjamin Spock

That is, if you can remember your childhood; if you can't,
check out a few good books on child development. When you
read about—and come to understand—what "normal" or
"typical" behavior is for children at certain ages, there is less
of a chance that you'll react to this behavior with irrational
fury. True, you may still be frustrated by your two-year-old's
tantrums, your four-year-old's incessant questions, or your

teenager's messy room, but there's comfort in knowing this too shall pass. However, we do not recommend that you excuse unacceptable behavior by writing it off as a stage your child is going through. Appropriate discipline is still the order of the day for behavior that's out of line.

But some parents take too hard a line, and in putting children through their paces are running an intellectual Iditarod. These parents push their children to be "well-rounded," popular, and accomplished in school, in competitive sports, and in "enrichment" activities like music, drama, dance, social clubs, and foreign language studies. Eventually, all this pushing produces tired, cranky children who rebel against their parental handlers and get embroiled in angry conflicts. But angry conflicts can be avoided if a child gets enough time to play and daydream, if she is allowed to choose her own extracurricular activities, and if the weekly calendar isn't a forced march through too many preplanned "fun" events.

Speaking of fun . . .

> *Are we having fun yet? No. In fact, we won't have any fun for about six years because our kids are teenagers.*
>
> **—Rochelle**

Conflicts with preteens and teenagers dominated the Women's Anger Study data. This was not surprising to members of our research team with teens of their own—which may be why some team members are glad to be working mothers.

> *I think we're seeing in working mothers a change from TGIF to TGI Monday. If any working mother has not experienced this feeling, her children are not adolescents.*
>
> **—Ann Diehl, *Vogue*, January 1985**

Adolescents. Just say the word and fathers run screaming for cover, siblings hide out in their rooms, and you wish you could change your identity and disappear for a few years. Why? Not since the "terrible twos" have children been so rebellious, so intent on gaining independence, and so vocal about it.

> *If I want your opinion, Mother, I won't just ask for it, I'll tell you what it is!*
>
> **—Jody, age sixteen, at a family picnic**

Suddenly our opinions, rules, values, politics, and lifestyle are seen as

> *. . . bogus, phony and Neanderthal*
> **—Mack, age fourteen, on his parents**

But the only thing bogus about the heartfelt, angry conflicts that are a way of life between parents and teens is the superficial excuse for the power struggle, and that changes from day to day:

> *Monday we fought because he wouldn't take out the garbage and it stank. Tuesday he canceled the barber shop appointment I made last week and he refuses to rebook. Wednesday he stayed out late and didn't call to say when he'd be home, and what makes me the maddest, he smiles at me when we fight and all I see is this lethal-looking overbite covered with braces that I'm paying for! It's too much! I want to run away from home!*
> **—Gretchen, Mack's mom**

Teenagers vent their anger at home because it's a safe place to rant and rave. Venting at home also prepares both you and your teen for the latter's imminent departure from the nest. This is usually one step ahead of his surefire eviction and the timing seems almost divinely ordained. Perhaps it's part of God's plan that teenagers become so obnoxious we can let go of them without much grief. Meanwhile, it's a real strain on you and your family for a number of years. In fact, research shows that couples are the least happy when they are the parents of school-age children and adolescents. But you and your spouse will make it through these times if you try to laugh about it.

Proactive Strategy: Get a Sense of Humor

Think of it like this:

> *The beauty of "spacing" children many years apart lies in the fact that parents have time to learn the mistakes that were made with the older ones which permits them to make exactly the opposite mistakes with the younger ones.* **—Sydney J. Harris, author**

But you will make fewer mistakes with all your kids if you teach them the positive side of their angry emotions.

Proactive Strategy: What Smart Moms Teach Their Kids About Anger

Smart mothers teach their children that anger is a natural emotion that must be expressed in a healthy way. Without this lesson, children may pass from "Amazing Grace" to disgrace, and even commit violence and murder.

> Nationwide . . . homicides by juveniles 16 and under during the period (1986 to 1992) jumped 96% while aggravated batteries grew by 74%. In Chicago, four youths under 14 committed killings with firearms from 1983 to 1990, but 24 did so during the next three years.
> **—F. McRoberts, J. Irwin, *Chicago Tribune*, October 16, 1994**

Why does this happen? Analyst Alice Miller says the potential for violence can be traced to strict child-rearing practices that squelch spontaneous feelings. Miller calls it the "poisonous pedagogy" because such an approach teaches children that strong feelings (like anger) are harmful and must be suppressed. She also contends that individuals who don't understand anger and can't accept it as part of themselves will have the need to strike out at others.

But it doesn't have to be this way, not if we teach our children to respect strong emotions and express those emotions in a healthy way. Madge (who always stifled her own anger because she feared her stepfather's violent temper) has started early with her two- and five-year-old girls:

> I've said to both of them, "You know you're really angry right now, aren't you? . . . it's okay to be angry and what can we do?" . . . this morning Colleen was upstairs with her Pop-Tart and her father brought it back down to the kitchen and she was screaming and crying . . . she came and sat on the kitchen floor and folded her arms and said, "I'm really mad. Daddy made me mad." . . . I thought, "Yeah, this is wonderful . . . just verbalizing is a good way to get it out."
> **—Madge**

Madge made a good beginning by letting her daughter say she's angry. Madge then reinforced to her child that it's okay to feel angry and it's okay to talk about it. It's even all right to be angry at a parent, something which, unfortunately, is taboo in many families. Later, Madge will add more lessons about expressing anger and will use sibling squabbles and other encounters as opportunities to teach her children about problem solving to resolve angry disputes.

You should try this too, but remember, no matter what you or Madge tell your children about problem solving and constructive anger management, actions speak louder than words, and your behavior will be the most powerful influence on your kids. Why? Because, as we've emphasized throughout this book, anger behavior is learned. Your youngsters learn what anger is and how to express it from your angry outbursts, whether these outbursts are directed at one child, all your children, or your spouse. In fact, children learn a lot from how you and your husband settle your own disagreements, whether those disagreements are a squabble, a skirmish, or a full-fledged fight.

Unfortunately, what your children learn from a full-fledged fight scares the dickens out of them. Indeed, compelling research evidence suggests that if your children fear they have somehow caused an argument between you and your husband, this fear can put a mental hammerlock on them years down the line:

> *When my parents were still married I was about four and my sister was two or three. They'd fight . . . It was awful. Me and my sister would stand in the hall and listen. And I would get scared, and so . . . we'd . . . go in our room. Sometimes we would move our mattresses and . . . jump up and down and try to play so we wouldn't have to hear.*
>
> **—Sally, now age ten**

Hearing and seeing parents fight affects boys and girls in different ways. Boys become more aggressive. Girls, like Sally, become more anxious and withdrawn. Neither response is very productive and both can create emotional problems for your children later in life. The situation is even worse if your disagreements with your mate go unresolved. Why? When the arguments continue, it just increases your kids' distress.

The upshot here is that you must avoid being goldfish in a Baggie and quit having shouting matches in front of your kids. However, if an argument does erupt, carefully explain that it solved a problem; that the children aren't to blame;

and that there's nothing to be afraid of. When your young-sters are old enough to understand all this, they'll actually start to benefit from observing how you and your spouse ex-press angry feelings yet still manage to love each other. They will also learn that anger does not mean terror, abandon-ment, or uncontrolled aggression.

Instead, your kids will discover that it is a normal part of living with other people, an emotion that requires mothers—and others—to be as tough-fibered as circumstances demand and as gentle as they allow.

PART NINE

D-I-V-O-R-C-E

29

_____

UNDERSTANDING AND RESOLVING YOUR ANGER

Do you want me to characterize divorce in one sentence? It's hell, sheer hell. The lack of financial stability is the worst part. It creates all sorts of fears and anxiety. The kids don't understand why I'm still so messed up. Somehow, I'm supposed to come out of this a whole human being, but I'm not sure how . . .

—**Bonnie**

Divorce often swallows us whole, then chews us up and spits us out in ragged little pieces. Unfortunately, the odds of ending up piecemeal are greater now than ever before because 40 to 55 percent of all marriages today are likely to end in divorce—and that estimate may be low since some studies put the figure at 70 percent or more. The upshot is that for many couples, the last act of marriage is a solo—even if one of you wants it to remain a duet.

In fact, in 85 percent of all cases, only one partner wants to take his or her act and hit the road. Often this dissatisfied partner is the wife. Indeed, women are twice as likely as men to initiate divorce, whether or not they've been auditioning replacements. By contrast, when men want out, there's usually a new woman waiting in the wings, but having an understudy ready to step into the leading role doesn't make divorce any easier.

This is true whether we're talking about the person who leaves or the person who's left because neither one gets off easy, starting with the partner who initiates the divorce. The initiator is afraid of damaging the children, feels guilty about inflicting pain on his or her mate, and has heavy angst about possible condemnation by the clergy or members of the couple's social network. Likewise, the person who's left or on whom the divorce is imposed may feel misused, neglected, unlovable, and reluctant to face friends and neighbors, not to mention highly mistrustful of future involvements. Obviously, divorce is a profound life crisis for both partners, and for each one, it causes emotional upheaval, radical changes in daily routines and habits, and major lifestyle, social, and attitude adjustments that will take more years to work out than either partner cares to count.

> *My attitude would be much better if . . . my ex had just had the good grace to die. At least when someone dies people grieve alongside you. Divorce is much hairier—I mean, I was the only person mourning my marriage!*
>
> **—Dorthea, divorced seven years**

There are more guidelines for mourning the locks of our hair on the salon floor than for grieving over our marriages. Indeed, when we lose a partner through divorce, many theorists claim we go through the same emotions and the same adjustment steps Elisabeth Kubler-Ross describes for coping with the death of a loved one. But while divorce does involve grieving and while it is based on earlier experiences with separation and loss, there are several important factors that make mourning a marriage different:

1. Death is irrevocable—marriage and divorce are not. Often, partners wed new mates; others reconcile or at least hope to do so.

2. If reconciliation doesn't work out, the divorce becomes a living reminder of your terminated relationship, especially if you have children and if you must continue to interact with your ex-husband.

3. You might feel a sense of failure and rejection over your divorce that you wouldn't ordinarily experience if your spouse "just" died.

4. When a loved one dies you're the beneficiary of sympathy and considerable community support as well as home-cooked meals, free baby-sitting, and volunteers to run errands. By contrast, divorce creates awkward social situations because your friends and relatives aren't sure how to behave toward you or "that beast."

But one thing is sure: From the very beginning, anger is a prominent factor in the divorce process. For example, it can be a catalyst to divorce if you're mated to one of the damned, fear your marriage is in a coma, or is otherwise harmful to your psychological health. Likewise, divorce is an act of courage if you're smothered by daily injustices or degradation and you use your anger to set yourself free, to win

> . . . *a feeling of needed relief from the demands of an unjust, unequal relationship.*
> **—Most common reason cited by divorced mothers**

Dorothy got relief from her unjust, unequal relationship when she finally mobilized her anger and divorced her husband of thirty-one years:

> *I was angry at these things: Angry when the promise not to smoke again was broken right after we were married . . . [when] the promise not to drink again was broken four months after we were married. Anger later when I realized he probably was never going to change . . . I look back on it now and realize how enabling I was for that patterning . . . in other words, going along with someone else enabling them to do that.*

*This was especially true in terms of moving to accom-
modate his career. "I've moved with you eighteen times,"
I told him, "when's it my turn?" Finally, as I took on a
more professional, separate life [as a Ph.D. on tenure
track in a university faculty position], I realized I was a
separate identity from this man. I was someone who was
myself and not just a person who was a wife. I told him
however he wanted to do it, I'd be glad to file [for divorce]
or he could file. But it had to be one or the other.*

—**Dorothy**

For many of us, this is what marital anger finally comes
down to—one partner or the other files for divorce—but
anger doesn't end at the beginning of the divorce process or
even somewhere in the middle. Instead, it actually carries
over into four of the five phases of divorce adjustment and,
as Sandra has found in conducting dozens of divorce adjustment workshops, you can get through these phases more easily if you know what they are. It also helps to know that you
can skip a few stages or experience them in a different order,
but most women will probably go through all five in the se-
quence identified by divorce researchers. Most women will
probably go through similar emotional reactions too, and
that's all right because it helps to realize that you're not the
only one who feels irrational, panicky, or unglued! Also, recognizing the phases of divorce adjustment will help you to
fathom when you've crossed the finish line into acceptance
and recovery, and that's the biggest payoff of all. Of course,
before you can cross this line, you need to know how far
away it really is.

Proactive Strategy: Understanding Where You Are in the Divorce Adjustment Process

Phase 1: Alienation and the Erosion of Love, Otherwise Known as Emotional Divorce

The angrily separating oils and waters of a dying marriage
may force you to seek an emotional divorce long before you
file for a legal one. Indeed, "emotional divorce," the withholding of emotion from the relationship, can take place months
or even years before your marriage actually ends.

I look at him and I feel nothing, so I just give him the silent treatment year after year after year.

—Mercedes, married eighteen years

But when you're living under the same roof with your emotionally estranged spouse, it's usually anything but silent. While you may spend less and less time in shared activities, when you are together, fights, insults, and complaints are often the order of the day. So is denial. Whoever doesn't want the divorce might employ a whole raft of reasons to avoid dissolving the marriage. But whether he or she uses money, the children, or anything else as a stalling tactic, the bottom line is always this:

I doubt if there is one married person on earth who can be objective about divorce. It is always a threat . . . such a dire threat that it is almost a dirty word.

—Nora Johnson, author

When my first marriage was crumbling, the most obscene word was m-a-y-b-e. "Maybe I'll be home for dinner. Maybe I won't. Maybe we'll make love. Maybe we won't. Maybe we'll stay together. Maybe we won't. Maybe . . ." The ambivalence was what finally did us in.   **—Cara**

In Phase 1, you and your partner are ambivalent about maintaining your relationship. At times you desperately desire freedom and at other times you cling to the security and benefits of marriage:

Although I teach psychiatric nursing and I teach . . . the concept of ambivalence, I never fully understood ambivalence until I began to contemplate my divorce. I vacillated . . . for about two years trying to make the decision. Some days I was absolutely sure that I should file for divorce; I was suffocating in that marriage . . . then a fairly pleasant social event would occur, or a nice family outing with the kids, and I would think, "He's not so bad after all, he's probably better than most men."   **—Kassie**

But "better than most" doesn't always cut it. Even if the person who wants the separation feels guilty about leaving and even if the person who's about to be left feels guilty about failing to please his or her mate, eventually the marriage becomes intolerable for both. Why? All human beings need love and esteem, and these needs can't be met in a dying relationship. In addition, both partners soon realize that you don't have to compete in a daily tug-of-war if no one's at the other end of the rope.

Phase 2: Anger/Depression/Detachment—The End of the Marital Rope

Unfortunately, by the time you reach Phase 2, there's enough of that rope for you and your spouse to hang yourselves, or at least to hang your marriage, and often one of you does. Frequently, it's the wife who files for divorce, but no matter who does the filing, both partners are likely to go on an emotional bender. For instance, you might be angry or overwhelmed with depression, and often will find yourself alternating between these two feelings because they're both sides of the same coin. The experience is most intense for whoever has the biggest investment in and commitment to the relationship. If this describes you, you may find the situation unbearably bleak, dangerously insecure, and absolutely infuriating, especially if your soon-to-be-former mate is coping rather well.

> *Sure I hate him. Sure I love him. And sure I'm going nuts. I alternate between using my son's punching bag and using cases of Kleenex.* **—Pam, divorced one year**

When some of us divorce we become Kleenex people because we feel so used up and thrown away. This might apply to you if you're the rejected partner, if you're focusing on your "de-selection," or feel your spouse's abdication is undeserved. Your litany may well be, "Why me? What have I done to deserve all this?" especially if your husband's young lover is built like a Ferrari and you have a body by Meals on Wheels.

Unfortunately, some of us feed our rage long after it's healthy to do so. We continue to play the blame game, telling everyone what #@!^&* our husbands are and maintaining our fury until we become hostility junkies who are stuck in a psychologically angry state.

> *The angriest I ever was, was when he first told me he was leaving. He'd been seeing another woman for two and a*

half years. Of course, I cried most of the night and then I got angry the next day. He went to bed and was snoring in five minutes. From then on, for a year there we couldn't see each other without screaming and hollering. I was angry the whole time. I kept finding out more and more things he'd done and I would get madder and madder . . . Other women he'd seen . . . the last few years he was supposed to have been working a lot of overtime at the plant and everybody thinks I was stupid because I didn't see things earlier. But I trusted him . . . I've had ministers tell me that as long as I hate him, as long as I can't forgive him, that I can't be right. And I just said, "If I have to forgive him, if I have to get over my hate for him in order to be right, then I'll never be right because I'll never do it." —**Ingrid, divorced three years after a thirty-eight-year marriage**

Like Ingrid, many long-divorced women spit venom when they describe their rejections, making their losses seem very recent and fresh. Alas, these hostility junkies are not unique in their refusal to move beyond the anger and depression of Phase 2.

Judith Wallerstein, a California psychologist, has studied a group of divorced couples and their children for over a decade. In periodic interviews she's found that both the men and the women have persistent, intense anger toward their former spouses—even ten years or more after their divorces took place! In fact, this never-ending fury characterized half the women and fully a third of the men in the research group. Unfortunately, while short-term anger is normal and justified, this long-term anger is highly destructive, but there are ways to recover from it, as you'll see.

For the majority of us, some slight recovery begins when anger and depression are replaced with detachment. This usually happens at the end of Phase 2, when our emotions are so dead or numb that our brains blot out all but the most practical side of divorce—who gets the house, who gets the dog, who pays child support, and who moves out—and when one partner moves out, it really means you're both moving into:

Phase 3: Separation Distress/Breaking Old Habits/Transition

Poof. Gone. Supernova. In Phase 3, it's pretty obvious that your nuclear family has exploded because physical separation has taken place. One of you now lives in a strange, unfamiliar apartment or hotel room. The other is in a home full of maimed memories, and because humans are territorial beings, the changes produce anxiety for everyone involved.

For these reasons, many researchers believe Phase 3 is the most traumatic, anxiety-ridden phase in the divorce adjustment process, especially if it comes after a marriage of long duration. After all, divorce is second only to the death of a loved one in terms of its psychological impact, and that impact is never more keenly felt as when physical separation first takes place.

In fact, the physical separation might be so difficult and so stressful (especially if the divorce action was sudden and unexpected) that one or both of you undergoes "separation distress syndrome." Your symptoms may include panic; tension; apprehensiveness; a loss of self-confidence; vigilance; insomnia; an erratic appetite; an increased use of alcohol, cigarettes, and/or drugs; an inability to concentrate on your tasks or job; sudden anger or crying; regret over lost happiness; bewilderment; vulnerability; an inability to control your life; a sense that life is rushing by too fast; yo-yo mood swings ranging from occasional spurts of euphoria, exuberant self-confidence, and the energetic pursuit of new projects to the very depths of depression, despair, distress, and loneliness.

For many of us, sitting down to breakfast (and lunch and dinner) with loneliness is the worst symptom of all. Often this loneliness is a double whammy because we're not only emotionally isolated, but socially isolated as well. Our entire life support system is in flux because we're no longer included in the activities of our married friends, yet there is no new social circle to welcome us. In addition, we might have trouble telling our families about the divorce because they express disapproval and disappointment, while, at the same time, our friends are uncomfortable because of divided loyalties or out of fear that their own marriages will fail. To top it off, people can't resist getting the skinny on the situation and asking that nagging, $64,000 question: "What happened?" If we don't exactly know what happened (or can't fake a good answer), we feel even more lonely and depressed.

Eventually, after a few weeks or months, this suffocating loneliness can leave us begging for air, or begging our ex-husbands to reconcile. Likewise, living in an impersonal hotel room or apartment may "inspire" our former mates to seek the comforts of home. In addition, we may still be drawn to our old partners, and even though the love has faded, we find numerous excuses to "drop by."

> *David's timing was rotten. He would always come by just as I was getting ready to go to class or to work. He seemed shocked at the changes in my schedule, but it was just that I was finally arranging my lifestyle to meet my needs, not his.* —**Jen, divorced one year**

Many of us do a ruthless edit of our old habits to accommodate our new lifestyles. We might break established patterns of eating, sleeping, and the daily routine—sometimes out of necessity and sometimes as a way of coping with emotional and social isolation. For instance, you may find your bed is suddenly too big, and rather than sleep alone, you doze on the couch with the TV blasting so you can hear human voices. Likewise, if you've never worked outside the home, you might seek employment or return to school—tough assignments at any time, but more difficult when your self-confidence is low. The situation is even worse if your pocketbook is in the same state. Lawyer's fees, moving expenses, and establishing a new life can flatline your budget, causing you to reassess your priorities and goals and to revise your whole identity, a necessary step if you are to enter Phase 4.

Phase 4: Revising Identity/Finding New Friends/Dating

Plucking off the identity that's been Velcroed to your hide since you were a bride is no mean feat—but it has to be done. Why? Because you need to know who you are if you are no longer "his" wife. This is especially important if you took your whole persona from your marriage. The solution to this identity crisis is to experiment. In other words, since your old role is lost, shop for a new one that's a better fit. In the process, check out different wardrobes and hairstyles, explore fresh job opportunities, and date a variety of people. Of course, "people" might be stretching it a bit . . .

Indeed, dating is strange at any time, but it's especially bizarre if you've been out of circulation after a lengthy marriage. Why? Not only do you fear igniting a displaced erotic charge, but many of the social rules you—and the rest of us—have relied upon since girlhood have long since imploded. In addition, there are difficulties arranging for baby-sitters, the possibility of a backlash from your ex-spouse, and awkward moments when the kids ask the latest hunk-of-the-month if he has honorable intentions toward Mommy. But despite these obstacles, dating and participating in social activities are an important part of postdivorce adjustment because they can build your self-esteem. In fact, researchers have found that the more self-esteem and confidence-building interactions you have, the fewer adjustment problems you'll encounter down the road—even if your ex-husband has made temporary roadkill of your confidence:

> *My self-confidence was nil by the end of my sixteen-year marriage. When I filed for divorce, I had no idea if I would ever have a man in my life again . . . I did not think of myself as attractive, after years of hearing about my "big butt" and other flaws. It was absolutely amazing to me that I became quite popular after my divorce. I remember how shocked I was when I heard someone refer to me as a "pretty woman." It was good for me to date a variety of men before settling in a one-to-one relationship again. I revised my body image and, more importantly, my image of myself. It was great to feel attractive and desirable again.* **—Melissa**

When you feel attractive and desirable again, when you've reestablished your identity and your life, you are ready to meet the world—and Phase 5—head-on.

Phase 5: Psychic Divorce/Acceptance/Recovery

When you finally head into "psychic divorce," you've reached the final stage of divorce adjustment and you're on your way to becoming a healed and fully autonomous person again. How long does this take? Some women move at warp speed. For the rest of us, cobbling together a new life takes several years. Many factors influence the length of the process including your age and personality, the number of years you were married, your children, any financial difficulties you're still facing, and interactions with your ex-spouse, relatives, and friends. In addition, if you continue to focus your anger on your ex and wage never-ending battles over money, child custody, or visitation, ask yourself this: Are you using these actions to hang on to "him" and in so doing, delaying your own recovery?

Your recovery will also be delayed if you remain double-parked on memory lane. While it's perfectly normal to be temporarily preoccupied with your marriage and to review what happened in great depth, the danger is getting stuck in this stage—and many people do. They ruminate about their "mistakes," rerunning every incident and telling themselves "if only this, if only that." To get back to the "on" (with life) ramp, these stalled-out individuals must develop a satisfactory "account" of their marital demise—and you must do the same thing. In other words, you need to know what went wrong, whether it's "we were too young," "his family just never accepted me," "he was never the same after Vietnam," or whatever. And although just about any honest explanation will do, remember that an account that lays the total blame on your former mate is almost never justified.

When you finally do come up with a satisfactory, justified account, you won't dwell on your marriage anymore, and gradually, optimism about the future will replace anger, depression, and a longing for the past. This is shown in a study we conducted in which 78 percent of the women and 71 percent of the men rated themselves as "much happier" or "somewhat happier" after their divorces than they were during their marriages. In fact, the majority of women reported that they were much happier. Why? Divorce, like other painful events, presents numerous opportunities for personal growth. Surviving this life crisis can produce greater self-awareness and self-confidence. In addition, it can strengthen our ability to make a successful adjustment to a difficult situation. But how do you know if you've successfully adjusted or not?

Mel Krantzler, author of *Creative Divorce*, says you know you've made it when any resentment and bitterness toward your ex-spouse have subsided; you spend more time solving problems than complaining about them; you create new friendships and reestablish old ones; you make decisions based on your own best interests; you no longer find the opposite sex despicable and you actually begin to look upon them in a favorable light; it dawns on you that many other people are divorced too; you reach acceptance. To achieve these goals, we recommend the following:

Proactive Strategies: Constructive Steps for Adjusting to Divorce

Step 1. During early separation distress, stick with your daily routine as much as possible. Although you may not feel like eating, going to work, or seeing people, it's crucial that you do so because withdrawing and dwelling on negative thoughts will block your recovery process. Also, remember to build rewards into your day. Treat yourself for having a good breakfast or doing your exercises, even if you don't feel like it. Finally, be sure to get enough rest and if necessary, include a nap in your afternoon or evening schedule.

Step 2. Examine the messages you're giving yourself about the divorce. Are you equating the failure of your marriage with total life failure? Are you saying, "I can never be happy again," or "I don't have anything to offer anyone"? These, plus any thoughts beginning with those fatal words "if only" can prolong sadness and make you feel much worse, so give the negative ideas a rest! Remember, much of how you feel about the loss of a relationship depends on how you think about it, so to change one, change the other!

Step 3. Establish a support network pronto! Let friends and relatives give you a helping hand. Allow yourself to ask for nurturing. Have at least two people you can call when you're in the pits. If married friends make you uncomfortable (or vice versa), find other divorced individuals who've "been there" and can offer empathy and support. Where do you look? Try churches with social groups and Sunday School classes for single and divorced adults; Parents Without Partners, which has chapters all over the country; community groups; or ask your company's employee assistance counselor about groups in your area. Now, attending these groups is hard at first, but the benefits are twofold. First, you'll meet people who understand what you're going through. Second, you'll find some good "safe" company—"safe" because you can be part of a group attending concerts and plays, taking dance lessons, etc., without any pressure to pair off with a member of the opposite sex.

Step 4. Limit the use of alcoholic beverages, tranquilizers, and over-the-counter medications that are supposed to relax you or make it easier to sleep (see Chapter 16). Remember that indulging in pharmaceutical experiments or drowning your sorrows will plunge you into greater emotional depths and stopping for "happy hour" practically guarantees you'll wind up feeling miserable and depressed. Instead, try meeting a friend for a game of tennis or a salad, either of which will have a more positive effect.

Step 5. Avoid glamorizing or romanticizing your lost relationship. In other words, get real. Stop giving your former mate more credit than he's due. This happens when you only remember the good stuff and none of the bad, and that's when you have to wake up and smell the coffee, to realize that:

> *I am missing you far better than I ever loved you.*
> **—Melba Colgrove, Harold H. Bloomfield, and Peter McWilliams, from *How to Survive the Loss of a Love***

If you miss him more than you loved him, your anger can be quite beneficial to regaining your mental health. Just force yourself to remember some of the rotten things your ex-husband did. Not only will it dispel any sentimental illusions you have

> *He left me when I was pregnant. Whenever I think, "Oh, he's really all right," all I have to do is remember that!*
> **—Kate, divorced eleven years**

it will allow you to become actively involved in your own recovery instead of wallowing in guilt, self-pity, and hopelessness:

> *Probably the first time I really got in touch with my anger was when I went through a divorce at age thirty. My ex-husband behaved badly in the process of our parting, but for months I put up with his behavior and tried to be un-*

derstanding and caring. In retrospect, I now realize that at one level my sense of self was so tenuous that I found my own anger "unjustified" because perhaps I somehow deserved the bad treatment. One day I hit my limit and marched over to his apartment and confronted him. I think this was a real turning point for me because the intensity of my anger was frightening, but I expressed it without physically attacking him!

—Samantha, on confronting her husband over leaving her for another woman

When you hit your limit, it's important that you remember to use your anger productively instead of just striking out, like Lydia. Lydia struck out literally and figuratively. During a discussion of child custody problems, her husband insulted her. She lost control and punched him. He did not hit her back, but instead had her arrested and used this incident, along with Lydia's loss of control, to beef up his case for custody. This is why it's crucial to use your anger wisely and in a way that facilitates your own recovery. Vengeful or violent acts do not help you heal, so avoid them like the plague!

Step 6. Focus on the benefits of your new freedom:

The best thing is that I don't have to be on any schedule . . . I don't have to answer to anyone. I can be more relaxed. No one says, "You goddamn slob, why isn't the floor clean?" I can make my own time. I'm my own boss.

I can spend more time with the children because I don't have him to contend with. I don't have to share myself—I'm mother and father. There is less [of a] problem with discipline because there's only one authority.

It's easier now. You can do so much when your mind is free and you don't have any aggravation . . . I have to live up to my own expectations, no one else's.

I have more sex, and I might add, a lot better than before.

—Boston-area women interviewed in a recent study

Step 7. Get involved in counseling or a divorce adjustment group, especially if you are stuck in an early phase and feel too paralyzed to go on. You can locate these groups through local colleges and universities, women's centers, community mental health centers, child or family service agencies. Usually, the meetings are scheduled for a limited period of time (eight to ten weeks) and are inexpensive to boot. The big plus is that these meetings provide a setting where you can vent your anger, share your grief, and engage in a little realistic retrospection. In addition, knowing you are among friends, that is, people who are in the same boat, can help you eliminate self-pity and create a common bond, even if it's only short-term. But you don't need a short-term group if your anger is long-term. Long-term, entrenched anger (like Ingrid's, described earlier in this chapter) indicates a need for individual psychotherapy rather than a short-term group. In a similar way, if your sadness is prolonged over many years, professional help is necessary (see Chapter 11).

Step 8. Most people begin dating about six months after their divorce. When you're ready to start, make sure you're in the right place at the right time. In other words, put yourself in appropriate locations for meeting the kind of people you like. Singles bars can be limiting—not to mention disappointing—so instead, choose activities that appeal to you and dive right in. The odds are that you'll discover some attractive people who share your interests. For instance, if you heed the call of the wild and like the great outdoors, join a ski, scuba, or hiking club. If fellow professionals are more your style, sign up for civic or academic organizations. In addition, boldly go where you've never gone before—to gourmet cooking school, photography class, or a wine appreciation seminar. As you discover new activities you enjoy and really get into them, you will appear even more appealing to the opposite sex. Above all, don't look too desperate because desperate women send men running for the hills. Finally, don't become part of another "we" until you are fully independent and functional as a "me."

Step 9. Remember that mum's the word and as you get into new relationships, you shouldn't kiss and tell—at least not right away. Avoid the temptation to unload all the grimy details of your previous relationship on your new beau and tell it to your therapist or support group instead. Likewise, try to concentrate on being a fun date and on enjoying the activity at hand. Also, don't view your new guy through rose-colored glasses just because he is so unlike your ex-husband. Evaluate his sense of humor, promptness, love of music, or any other appealing characteristics on their own merits. In other words, relate to the new man as a unique individual. Don't be blinded by the glare of the "halo" you've placed on his head. In fact, wait a good two months before you make any judgments at all. This gives you time to overcome any illusions and decide whether the guy just looks good on paper because he fills the void or because he might possibly be a substitute father for your children.

Step 10. Find innovative ways to deal with being child/time challenged—otherwise known as baby-sitting problems. If you're the custodial parent (and the mother usually is), you may find that you barely have time to breathe, let alone a free hour to pursue the social activities that speed divorce adjustment. Also, child care is expensive and hard to arrange. When faced with this problem, many single parents go the exchange baby-sitting route. In other words, Diane baby-sits for Barbara on Friday night, and on Saturday night, the favor is returned. This allows each mother to relax and have a fun time because she knows her children are in good hands. Other solutions for single parents include sharing the cost of baby-sitters or planning outings that include children, such as pot-luck picnics where kids an play together while their parents get a much needed fix of adult conversation.

Step 11. Develop strategies for combating unpleasant emotions. Use your journal to note any circumstances that trigger outbursts of anger or sadness, then make needed changes in your behavior or environment. For instance, if your trek to work takes you by the restaurant where you and "he" met, change your route. If you get bummed out at the sight of "his" favorite chair in the den, have it reupholstered or put it in your next garage sale. You can also use some of the strategies you learned in previous chapters, including meditation, calisthenics, gardening, playing a musical instrument, slam-dunking a basketball, or filling out your journal, and if you want to yell or cry, go for it, because that kind of venting is perfectly all right!

Of course, some days you'll vent more than others because the road to recovery is studded with potholes and, occasionally, you fall into one. Like when a wedding anniversary or special date comes along and you get that depressed, refugee-from-a-love-safari feeling, or so ticked off you could wreak some major havoc. And if your ex-spouse gets remarried, it may reactivate the anger and depression of Phase 2 in a major way. You might even be afraid you're regressing and taking one giant step back for every puny, baby step forward, but you're not. These ups and downs are perfectly normal and it will help if you learn to be patient with yourself, acknowledge that it takes time to grieve, to alter ingrained habits and rebuild self-confidence. Then, use your loneliness as a constructive opportunity to reflect on your life, your goals, and your future (remember, you have already survived the loneliness of being married to an unloving, insensitive mate and if you made it through that, you can make it through anything). Pamper yourself and do what you would do for a friend who was down—cook your favorite foods, see a comedy, go on a vacation, or buy that beautiful bracelet. You should also make specific plans with your family and friends for the holidays and weekends, turning these worst of times into the best of times. Finally, reward yourself for making it through the day, the week, and the month, and remember:

> *No one relationship can give you life or take it away from you . . . If you live and grow, your commitment is to life, and love comes in that same spirit—love that is a joyous desire to share all that is best in yourself and others.*
>
> **—Stanton Peele, author**

But when those "others" are your children, getting the best out of them can be a challenge because when you get divorced, they get divorced, and they have to work through their anger too . . .

30

HELPING THE KIDS
HANDLE THEIR ANGER

I overheard my eight-year-old son tell my six-year-old daughter that since mommy and daddy were failures at being married, they would be failures at being divorced. This, he explained, meant that we would get back together again. I didn't have the heart to tell him his father had just gotten engaged.

—Kelly, divorced one year

More than 60 percent of all divorcing couples have children at home, and many of these children desperately want their parents' divorces to fail. Often, the children don't get their wish, and they react with anger and sadness, especially at the moment of separation:

I sat on top of my dresser and cried and refused to leave my dad's house. I thought it was wrong of my mother to move. Even worse, she had lied to me. She had promised me she wouldn't get a divorce. **—Joanne**

To many children, promises made in the twilight of a marriage were meant to be broken, and that's just one of the problems. Bitter battles over custody, visitation rights, and child support payments can keep your kids embroiled in tension and fear and hinder their adjustment to the divorce. In addition, no matter who has custody, salt is continually poured into the wound as youngsters are shuttled back and forth for weekends, holidays, vacations, and family reunions. It's even worse if all this shuttling is done in a haphazard or insensitive way. For instance, some individuals, thinking only of their own anger and resentment, refuse to let the non-custodial parent visit. Others bombard their children with negative remarks about the ex-spouse.

> My mother thought of my father as half barbarian and half blunt instrument, and she isolated him from his children.　　　　　　　　　　**—Pat Conroy, author**

A few parents even try to coerce children into taking sides in the dispute, tearing the kids apart psychologically and putting them in a no-win situation:

> In matrimonial battles . . . the children all too often become the battlefield. I remember a . . . boy, barely into his teens, absently rubbing the fresh scars on his wrists. "It was the only way to make them all happy," he said. His mother and father were locked in a bitter divorce battle and each was demanding total loyalty and commitment from the child.　　　　　　　**—Andrew Vachss, attorney**

> His mother had arrived at his father's home to pick him [Mark] up. Believing that she was thirty minutes early, his father . . . told her to wait half an hour. Instead of returning later, she continued to ring the doorbell . . . calling Mark to come out. Inside the house his father told [him] to ignore her calls and continue playing.
> **—C. Garrity, M. Baris, authors**

Of course it's hard for children to feel playful when they're in the middle of their parents' divorce. It's even harder if the family's standard of living is reduced and kids are forced to realize that the piggy bank is no longer full. This realization usually sets in right after you split up and your children are moved from a comfortable suburban home to a cramped apartment, or when they find themselves wearing hand-me-downs instead of the latest fashions, replacing restaurant meals with budget menus, or discovering that there's no money for extras like dance lessons, summer camp, or family outings. Such a drastic change in lifestyle makes kids mad. It doesn't do much for mommy either. Unfortunately, a decrease in income is a common fact of postdivorce life:

- The income of a divorced woman (usually the custodial parent) declines by 73 percent the first year after the divorce.
- By contrast, the income of a divorced man (usually not the custodial parent) increases by 42 percent the first year after the divorce.
- Only one third of divorced mothers actually receive the child support payments awarded by the courts, and it is the children who suffer most from their fathers' irresponsibility.

It's easier to nail Jell-O to the wall than to get some divorced fathers to accept responsibility for their children. Children correctly interpret this as parental neglect, and it's just one form of the neglect that makes your kids mad. And the others? Compared to when you were married, you (like many newly divorced parents) might be less affectionate with your children. You don't communicate as well either, because you're preoccupied and distracted. In addition, your household may be totally up for grabs with erratic meal schedules (especially if you forget to cook dinner because you're in the bedroom crying); bedtimes that change more rapidly than the evening news; and discipline that's all but flown out the window—especially during the first year after the divorce. With all this going on, it's no wonder your kids feel bewildered, unsettled, neglected, and become more demanding, clingy, and unruly, all of which can irritate the hell out of you and make you respond in kind—or maybe "unkind" is more like it.

I feel like I yell at my daughter all the time, like I'm a terrible mother. She needs a lot from me, and she deserves a lot, but by the end of the day I just don't have it to give. **—Iris**

Many of us who are divorced parents feel the same way. Although we're doing our best to regain our equilibrium, our kids just don't understand. They feel rejected and abandoned by us and their fathers, and this justifiable anger is perfectly legitimate, which is why mothers who are themselves too legit to quit, acknowledge their children's anger and help youngsters deal with the pain.

But how do you do it? First, accept the fact that your kids are mad at you, at Daddy, at themselves, and at the cold, cruel world. Then allow them to express these feelings. Tell your youngsters that it's all right to cry or get mad. Let them know you understand things are tough for them too. It's important to do this because if your children can't express their anger directly, they may do it indirectly through acting out at school (see Part Eight) or other rebellious behaviors. Finally, remember that your kids' adjustment to the divorce, like your own, will just take time, but there are ways you can help the process along.

Proactive Strategies: Helping Children Adjust

Divorced parents don't come with a warranty and it's a good thing, because if they did, you and your ex-spouse would be traded in for more competent models—or at least this is what you're afraid might happen. And you're not alone. After a divorce, many of us feel incompetent and like we've failed as parents and mates. In addition (as if this jolt to our self-esteem isn't bad enough), divorce forces us to make some radical changes in our parenting roles. We also are forced to make decisions about child care and discipline without support from another adult, which can be a grueling process because we're flying solo.

> *I'm raising my kids alone, so I'm the mother and the substitute father, and right now, I'm ashamed to say, I do both jobs very badly.* **—Marisa**

When you're the mother and the substitute father, you might feel so insecure in your role(s) that you replace more balanced parenting with rigid discipline and authoritarian control. Or maybe you go to the opposite extreme and your guilt over the divorce makes you bend over backward to indulge your child's whims. Obviously, neither extreme helps your kids, but these guidelines will:

1. Be honest. Help your children adjust by telling them the truth from the very beginning. Although youngsters don't need to hear all the smarmy details of your marital breakup, they do need accurate information instead of half-truths.

Most important of all, reassure your kids that they did not cause the divorce.

2. Create some quality time. Spend a few unhurried minutes alone with each child, each day. Answer questions about where he or she will live and go to school, when Daddy will visit, and so on. If possible, try to keep your children in the same home or school at first since this holds down the number of major adjustments your kids will have to make.

3. Don't substitute your child for your former spouse because this isn't fair to you or your kids. Now that Dad is gone, your oldest son shouldn't be forced into—or encouraged to assume—a surrogate father role. In addition, he should not be disciplining younger children and taking on his absent father's household maintenance chores. Likewise, don't make your daughter a confidant, pressing her into service when you want to unload about your new boyfriend or your ex-husband. Why? Even though they're teenagers, children still need to be children and they have enough problems of their own without taking on all of yours. The upshot here is that if you need adult sympathy and emotional support, get it from other grown-ups.

4. Give your children an accurate picture of your ex-husband's strengths and weaknesses. Resist the urge to totally trash your ex or to put him on a pedestal because:

> *The child knows quite well that each of his parents believes the other to have serious personality flaws, for why else would they be divorced? It's reasonable that a child whose parents speak only of the ex-partner's assets and merits should ask, "If he was so great, why did you divorce him?"*   **—Richard Gardner, therapist**

The bottom line is, be truthful. If Dad has abandoned the family, visits infrequently, breaks promises to the kids, and is a continual source of disappointment, don't tell your children what a loving parent he is—they know better. Instead, in a very compassionate and calm way, explain to your youngsters that their father has some serious weaknesses. In addition, you can soften the blow of an unloving parent by pointing out all the friends and family members who truly love the child, then make sure your son or daughter gets to spend lots of time with these caring people.

5. Be patient when your children's sunny smiles melt down into searing sneers of hate aimed right at the men you're dating. Children often display open hostility toward new romantic figures in Mommy's (or Daddy's) life because they fantasize—almost universally—that you and your ex-husband will get back together again. In fact, your children may even try to engineer the reunion, and they're not going to warm up to anyone who might interfere with their plans. You also need to remember that hostility is a form of denial youngsters use to ward off the painful shock and grim reality of divorce. This is why your kids deserve an honest explanation of the situation including your need to date. ("Mommy needs friends too. I feel pretty and lovable when I go out with John.") Just move at a tortoise pace before you involve any new lovers in your children's lives. Why? It can be extremely distressing and confusing for youngsters to meet a parade of men, especially when some spend the night or take you away for the weekend. We recommend that you meet your casual dates someplace outside your home and introduce them to your children only if and when you establish a committed relationship.

6. Help your children find healthy outlets for the anger and resentment they feel over the divorce. Encourage them to participate in active sports, which can discharge physical tension and provide opportunities to boost self-esteem. In addition, don't tolerate temper tantrums, fighting with siblings or peers, yelling at parents, damaging furniture, or indulging in delinquent actions. Say

> *I can see how angry you are about Daddy leaving. You can be as angry as you want, but you can't go around the house breaking things.* —**Richard Gardner, therapist**

In order for children to break new ground and get on with their postdivorce lives, therapist Judith Wallerstein says they must master six interrelated "coping tasks." This means your kids have to face the reality of your divorce; keep a distance between themselves and the conflict between you and your ex-husband; resolve any feelings of rejection and loss; resolve any anger and self-blame; accept the permanence of the divorce; and build their own hopes for the future. Now, how long it takes your children to do this depends on their ages and emotional maturity, but generally, most youngsters are back to normal development within a year or two. Of course, that year or two can practically do you in.

Indeed, one research group found that in the aftermath of divorce, children exhibit more negative behavior with their mothers than their fathers, and this is especially true for boys. Boys become highly oppositional and aggressive after divorce, whereas girls complain and whine. Both responses can cause you stress. The situation usually comes to a head about one year after the divorce, which is about the time most children max out on their negative behavior. Divorced mothers who've been through this (and lived to tell the story) describe the period as "declared war," "a struggle for survival," or the old "water torture," but thankfully, there's a light at the end of the tunnel.

By the second year, things usually settle down. You and your children have learned to adapt and you lighten up a bit. In addition, you're more consistent with your discipline and more confident of your ability to control your offspring. With a little postdivorce experience under your belt, you feel more nurturant and communicate more effectively. Your children can see the difference and will usually meet you halfway, especially your sons, whose aggression level—while still higher than your daughters'—drops significantly during the second year.

Something else that's significant is the attitude and behavior *you* exhibit toward the divorce, because your mindset greatly influences your children. If you're deeply into revenge, despair, or heavy-duty victimology, your kids will be miserable. On the other hand, if you function pretty effectively and establish a stable home, studies show your children will not be unduly disturbed. In fact, one research team found that five years after divorce 34 percent of the children studied were resilient and happy and 29 percent were doing reasonably well. Unfortunately, 37 percent were depressed and looked back on their predivorce life with great longing. The situation was hardest for youngsters ages seven to eleven, while older adolescents and very young children handled the situation in a more positive way. In addition, some studies show that regardless of age, daughters suffer more lasting emotional harm than sons. So what's a mother to do?

The most crucial factor in circumventing harm for girls and boys is a loving relationship with both parents. For this to happen, you must call off the ground war between you and your ex-mate, and you have to establish frequent, regular visiting patterns. In addition, no matter who's the custodial parent (in 90 percent of all cases, it's the mother) it's important for children to have continuing contact with the noncustodial parent. These contacts can take the form of going out to eat, visiting the other home, various shared activities, or just shooting the breeze on the phone. Of course, this is easier if you and your former spouse establish a truce, and you owe it to your kids to do so. Despite the anger and resentment you feel toward each other, you and your ex need to develop a reasonably amicable—or at least a neutral, noncombative—working relationship. You also need to present a united front on child rearing and give each other your full support.

Unfortunately, some women's backup troops never arrive. Only one third of the children of divorced parents see their fathers regularly and half have not seen their dads in a year or more. Sadly, this father loss can have profound negative consequences (see Chapter 9), but it doesn't have to be this way, especially if a new, loving father and stepsiblings are brought into the fold. Of course, some members of the fold might be a bit miffed at this arrangement and their anger could prove to be a wolf in tiny sheep's clothing . . .

31

GREAT GUIDELINES FOR STEPMOTHERS

. . . our wedding was perfect except for one thing. My new, eleven-year-old stepdaughter—who was all smiles to my face—used the video camera to take really unflattering shots of me, like close-ups of my butt or my body without my head. Even though I know Charles and I will be happy, I'm beginning to think I'm in for a rough time with his kid. **—Masey, age thirty-five**

Once you've played a part in the buddy movie from hell— otherwise known as your defunct marriage—you might promise yourself that you'll never do it again, but the odds are that you will. In fact, three fourths of all divorced women and five sixths of all divorced men take another walk down the aisle, and this time, they don't trip. Despite dire predictions about stumbling over the same mistakes, most second marriages are successful. Why? Maybe we choose more carefully, modify our unrealistic expectations, benefit from previous experience, resolve that "things will be different," or simply learn that:

When two people love each other, they don't look at each other, they look in the same direction. **—Ginger Rogers**

Often it's easier to look in the same direction if you're with a man who appreciates your perspective, and this usually means a man who's been through a divorce. Indeed, divorced people are more likely to marry other divorced people, and often, both of you will have kids. This makes your marriage incredibly complex. Why? If you have children, you're still connected to your ex-spouse, if your new groom has children, he's still connected to his, and the numbers game can get more complicated than playing the lottery. Just consider what a "normal day" with this many people is like.

Martha is attending her daughter Karen's ballet recital with her current husband, George; her former spouse, John; John's new wife, Carolyn; her other children by John; her children by George; her stepchildren; John's stepchildren; assorted aunts, uncles, and sets of grandparents; and, if there's still room in the audience, other miscellaneous relatives. But is it just another happy family outing? That depends.

While it's possible for Martha to be on good terms with Carolyn, it's equally possible that the two women will be mortal enemies. In addition, although Martha tries hard to keep a good relationship with George's children (her stepchildren), George's ex-wife, Amy, is possessive and uneasy so there is rivalry, jealousy, and tension between the two women. To complicate the situation (as if it could get any more complicated), Amy is the custodial parent of George's children, and she frantically calls George whenever she can't manage the kids. Martha resents this and she isn't crazy about Amy's requests for more child support, help with household repairs, and other demands on George's time and energy, either. And the situation is far from uncommon.

> *Your basic extended family today includes your ex-husband or wife, your ex's new mate, your new mate, possibly your new mate's ex and any new mate that your new mate's ex has acquired.* **—Delia Ephron, author**

No matter how insightful, committed, and compatible you and your new mate may be, at any given moment, life can erupt into a giant stepfamilial free-for-all, especially if you both bring children from previous marriages to live under one roof. Some—or all—of these kids might be extremely unenthusiastic about your new union. They might be overtly hostile and even try to sabotage the entire undertaking, especially if they can't stand your face.

> *Life consists entirely of people who are not related by blood, many of whom can't stand each other.*
>
> **—Delia Ephron**

While your stepfamily might not be related by blood, your stepchildren might try to draw some. Since they probably had no voice in your and your husband's decision to marry, they may feel resentful toward you and disloyal to their biological parents if they show you any affection. In addition, competition for your love and attention may cause some intensive rivalries with your natural children. As a result, household rules and routines will have to be renegotiated including chores, mealtimes, and bedtimes. But when you lay down the new law, stepkids often try to divide and conquer, insisting that their past lives were an endless round of chocolate sodas and total freedom from baths, tasks, and schoolwork. The stepchild posse is also quick on the draw when it comes to challenging your parental authority with this reasounding shot to the heart: "You're not my mother! I don't have to do what you say!"

> *If I would say, "Come here and help me fix supper," she [my stepdaughter] would say, "I'm busy—I'm talking on the phone right now." Now I know that's what thirteen-year-old girls do—they live with a telephone in their ear, but I took it personally. I thought, "Well, she's trying to make me miserable." It finally got to the point where I could not tell her to do anything or even recommend—I was in limbo. I was too old to be her friend and I wasn't her mother.* **—L. Williams, age thirty, on her thirteen-year-old stepdaughter**

These forms of verbal sniping make every stepmother alive grit her teeth and pray for patience, or for a minor victory.

But even a minor victory is hard to achieve if the pint-sized forces of darkness are allied against you and your new husband is playing Darth Vader, or if your natural children and your stepchildren join together to take you on, or if your new husband and his natural children form a coalition, or it's you and the stepchildren versus their natural father, or whatever. In fact, whole slews of confederacies are possible, and whether they're permanent or temporary, any one of

these combinations can send you off the deep end, as June
discovered:

> *I suppose the most angry I've ever been was the time*
> *when I had that tremendous scene with my stepdaughter*
> *and my husband . . . I felt very isolated . . . I left the apart-*
> *ment and I walked the [city] streets aimlessly. There were*
> *several occasions where Bob and I did not see eye to eye*
> *and he was siding with [his] daughter. I did not know*
> *how to handle it. I just felt relief when she went on to*
> *college. When I think about her and all those things I*
> *tried to do, I have some anger there, I really do. Of all the*
> *children, she is the one that still makes me angry. I still*
> *carry that in my heart. I don't think she appreciates all*
> *that we did for her.*   **—June, age sixty-two**

A lack of appreciation by stepchildren is a common anger
trigger (as is a lack of appreciation by natural children), and
many women complain about it.

> *The stepchildren come on weekends and eat, slop, de-*
> *mand, and take, take, take—there's never a "thank you"*
> *or one word of appreciation.*
> **—As reported to Richard Gardner, therapist**

> *I don't appreciate how my husband always sides with his*
> *own kids, especially when I discipline them and he tells*
> *me I'm picking on them even when he knows I'm right!*
> **—Colleen**

Your new husband might feel his own kids are the winning picks in genetic roulette, particularly if he sees them as
extensions of himself. This is why any criticism you make of
your stepchildren may put your spouse on the defensive or
provoke counterattacks on the habits and personality traits
your children have.

Now, as you have at each other and try to negotiate these
minefields, it can put your new marriage under a tremendous
strain, and most of this strain is due to your conflicts over
the children.

> *The first year was awful; our marriage almost went*
> *under. But, in time, the kids realized that no one was try-*
> *ing to replace anyone else, that they could have natural*

*parents and stepparents as well. I'm not quite sure how
or why, but it does seem to be working.*   **—Ruth**

*My little stepson and I developed a good relationship, but
suddenly he asked me to quit calling myself his stepmom
because in school he'd discovered that the only famous
stepmothers were in fairy tales, and they were all cruel.*

—Tasha

Fairy tale stepmothers are a hard act to follow—unless
you're trying to be mean, nasty, and vengeful. Unfortunately,
this legacy of wickedness and cruelty haunts stepmothers to
this very day. In addition, researchers have found that being
a stepmother is a more difficult, demanding adjustment than
being a stepfather (surprise, surprise). The problem is that
you must become an instant parent

*Just all of a sudden, pop, and they're in your lap and
you've got these children.*   **—Josie**

to a child reared by someone else while simultaneously getting used to your new spouse. In your determination to overcome your honorary position in the Evil Stepmother Hall of
Fame, you may hesitate to discipline your stepchildren,
which, of course, royally ticks off your own children, who
then accuse you of letting the stepchildren get away with
murder. And the fun builds from there, especially if you put
pressure on yourself to blindly follow your gender-role socialization and make sure your household is as cheery as the
Good Ship Lollipop. Alas, when that ship hits rough seas, you
might take your stepchildren's conflict and misbehavior as
signs that you're a failure, even though you tried your best.

This was Carla's situation. Carla became a stepparent to
her husband's very young children and tried to fill the void
caused by their biological mother's death. She gave her stepchildren all the love she was capable of and hoped for their
love in return, but the smooth sailing ended when her youngsters hit adolescence:

*. . . what I tried to do was become the "real" parent to my
very young stepchildren because I truly believed that was
what they needed from me. Deep inside of me has always
been the fear that they would not see me as their mother
or love me as their mother. If that were true I would then*

be "inadequate" as a mother. The result of this faulty reasoning is that on a few occasions when my stepchildren might suggest either through their comments or behavior that I was not "a good mother" this triggered incredible rage in me. I . . . just would not hear it. It was the unspeakable and I would not allow this. It was when my stepchildren became adolescents and began to do things I was not particularly happy about that this anger made itself so apparent. But in this situation what felt like anger was really fear and hurt. The anger somehow was protecting me from other feelings.   **—Carla**

You can protect yourself—and your stepchildren—from unnecessary anger, fear, and hurt if you follow a few basic rules found in these guidelines for stepmothers.

Proactive Strategy: Guidelines for Stepmothers

1. Don't come on too strong. Feelings of love and trust between you and your stepchildren can't be forced and will need some time to grow. Remember that the children's past experience makes them wary of adults, and this is perfectly understandable. It's especially important to go slowly if you don't have kids of your own. Why? If you're eager to play mom for the first time, you might be terribly disappointed in your stepchildren's lack of responsiveness. Give them—and yourself—some space and let things develop naturally.

2. Don't take all of your stepchild's anger personally. He or she may still be adjusting to the divorce and anger is a normal, legitimate response to the profound disruption the child has experienced. You, as stepmother, often get the brunt of the youngster's displaced anger toward his natural mother, his father, the divorce, and the world at large. Also, if the child believes you played a role in the breakup of his natural parents' marriage, he may despise you. Often there's no real reason for this belief, but at the very least, your agreement to marry his father put an end to any childish hopes of reconciliation, and hope is a hard thing for anyone to give up—especially a child.

3. Revise any unrealistic expectations you have. Therapist Aaron Beck challenges you and other members of your remarried family to deep-six the myths you're carrying around, including: "Our new marriage should be conflict-free." "We should try to be perfect parents and stepparents." "My stepchildren should view me as their new mommy (or daddy)." "My children are disloyal if they become attached to their new stepparent." "If my children care about their natural mother (or father), they can't care about me."

4. Let the biological parent discipline his or her own children for the first few years. This circumvents one of the major pitfalls in stepfamilies.

5. Take heart. Research shows that remarriage improves the lives of many children, especially those of preschool and elementary school age. As a loving stepmother, you can help repair your stepchild's damaged sense of self-worth. If she feels rejected or abandoned by her natural mother, you can assure her that she is lovable. Your natural children can do the same. In fact, relationships with stepsiblings and extended family members can be invaluable to a child's well-being and provide great benefits. In addition, most stepkids eventually learn that it's cool to have so many people care about them and influence their lives in so many positive ways. What's even better is that children discover they can easily enjoy more than two parents and four grandparents, especially if you teach them

There's not only life after divorce, but love.
**—Sandy, divorced ten years, remarried for
thirteen years, stepmother of eight**

PART TEN

ANGER THAT EMPOWERS

32

HOW YOU CAN TURN ANGER INTO ACTION

If you think you're too small to have an impact, try going to bed with a mosquito.

> **—Anita Roddick, author, entrepreneur**

I am not an animal in my personal life. But in the ring there is an animal inside me . . . I can always feel it there, driving me and pushing me forward. It is what makes me win. It makes me enjoy fighting.

> **—Roberto Duran, world champion prizefighter**

When anger drives us forward to do something, to take action and go pow, right in the kisser of injustice, powerlessness, and irresponsibility, we not only feel empowered in our personal lives, but we can become catalysts for tackling tough social problems as well. And when you become a catalyst for yourself or for others, you may find you enjoy the energetic rush your anger provides, like these participants in the Women's Anger Study:

> *It's a rush . . . almost attractive because it . . . is occurring physiologically. I think it does operate as a stimulant.*
> **—Treena**

> *I felt a real buzz . . . I felt strong. I felt like someone was listening to me. If I have to raise my voice to finally get someone to listen to me, that's fine. I felt in control. I felt like I had someone's attention.* **—Gayle**

> *I got an attitude and with it, I learned to get some attention and some much needed action. It was beautiful.*
> **—Carlotta**

When you recognize the beauty of the angry beast in you, you can use your anger to learn, to illuminate the issues, and to find solutions, like these women who are each the stars of their own:

Anger Success Stories

> *Basically, I'm shy, but when I believe in something, I become a different person . . . I was angry.*
> **—Ree Adler, attorney**

After Social Security refused to pay for the vital medication a thirty-two-year-old kidney transplant patient needed to prevent organ rejection, attorney Ree Adler used her anger to address the rigid, catch-22 government bureaucracy and find a solution for her client. First, Adler contacted Social Security officials and a powerful congressman, but all merely regurgitated the ironclad regulations. That's when Adler decided to kick some ass, an attitude that not only transformed her, but transformed the situation:

> *I called up the president of the company that makes the drug and told him the story . . . he said, "We can't do this for everybody." I said, "I'm not asking you to do it for everybody. I'm asking you to do it for this one person. It will save her life." Something about the way I said it must*

have taken him off guard, because now she has a lifetime supply of the drug. —**Ree Adler, attorney**

Wanda went through a lifetime supply of anger in a single experience when she was unjustly canned from her administrative position as a university department head and decided to file a lawsuit:

I had an unscrupulous dean who manipulated me—or tried to. She told me I could resign or she would fire me when I did not cooperate. Because of the support of my husband coupled with the outrage I felt at her unethical behavior, I said I had done nothing to necessitate resigning so she could fire me . . . this was a courageous act in an academic setting where the rule seems to be "go along to get along." It was very anxiety producing to buck authority [and] . . . the norms of my professional setting. This process helped me learn to deal with disapproval from . . . authority figures as well as professional peers since I filed a lawsuit when she did fire me.

What helped sustain me during this process was the outrage I felt both at her [and] . . . an institution that would allow such an unethical misuse of positional authority. It helped me learn to channel my anger in appropriate ways and to realize that capitulation, while less anxiety producing in the short run, diminishes your self-respect over time. —**Wanda**

As you've learned, anger is often a sign that you're not getting enough respect from yourself, your colleagues, your friends, or your family. Catherine's family made her so mad that she finally took effective action:

Ten years ago I became more involved professionally. This meant increased travel. My husband and twelve-year-old son were upset that I would leave them to fend for themselves. One way they expressed their resentment was to do only the barest of essentials when it came to housekeeping . . . This time I came home early, which was fortunate for them. I walked into the living room and there, on the Oriental rug, was a pile of dog poop ground in and dried to the carpet. It had my husband's footprint, which included his sock dried into the poop. He simply walked out of his sock and closed the living room door behind him.

> *I screamed and screamed. In fact, I hoped that I would not run out of scream before they came home. Even though the first barrage of expressed rage abated prior to their arrival, I had enough effective input and rational screaming to get the point across . . . We discussed my anger and hurt. They both blamed each other, but resolved to care for the house in my absence. Since then, I usually see glistening floors damp from a very new washing and steam coming from the dishwasher. I smile, and I never come back early.* **—Catherine**

Sometimes your family forces your hand early in a situation, other times this occurs after things have been going on for a while and you finally can't take it anymore. For Evelyn it took a year, a year of her husband Steve's unemployment, his "style of looking for work," and dipping into savings to feed, clothe, and house their family of four:

> *I was really frustrated with him. I spent time really internalizing a lot of stuff and stewing about it and making myself madder and madder and madder, . . . finally . . . I decided, "Well, I've just got to talk about this." I didn't explode and yell and scream exactly, but I just kind of let it all out and it was a very emotional experience for me. . . . I was very frank and I said . . . in almost a brutally honest [way] . . . "I'm not telling you I want a divorce right now. I'm just saying I feel sort of desperate and I feel like things have got to change. I can't keep living the way I'm living right now." . . . and although I was crying and emotional I was also pretty "with it," you know, as for my thoughts.* **—Evelyn**

With this conversation and the anger that provoked it, Evelyn was able to dissolve the "big black cloud" hanging over her head. In fact, expressing her anger proved to be a real turning point in Evelyn's marriage because Steve acknowledged what she was saying and did something about the situation:

> *He took it [my anger] seriously and said, "You know, Evelyn, for us to have a good marriage is the most important thing to me." I woke up the next day and the next feeling pretty much better. That doesn't mean I don't still have little fits of anger at him, but not this big black cloud thing hanging over my head.*

Right before I had this conversation with him, well probably for about two weeks before that, I had been in a real funk. That experience was good. It lightened the load and so I've been more content with things. I've just calmed down about it. And I think that's not an experience I've often had. I feel more peace now.

One thing that has changed . . . as a result of this conversation, is that he's been sharing a lot more of what he is doing . . . It makes me feel [less] desperate about it . . . like there is action being taken . . . progress being made and . . . this isn't going to go on forever . . . **—Evelyn**

As Evelyn discovered, when you mindshare your anger, you get results, and one of those results is that your angry feelings start to disappear. In fact, Evelyn's anger began to diminish the minute Steve heard her out. Likewise, Kara's anger at her college president boss subsided after she had a second meeting with him (see Chapter 19). Kara used this meeting to make sure the president stopped ignoring her and wasn't fuzzy around the edges where her needs were concerned. This was important to Kara, who was so bent out of shape in the first meeting that she wanted to grab her boss's face and shout, "Look at me. Do you hear what I'm telling you?" In the second session, Kara made sure her anger was not only heard, but understood.

About three weeks later we had another meeting that I requested, and this time, he did listen to me. But it took a second meeting. He finally sat down and said, "You know, I don't really understand what your job entails. Everybody keeps telling me that you have too much to do. So tell me about your job."

And he sat there and he listened and he did acknowledge that my job entailed a lot more than he originally thought it did. That just made all the difference in the world to me. I had asked for additional help. He did say that next year he would really look at budgeting [for help]. I got his attention. **—Kara**

Anger not only helps you get attention, it helps you resurface when you're feeling demoralized and are trolling in the depths of depression, as Mary Catherine Bateson discovered after being asked to step down as the dean of faculty at Amherst:

I was shattered. It took me a year to recover a sense of myself as worth defending and to learn to be angry both for myself and for the college as I watched a tranquil campus turned into one that was truly tense and unhappy. Anger was an achievement, a step away from the chasm of despair. **—Mary Catherine Bateson**

Even if you feel you've homesteaded on the chasm of despair, you can uncover your anger and learn to use it effectively. This is especially true if you've been severely abused like Judith, the rape victim (see Chapter 9),

I am much more open about talking about having been raped . . . to overcome the anger . . . Because by telling other people, you sort of allow them to take on some of the anger . . . If people, men as well as women, know I have been raped, they will sometimes come to me . . . so I am engaged in my own therapy and in giving out my own therapy. I do not charge for it. I'm not a therapist, I just offer it to people. It's probably as much for myself, certainly maybe more, in terms of helping me handle the feeling of outrage and therefore, at least one level of anger. **—Judith**

or denied the anger experience, like Lynne.

As a young girl, Lynne was not allowed to show so much as a "flicker of anger" in her eyes, much less to verbally express it. Nor (as an adult) did she express it to her first husband, until this incredible moment of relief and joy:

I was very angry for twenty-five years and didn't even know it. I was raised with an alcoholic and domineering father and an extremely passive and submissive mother . . . One episode that comes vividly to mind happened when I was a senior in high school. My dad was yelling, shaking his finger and berating me for something, I don't recall what, but in a moment of recklessness on my part, he spotted a flicker of anger in my eyes. He immediately pointed his finger in my face and said, "Don't you dare look at me like that." And truthfully, I don't know what possessed me to show emotion in the first place because I had learned from a very young age that the less emotion I showed the better it would be for me.

He criticized everything I did from the way I walked, talked, laughed, my friends, or lack of friends—

everything. He trained me well to accept criticism, degradation, and emotional abuse. I married at eighteen, a man who was a lot like my father. And because I was accustomed to being emotionally and verbally abused I didn't know that it wasn't normal. I was married to this man for seven years and until we were divorced, I didn't realize that I was angry. He had always been insanely jealous and accused me of doing all kinds of things (which I never did). I was totally devoted to him and our marriage. When I found that he had been cheating on me for years, it was like a dam bursting. All the rage that I had kept inside from my marriage as well as my years growing up started to surface.

I remember the first time that I verbally expressed anger to him. I had never verbally expressed my anger to him or anybody else. He called me one night after our divorce and was carrying on about "he couldn't believe that I would do something" and he "would never have believed" that I would do something else. And I was sitting there listening to him and all of a sudden I started to get angry, and the more he talked, the angrier I got, until finally, I felt like I was going to explode if I didn't say something.

I then proceeded to tell him things that I would never have dared to say before and I hung up on him. I admit I was a little nervous at first wondering what he would do to me. I thought, "Oh God, he's going to kill me." A few minutes later, I heard his truck pull up in front of my apartment and he knocked on the door. He told me that he was leaving some money in the door [that he owed me from the divorce] and for me not to let it blow away. And he left.

I can't describe the feeling of joy—accomplishment—relief . . . that was the beginning of my recovery—I expressed anger and the world as I knew it didn't end—a recovery of myself as a whole person. My right to feel and express anger as well as a lot of emotions that I had suppressed or just didn't know how to express. That was fifteen years ago and I'm still working on it. Being able to recognize my anger; being able to say "this makes me angry" and expressing this anger is a remarkable feat for me.   **—Lynne**

Likewise, the most remarkable outcome of publishing our research is enabling women like Lynne—and you—to find your own angry voices and to use them as mantle bearers for your dreams, your values, and your rights as human beings. But sometimes you can't take the action steps necessary to help yourself. You might be a prisoner of complicated life circumstances and any sudden, drastic moves—even speaking out—could cost you your job, your home, or maybe your life. If this describes your situation, you need a carefully thought out plan (see Chapter 26) to end your misery and powerlessness, but first make sure that your mind isn't an elephant's graveyard of inaction—the place where good plans go to die. And this pachyderm parallel isn't too far-fetched.

Just consider the elephant who was staked to the ground with a chain. As a baby, no matter how hard she struggled, she couldn't break away. Now, as an adult, although she's big enough and strong enough to gain her freedom, she doesn't bother to try. Does this story make you uncomfortable because you, like the elephant, have stopped trying? Good! Maybe the discomfort you feel is really lifesaving anger, and hopefully, the life you feel angry enough to save is your own. All it takes is a little courage.

The university of courage is to do what you believe in.
—El Cordobés, Spanish matador

But enrolling in the "university of courage" shouldn't become a stint in the college of hard knocks, which is why you should make major changes with care.

Proactive Strategy: Make Major Changes with Care

We've all known women who took one assertiveness class and were suddenly transformed from ninety-eight-pound weaklings into Hulkettes capable of decking everybody in sight. But trading one extreme for another is not healthy and it's not what we recommend. What we suggest is that you develop your own long- and short-term goals and consider how these can be supported by your new anger behavior. Why should you do this? Because it's not good enough to spew retorts faster than a speeding bully, to be more powerful than any local emotion, or to leap built-up feelings in a single bound—you have to know what to do with all this supercharged angry energy, and doing anything means making a change. Now change only happens if you hang tough through these four challenging steps:

Step 1. You act without insight into your behavior (we all do this because we're all saddled with old ideas and preconceived notions that cause us to act without thinking), but then:

Step 2. You see the light and come to understand that your behavior is causing you problems. Of course, this is in retrospect (hindsight is always 20/20) after you've acted the same old way.

Step 3. You continue to act the same old way but begin to break out of the dittohead mentality because now you see what you're doing while you're doing it.

Step 4. You decide you want a better outcome, so you start shedding your old ways. You begin thinking things through in advance—before you act—and when you do act, you act differently. You change your behavior to get a new, improved outcome.

Getting new, improved outcomes is what change is all about, and everyone who wants a change has to go through these same steps. Sometimes the process is frustrating because the steps seem rampantly puny, but successful change starts small and progresses in tiny increments before adding up to something big, as researchers and philosophers have found.

A journey of a thousand miles begins with a single step.

—Confucius

Of course, given the length of the journey, it's essential to reward yourself along the way, to acknowledge your own efforts whenever you modify your anger proneness or change your style of being angry. In addition, cut yourself some slack if you occasionally slip back into your old anger behavior. After all, you're only human, so don't waste any time feeling like a failure and don't abandon your attempts to change just because you have a bad day and fly off the handle at your kids (when you're really mad at your spouse) or give your office the silent treatment (rather than confront your co-worker's irresponsibility). Remember, studies show that the change process is a spiral and everyone who tries it relapses now and then, so just be patient, do your best to cope with the Slinky syndrome, and keep this thought in mind:

> *You can only fail if you quit or if you don't try.*
> **—Art Mortell, motivational speaker**

And you may have to put out a little extra effort when you find yourself in the especially trying position of:

Proactive Strategy: Dealing with Reactions to Your New Fighting Spirit, or Ambush in the Tunnel of Love

Don't be surprised if the people you care about think you've ambushed them in the tunnel of love. Your spouse, children, friends, and colleagues may consider your new fighting spirit a call to arms. They're not going to take it lying down, and this is to be expected. Why? Systems theory says that changes in one member of a family system will have reverberations throughout the whole system, so it's almost inevitable that your loved ones will try to force you back into your old, self-sacrificing pattern of behavior. It's not that they want to hurt you or keep you down, it's just that they don't have the foggiest idea what to do with the new you. Harriet Lerner calls these responses "countermoves" or "change back" reactions, and they can torpedo your fledgling efforts, especially if your family hurls the seven megaton word *selfish* right at your heart. When this happens remember that "selfish" is sometimes the most generous you can be, especially if your husband is insecure and responds very aggressively to your attempts at change:

> *This did seem to be the case with Anita's husband. When Anita began to voice even mild comments or questioning of him, he reacted with tyrannical anger and contempt. Although he appeared . . . to be a liberal, enlightened person . . . her husband felt very . . . frightened of feeling alone and unsupported by Anita.*
> **—As reported by Jean Baker Miller, psychoanalyst**

You, too, need to combat that alone-in-the-world feeling as well as the anxiety and doubt produced by your family's countermoves. One of the best ways to do this is to seek validation and to enlist support from other women, the support that can help you tackle big issues and win the fight for the future—your future.

> *Whenever I feel anger I try to say, "Okay, this is an emotion that's alerting me that there is a problem . . . If I keep getting angry like this, it's going to be an even bigger problem. What can I do now to diffuse the situation? What route can I take so this anger does not have to happen again?" . . . My anger lets me know it's time to take care of something, that there's a need to be taken care of, something that needs to be addressed.* —**Katya**

33

USING YOUR ANGER TO
WIN THE BIG FIGHT

*A woman is like a tea bag. You never know how strong
she is until she gets into hot water.*

—Eleanor Roosevelt

When you feel your anger ripening in the 5K heat, sometimes the only ones cheering you on are your female friends.
Sharing your anger experiences and feelings with other
women teaches you that some of your thorniest problems are
really feminine *causes célèbres*. In other words, you are not
alone. Many women have run the obstacle course of a rocky
marriage, impossible parents, and job stress, and the solid
support of fellow females who've been there/done that can
sustain you through these crises as well as the uniquely feminine rites of passage lurking ahead. Whether you're birthing
babies, experiencing your first hot flash, or waking up each
morning to find your butt a little closer to your heels in a
society that deifies the young and the firm, your women
friends can help you through.

Indeed, the first person you probably call with any kind
of news (especially bad) is your best female friend. Why?
While you might want to protect your family from reports of
any mess you've gotten into, it's easy to spill the beans to
good friends. Good friends let you be yourself and they don't
play judge and jury the way some family members do. Also,

with friends you can practice your new anger behavior. You can rant and rave about sexist bosses, lazy teens, overbearing mothers, or political Neanderthals without fear that lightning will strike. In addition, with a trustworthy friend as audience and adviser, you can rehearse what you'll do the next time you want to sink your teeth into someone.

Unfortunately, you might deprive yourself of this nurturant female companionship once you get a taste of beefcake. Why? Often when women marry or first become involved with a lover, they neglect their female friends. But most soon realize that an emotional diet is unbalanced unless it includes these close relationships. This is especially true if your husband can't or won't let you be yourself or if he doesn't want to share certain aspects of your life. Your same-sex friendships can fill the gap because they not only provide the missing ingredient, they actually serve as emotional "health food," and several studies bear this out.

According to one such study, married women who have one or more reciprocal friendships are significantly less depressed, have higher self-esteem, and are more satisfied with their lives than women who don't have these relationships. This is true regardless of the woman's level of marital satisfaction. In fact, in another study, 75 to 80 percent of the married and single women surveyed identified someone other than their spouse as a "best friend." In addition, at every life stage, women have more of these good friendships than men.

For most of us, good friendships are the soul food in the banquet of life, but all too often we females are turned away from life's table. Whether it's child care, federal aid for women and children, equal pay for equal work, equitable treatment under the law, or something as basic as personal respect, society has held a feeding frenzy, devouring feminine priorities until there are barely any crumbs left. This is why many of us.

> *. . . don't just want to have a piece of the pie. We want to make a whole new pie.* —**Gloria Steinem**

Now if you're thinking this pie-in-the-sky attitude is naive, think again. Many of the problems that make you angry, the problems that we've discussed throughout this book, can be solved, but only through collective action, and that's where the feminist movement comes in. Unfortunately, the term *feminist* might leave a bad taste in your mouth. Indeed, slick backlash propaganda (some of it by women!) has convinced many of us that being labeled a feminist is worse than sporting a man's biker tattoo:

> *I picture a feminist as someone who is masculine and who doesn't shave her legs and is doing everything she can to deny that she is feminine.*
> **—Linn Thomas, college senior**

> *Ask a woman under the age of thirty if she is a feminist and the chances are she will shoot back a decisive and perhaps, even a derisive, no.*   **—Claudia Wallis**

> *It is sad to see complaints about feminists, which originated with men on the Right, reiterated by women. It is merely a divisive backlash tactic—divide and conquer—to keep women bickering and under thumb. Some feminists certainly lack the tact or slick image required by the media to keep their arguments palatable, but it is disappointing that even observant women cannot get beyond the superficial to see that their ideals are valid.*
> **—Ellen Whitney Weihe, in a letter to *Elle*, March 1994**

If the word *feminist* makes you gag or catches in your throat sprockets, give this bolt-and-screw mentality a rest. This chapter is not a commercial for NOW or any other specific group, but it is a testament to the fact that organized activism is crucial for promoting female issues, which is why women's organizations need your help. Many of these organizations are working to get more females elected to public office. What difference do these elections make? In the last two years, female members of Congress have helped pass sixty-six measures important to women—and this is equal to the entire number passed during the last decade. Many of these bills authorize funds for major women's health studies, for domestic violence and sexual assault services, and for preventive screening tests for low-income women including mammograms, Pap smears, and high blood pressure exams. They are measures that, collectively, set a historic precedent:

> *This has been a historic session. We were able to undo two hundred years of neglect. Folks really became aware*

*of the fact that women do pay the same amount of taxes
as men, and they've been left out of medical research and
it's probably not fair.*

**—Representative Pat Schroeder, Co-chair,
Congressional Caucus for Women's Issues**

Something else that's "not fair" is the inequitable structure of the American workplace. More than six hundred women's organizations are dedicated to changing this situation including a group founded by Hilda, a fifty-one-year-old participant in the Women's Anger Study. Hilda became an activist when her anger over sex discrimination convinced her that she had to get involved:

I got a chance to speak at the state legislature with Phyllis Schafly. A real experience. You talk about getting my blood boiling, that did it . . . There's nothing I get madder at than this business of [her] standing up there and [saying] "The minute the ERA's passed, every man's got his bags packed and he's walking out of the marriage and going to leave these poor women . . ." yet here she is on the road 363 days a year. She has children. I'm sorry, it doesn't wash. This is a sham [I had to confront] and I don't confront anything other than straight off.

So I said to the legislature, "The people you ought to be concerned about are your mothers, your wives, your sisters, and your daughters. What effect are these laws that currently exist—this was 1973—going to have on them? Think about it." I saw my state senator slinking down in his chair 'cause he's sitting there with his arm around his bimbo. I guess the more you see, the longer it goes, the more cynical you get. But it can really make you angry, and to me, you just keep playin'. I mean, I'm not going to give up.

—Hilda, social activist for over thirty years

Other women aren't giving up either, and the message is ringing out loud and clear that things have got to change. For example, the American Nurses Association is winning stunning victories as it topples the barriers that prevent nurses from operating independent practices. In state after state, the antiquated laws that keep nurses under doctors' thumbs are being swept away and replaced with less restrictive regulations. One such victory was in Tennessee. After a massive smear campaign by the Tennessee Medical Association (the state branch of the AMA) and references by state legislators to keeping "the ladies . . . with beautiful hats" shackled, nurses suffered a major legislative defeat, a defeat that galvanized these suddenly angry women (and men) into action (see Chapter 19).

Furious over the physicians' demeaning, insulting propaganda, the nurses mounted a "comin' back at ya'" grassroots effort to revive and pass the bill. One year later, a standing-room-only crowd of nurses discovered what their collective anger could accomplish when they heard Representative Gary Odom proclaim:

> *Free at last, free at last, thank God Almighty, the nurse practitioners are free at last.* —**Gary Odom**

And nurses aren't the only ones who've learned that women can

> *. . . harness our anger and use it to change the world.*
> —**Erica Jong**

In fact, "harness" is exactly what Women's Action for Nuclear Disarmament (WAND) has in mind. The group uses workshops to empower its angry members, to move them from

> *Expressions of helpless rage, despair and confusion . . . to a sense of urgency and shared responsibility: . . . Through building the "we," that is, "seeing" together through creating an enlarged vision, participants transform their personal self-doubt and confusion into clarity and conviction. The sense of powerlessness of the individual is supplanted by the experience of relational power.*
> —**Janet Surrey, psychologist and member of WAND**

Empowerment through our relations with and connections to other women is the key to successful activism on women's issues, and if you don't think your anger can move mountains, just consider the story of Sojourner Truth. Born a slave and beaten with a whip, she was forced to bear the unspeakable grief of seeing most of her thirteen children sold into slavery. Yet, she overcame it all and found the strength to advocate for female rights at a time when even the most privileged women feared to speak out:

If the first woman God ever made was strong enough to turn the world upside down, all alone—these together ought to be able to turn it back and get it rightside up again! And now they is asking to do it. The men better let 'em. **—Sojourner Truth, to an Ohio convention, 1851**

And the world can only be truly rightside up when we use our righteous or moral anger to defy the gravity that holds social and political inequalities in place. In fact, our anger is key to these efforts, as several research studies show. In one such study, people were surveyed about their emotional reactions toward the less fortunate including migrant workers and the Third World poor. Survey participants were then asked about donating money or getting politically involved to help these individuals. What researchers found was that feeling sympathetic wasn't enough to get people off their butts. Instead, the participants had to get angry, to experience moral outrage before they would take any action.

A second study reinforced these findings. In this study, researchers found that people who supported a nuclear test ban only acted on their beliefs (by writing a letter to Congress, etc.) when their anger was aroused. In fact, one test subject who did not write a letter said:

If I had been more angered, moved, scared and sad, I believe I would have written.
—Nuclear test ban study participant

In other words, moral responsibility doesn't inspire action unless it goes hand in hand with anger, and taking anger by the hand is exactly what we women need to do to:

Confront Social Inequality

The grand pooh-bah tradition of social inequality won't end until we call upon our anger and:

. . . use [our] power . . . as men commonly do . . . within the political arena, to effect the change [we] want and need . . .
—Sherrye Henry

What changes do we women want and need? You name it. Many important, give-a-damn causes cry out for the energy and womanpower our anger generates, including:

1. Coming down on deadbeat dads. Forty-nine percent of all parents default on child support agreements, and 97 percent of those defaulting are fathers. In 1992, these fathers owed nearly thirty-four billion dollars to their twenty-three million children. What can you and your fellow women do? Lobby for legislation, like that enacted in Maine. In 1993, the state of Maine went after more than seventeen thousand delinquent parents, some of whom had never anted up a dime. The state spoke loudly and carried a big stick. The stick? Parents had—and have—to pay up or surrender their business, professional, and driver's licenses. And does the law get results? You bet! Some men wrote five-figure checks on the spot and one trucker coughed up nineteen thousand dollars rather than lose his driver's license. In total, the state of Maine collected almost thirteen million dollars within just a few months of the law going into effect. Similar legislation would benefit thousands of women and children in the other forty-nine states, so write your lawmakers and work for change!

2. Fighting for more battered women's shelters. We live in a nation that has three times as many animal shelters as battered women's shelters, and many women suffer crippling injuries—or worse—while they wait for shelter admission. We believe safe places must be available in all communities and women need to work together to establish these sanctuaries.

3. Working for equal pay. If you're thinking, "It's the nineties, this couldn't still be a problem," think again. Study after study confirms that women still don't receive equal pay for equal work—even when they work for the feds! In fact, female federal employees are paid just 63 percent of what men are paid, and in the private sector, it's worse—women who toil for corporate America make only 56 percent of the salaries earned by their male counterparts! The figures speak for themselves and hopefully they will inspire you to speak up, to join with other women (and men) in the massive lobbying effort required to confront this injustice and produce constructive change.

4. Combating gender bias in the classroom. A recently released study from the American Association of University

Women documents the gender bias running amok in our nation's schools—to wit, teachers show boys more and higher-quality attention than girls, they ask boys more questions, and give them more precise feedback. In addition, a new study found that teachers often give girls direct answers to their questions but teach boys a process for figuring out their answers. As a result, although children start school with approximately equal ability, by high school, girls fall behind—especially in math and science. The AAUW contends that this bias puts a spoiler on girls' futures because female students are systematically (although, perhaps unintentionally) discouraged from pursuing a broad range of academic opportunities. Or, to put it another way:

> *You get the idea that you can't do something because you are a girl, not because you don't have the ability.*
> **—A female high school student's**
> **comment to the AAUW**

Should this be allowed to happen in a country that needs all the talent and ability it can get? The answer is an obvious and emphatic *no*.

5. Challenging sex discrimination and sexual harassment in the workplace. Between 50 and 85 percent of all American women experience sexual discrimination and/or harassment in the places where they work, study, and teach. What can you do to help? Contribute to organizations that have legal advocacy funds, such as the AAUW, which provides support and funding for women in lawsuits like Diane Krause's. Krause, a clinical supervisor at a university dental school, is suing her employer after being denied seven and a half days off to give birth to her baby. In addition, her job was offered to someone else after she made this reasonable request.

6. Fighting ill-conceived legislation that impacts welfare mothers. If you, like us, are reeling in horror at recent proposals to jail welfare mothers and cut off their financial support, get mad enough to tell your representatives and senators this: A five-state study conducted at the City University of New York showed that women on welfare need education, and those who get education, get off welfare. The survey

showed that 88 percent of the welfare women who participated in college-bound programs got jobs after graduation—
and when they got jobs, they got off the government support
bandwagon. These same women told researchers that their
personal lives had improved a hundredfold, and all were
more confident about their futures.

The list of worthy causes goes on and on. Whether it's
pending federal legislation to cut food programs for disad-
vantaged women and children, daycare, eldercare, or the
need for equal medical treatment and research—using your
anger to fight social inequality always comes home to roost.

> *Andrea Martin was . . . diagnosed with breast cancer . . .
> when a golfball-sized lump showed up just four months
> after a mammogram . . . indicated she was clean. After
> completing chemotherapy . . . Martin discovered another
> lump. "After the first one I was scared," she recalled.
> "After the second, I was angry." That anger led her to cre-
> ate The Breast Cancer Fund to help finance education,
> advocacy and patient support, as well as research into . . .
> earlier . . . detection . . . "There's a device we've funded
> that can pick up cancer cells years before mammogra-
> phy," Martin told us . . . "By the time cancer shows in a
> mammogram, it's been growing six to ten years."*
>
> **—As reported in *Parade* magazine, January 15, 1995**

Andrea Martin is just one example of how using your
anger and womanpower can make a difference. Whether you
lobby for better health conditions, flextime, job sharing,
guaranteed family leave, or whatever is important to you,
your efforts will eventually translate into more time with
your children, more help from your husband, more professional and educational opportunities for your family, and a
better future for you and us all.

A Better Future for You and for Us All

So if you're tired of the materialistic, exploitative, screw-
them-before-they-screw-you mentality that has spoiled the
environment, fostered political corruption, fathered an epidemic of violent crime, and spawned a growing underclass
of the hungry, sick, and homeless, get mad, and remember,

you are not alone. Together we can pull the planet out of its nosedive and embrace a new spirit of compassion and strong human values. The moral or righteous anger that jump-starts our blood can defeat the status quo and win battles for clean air and water, for more effective government, and for a better quality of life. If we all care enough to be justifiably angry, we can transform our world.

◇ BIBLIOGRAPHY AND ENDNOTES ◇

Due to page constraints, the following bibliography has been abbreviated, and article titles and authors have been omitted in some cases. A complete list of references is available upon request from Dr. Sandra P. Thomas.

MAJOR SOURCES

Page xv. "The Women's Anger Study . . ." Led by Sandra Thomas, an all-female team of fourteen researchers at the University of Tennessee, Knoxville, with collaborators from several other universities, collected data for three years on more than five hundred women between the ages of twenty-five and sixty-six. Recruited by the research team from work sites and educational settings, women's groups and organizations, the participants represented a wide range of marital experience, income, educational backgrounds, and occupations. Eighty-five percent of the women were Caucasian, 13 percent African-American, and 2 percent Asian or other races. Both quantitative data (using well-established questionnaires) and qualitative data (women's own narrative descriptions of situations) were collected.

A new phase of the study, using the phenomenological method, is in progress. In-depth interviews have been completed with approximately sixty American women and a small sample of French women. Some of the quotations in this book were taken from the transcriptions of the American interviews. Future directions for the project include purposive sampling from other ethnocultural groups and residents of non-Western nations. One cross-cultural comparison, involving women living in Istanbul, Turkey, has already been completed in collaboration with the late Semiha Atakan, of Bogazici University.

Throughout the book, the term *we* refers to the research team led by Thomas. Members of the original team included Kaye Bultemeier, Gayle Denham, Madge Donnellan, Patricia Droppleman, June Martin, Mary Anne Modrcin-McCarthy, Sheryl Russell, Pegge Saylor, Elizabeth Seabrook, Barbara Shirk, Carol Smucker, Jane Tollett, and Dorothy Wilt.

Principal investigators in the current phase of the study are Sandra Thomas, Patricia Droppleman, and Carol Smucker. Other team members are Janet Crooks, Janet Deese, Lucy Gasaway, Mary Pilkington,

Donna Saravi, and Marilyn Smith. Pseudonyms are used for the quotations from study participants found in this book. Some individuals who contributed additional anecdotes to the authors granted permission for their real names to be used, and signed consent forms for that purpose. Questionnaires reprinted in the book are used with permission of the copyright holders; specific documentation appears throughout the chapters and/or in the Endnotes.

Page 4. "Western civilization has retained anger . . ." This assertion is from J. R. Averill, *Anger and Aggression: An Essay on Emotion* (New York: Springer-Verlag, 1982).

Page 4. ". . . Carol Tavris, puts it . . ." C. Tavris, *Anger: The Misunderstood Emotion* (rev. ed.) (New York: Simon & Schuster, 1989).

Page 9. "Psychiatrist Willard Gaylin . . ." W. Gaylin, *The Rage Within: Anger in Modern Life* (New York: Simon & Schuster, 1984); ". . . nationwide studies consistently show . . ." A. Siegman and T. Smith, eds., *Anger, Hostility and the Heart* (Hillsdale, N.J.: Lawrence Erlbaum, 1994), pp. vii–xv.

Page 11. "Author Anne Campbell . . ." A. Campbell, *Men, Women, and Aggression* (New York: Basic Books, 1993).

Page 13. "the experience of being moved." L. Temoshok, C. VanDyke, and L. Zegans, eds., *Emotions in Health and Illness: Theoretical and Research Foundations* (New York: Grune & Stratton, 1983).

Page 24. J. R. Averill and E. P. Nunley, *Voyages of the Heart: Living an Emotionally Creative Life* (New York: Free Press, 1992).

Page 34. "proneness to step up to the firing line . . ." C. D. Spielberger, G. Jacobs, S. Russell, and R. Crane, "Assessment of Anger: The State-Trait Anger Scale," in J. N. Butcher and C. D. Spielberger, eds., *Advances in Personality Assessment,* Vol. 2 (Hillsdale, N.J.: Erlbaum, 1983), pp. 161–189.

Page 39. "Most boys also learn . . ." J. B. Miller (1983). The Construction of Anger in Women and Men. *Work in Progress, Stone Center for Developmental Services and Studies,* Wellesley College, Wellesley, Mass.

Page 42. ". . . Lyn Brown and Carol Gilligan . . ." L. M. Brown and C. Gilligan, *Meeting at the Crossroads: Women's Psychology and Girls' Development* (Cambridge, Mass.: Harvard University Press, 1992).

Page 47. "As we become truly clear . . ." H. G. Lerner, *The Dance of Anger* (New York: Harper & Row, 1985).

Page 51. ". . . three major themes . . ." This part of the research is discussed in "Anger Targets and Triggers," (Chapter 4 of *Women and Anger,* S. P. Thomas, ed., 1993) by Gayle Denham and Kaye Bultemeier, doctoral students who were part of our fourteen-member research team. They conducted the qualitative data analysis.

Page 63. "In the last thirty years, . . . an increase . . ." This statistic is from C. Taeuber, ed., *Statistical Handbook on Women* (Phoenix, Ariz.: Oryx, 1991).

Page 66. ". . . self-in-relation . . ." J. V. Jordan, A. G. Kaplan, J. B. Miller, I. P. Stiver, and J. L. Surrey, *Women's Growth in Connection: Writings from the Stone Center* (New York: The Guilford Press, 1991).

Page 93. H. Weisinger, *Dr. Weisinger's Anger Work-Out Book* (New York: Quill, 1985), pp. 153–154.

Page 95. "One deep form of forgiveness . . ." C. P. Estés, *Women Who Run with the Wolves* (New York: Ballantine Books, 1992), p. 372.

Page 106. ". . . one fourth of all women . . ." E. McGrath, G. Keita, B. Strickland, and N. Russo, eds., *Women and Depression: Risk Factors and Treatment Issues* (Washington, DC: APA, 1990).

Page 118. "the potential to become enlightened . . ." G. O. Higgins, *Resilient Adults: Overcoming a Cruel Past* (San Francisco: Jossey-Bass, 1994).

Page 122. ". . . anger is a key . . ." H. S. Friedman, and S. Booth-Kewley, "The 'Disease-Prone Personality': A Meta-analytic View of the Construct," *American Psychologist,* 42 (1987), 539–555.

Page 122. ". . . how anger and hostility relate . . ." T. W. Smith and A. J. Christensen, "Hostility, Health, and Social Contexts," in H. S. Friedman, ed., *Hostility, Coping, and Health* (Washington, D.C.: APA, 1992), pp. 33–48.

Page 131. C. D. Spielberger, E. H. Johnson, S. F. Russell, R. Crane, G. A. Jacobs, and T. J. Worden, "The Experience and Expression of Anger: Construction and Validation of an Anger Expression Scale, in M. Chesney and R. Rosenman, eds., *Anger and Hostility in Cardiovascular and Behavioral Disorders* (New York: Hemisphere, 1985), pp. 5–30.

Page 135. "In the last fifteen . . ." J. A. Horton, ed., *The Women's Health Data Book* (Washington, D.C.: Jacobs Institute for Women's Health, 1992).

Page 136. ". . . Lydia Temoshok . . ." L. Temoshok and H. Dreher, *The Type C Connection: The Mind-Body Links to Cancer and Your Health* (New York: Plume, 1992).

Page 139. ". . . to Alice Epstein." A. H. Epstein, *Mind, Fantasy, and Healing: One Woman's Journey from Conflict and Illness to Wholeness and Health* (New York: Delacorte Press, 1989). The directly quoted material is from page 201.

Page 154. "Between 30 and 50 percent . . ." S. S. Russell and B. Shirk, "Women's Anger and Eating," in S. P. Thomas, ed., *Women and Anger* (New York: Springer Publishing, pp. 170–185.

Page 216. "As late as 1850 . . ." C. Stearns and P. Stearns, *Anger: The Struggle for Emotional Control in America's History* (Chicago: The University of Chicago Press, 1986).

PREFACE

Page xv. The first phase of the Women's Anger Study was reported by Sandra P. Thomas in *Women and Anger (WA)* (Springer Publishing, 1993). A new phase of the study, involving in-depth interviews, is in progress. Pseudonyms are used for the quotations from study participants found in this book.

CHAPTER 1

Page 3. Z. Kövecses, *Emotion Concepts* (1989), p. 61.
Page 4. "Anger," cited in the July–August 1993 issue of *Psychology Today (PT)*; studies published in *American Psychologist (AP) and Nursing Research (NR)*, C. Malatesta and C. Izard, eds., *Emotion in Adult Development*, pp. 175ff.); see J. R. Averill (1982), in Major Sources.
Page 5. Averill, op. cit.

CHAPTER 2

Page 11. Health Psychology (HP), 10 (1991), 18ff.; *Psychological Bulletin (PB)*, 100 (1986), 309ff.
Page 14. Journal of the American Medical Association (JAMA), 242 (1979), 1504ff.

CHAPTER 3

Page 16. J. G. Goldberg, *The Dark Side of Love* (1993).
Page 18. L. B. Rubin, *Just Friends* (1985), pp. 20, 183.
Page 25. E. Brondolo, Society of Behavioral Medicine (SBM) paper (1992); S. P. Thomas *Research in Nursing and Health (RINAH)*, 12 (1989), 389ff.; S. P. Thomas and R. Williams, *NR, 40* (1991), 303ff.; S. P. Thomas, et al., SBM paper, San Diego (March 1995).

CHAPTER 4

Page 33. See W. Gaylin (1984), in Major Sources; see C. D. Spielberger (1983, 1985), in Major Sources.
Page 36. S. P. Thomas *(WA)* (1993); *HP*, 8 (1989), 403ff.
Page 37. C. Tavris, *Anger*, 2nd ed. (1989).

CHAPTER 5

Page 38. The Emergence of Personality (1987), pp. 13ff.
Page 39. Sex Roles (SR), 10 (1989), 677ff.
Page 40. Social Problems, 23, 478ff.; *Journal of Child and Adolescent Psychiatric Nursing (JCAPN)*, 4, 9ff.; *Signs*, 12 (1976), 23ff.

Page 41. SR, 20 (1989), 295ff.; *Motivation and Emotion, 12* (1988), 171ff.; *JCAPN,* 4 (1991), 9ff.

Page 44. Paper by M. MacGregor and K. Davidson, presented at SBM, Boston, (1994); J. Bardwick, *In Transition* (1979), p. 48.

CHAPTER 6

Page 46. S. P. Thomas, *WA* (1993).

Page 53. Judith Avis in T. J. Goodrich (ed.), *Women and Power* (1991), pp. 183ff.

Page 54. R. Bly, "Where Are Men Now?" Paper presented at American Psychological Association (APA), Los Angeles (August 1994).

CHAPTER 7

Page 59. C. M. Aldwin, *Stress, Coping, and Development* (1994), p. 128.

Page 62. Shown in studies in *The Nurse Practitioner, RINAH, Journal of Behavioral Medicine, The Handbook of Stress, Journal of Health and Social Behavior (JHSB),* and *APA Monitor.*

Page 64. G. Witkin, *The Female Stress Syndrome* (1991).

Page 65. F. Crosby, *Juggling* (1991), p. 27.

Page 66. R. C. Barnett, et al., eds., *Gender and Stress* (1987).

Page 67. "Midlife Americans Glum about Prospects," *AARP Bulletin,* 34(8) (September 1993).

Page 68. American Journal of Health Promotion (AJHP), 5 (1989), 266ff.; *Psychology of Women,* 16(3) (1991), 4ff.

Page 69. JHSB, 22 (1981), 337ff.; *Journal of Nervous and Mental Disease (JNMD),* 177(8) (1989), 443ff.

Page 70. The Inner American (1981); D. Belle, "Gender Differences in the Social Moderators of Stress," in R. C. Barnett, et al., eds., *Gender and Stress* (1987); see M. G. Ory and H. R. Warner, eds. (1990), *Gender, Health, and Longevity,* 119ff. *Family Perspective (FP),* 20(1) (1986), 27ff.

Page 70. C. Turkington, "What Price Friendship?" *APA Monitor,* 16 (1985), 38ff.

Page 71. F. Crosby, *Juggling* (1991).

Page 72. Journal of Personality and Social Psychology (JPSP), 62(4) (1992), 634ff.

CHAPTER 8

Page 76. PB, 90(1) (1981), 89ff.

Page 85. S. Hobfoll, *The Ecology of Stress* (1988).

Page 85. F. Crosby, *Juggling* (1991).

Page 86. R. A. Dientsbier, *PB,* 96 (1989), 84ff.; L. Goldberger and S. Breznitz, eds., *Handbook of Stress* (1993).

CHAPTER 9

Page 93. T. Moore, *Care of the Soul* (1992).

Page 94. J. Viorst, *Necessary Losses* (1986), p. 232.

Page 95. R. L. Williams and J. D. Long, *Manage Your Life* (1991), p. 215; A. Miller, *For Your Own Good* (1983).

Page 95. J. Pennebaker, *Opening Up: The Healing Power of Confiding in Others* (1991).

Page 96. M. Woodman, *Addiction to Perfection* (1982), pp. 99ff. S. Lippsett, *Surviving a Writer's Life* (1994).

Page 96. C. Tavris, *Anger,* 2nd ed. (1989).

CHAPTER 10

Page 98. L. T. Sanford, and M. E. Donovan, *Women and Self-esteem* (1985).

Page 102. V. Secunda, "Victim Trap," *New Woman* (July 1994), pp. 91ff.

Page 103. L. Povich, *Working Woman* (January 1992), pp. 66ff.; see Sanford and Donovan (1985).

CHAPTER 11

Page 105. G. Klerman and M. Weissman, "Increasing Rates of Depression," *JAMA,* 261 (1989), 2229ff.

Page 106. See articles in *General Hospital Psychiatry* and *JAMA;* see McGrath (1990), in Major Sources; S. Nolen-Hoeksema, *Sex Differences in Depression* (1990).

Page 107. Research reported in *Psychological Reports (PR)* (1981, 1987), *Archives of General Psychiatry (AGP)* (1970), *(JNMD)* (1989); research reported in M. Weissman and E. Paykel, *The Depressed Woman* (1974); *Journal of Abnormal Psychology* (1980); *Journal of Personality Assessment (JPA)* (1993), 511ff; S. P. Thomas, *WA* (1993).

Page 107. D. C. Jack, *Silencing the Self* (1991).

Page 109. K. Wells, et al., "The Course of Depression in Adult Outpatients. *AGP,* 49 (1992), 788ff.

Page 112. R. Munoz, et al., "On the AHCPR 'Depression in Primary Care' Guidelines." *American Psychologist (AP),* 49 (1994), 42ff.; *AGP,* 49 (1992), 782ff.

Page 113. JAMA, 268 (1992), 3441ff.

Page 114. S. Nolen-Hoeksema, *Sex Differences in Depression* (1990).

Page 115. PT, 22(10) (October 1988), 50ff.

Page 117. R. Nozick, *The Examined Life* (1989).

Page 118. V. E. O'Leary and J. R. Ickovics, "Women's Resilience," paper presented at APA Conference, Washington, D.C. (May 1994).

CHAPTER 12

Page 121. C. B. Pert, *Advances*, 3(3) (1986), 8ff.

Page 123. Journal of Women's Health, 1(1) (1992), xv.

CHAPTER 13

Page 126. R. Rosenman, et al., *JAMA* (1975), 872ff.

Page 126. See studies published in *Psychosomatic Medicine (PM)* in 1980, 1983, and 1989; P. T. Costa, *PM*, 48 (1986), 283ff.; studies in *HP* and *PM* (1991); *HP* 12, (1993), 301ff.

Page 127. D. Lerner and W. Kannel, "Patterns of Coronary Heart Disease Morbidity and Mortality in the Sexes," *American Heart Journal (AHJ)*, 111 (1986), 383ff; D. Foley and E. Nechas, *Women's Encyclopedia of Health and Emotional Healing* (1993); see studies in the *British Journal of Medical Psychology (BJMP)* (1984) and *The American Journal of Cardiology* (1993); Oregon study cited in G. Witkin, *The Female Stress Syndrome* (1991); studies reported in *PM* (1989, 1990) and *HP* (1993).

Page 128. See Siegman and Smith (1994), in Major Sources; S. F. Anderson and K. A. Lawler, "Type A Behavior in Women and the Anger Recall Interview," paper presented at SBM, Boston (April 1994).

Page 128. American Journal of Epidemiology (AJE), 111 (1980), 37ff.; "Differential Impact of Suppressed Anger on Cardiovascular and Cancer Mortality for Married Pairs (Tecumseh 1971–1988)," paper presented at SBM, New York (March 1992); *PM*, 55 (1993), 426ff.; *AJE*, 130, (1989), 646ff.

CHAPTER 14

Page 130. J. A. Horton, ed., *The Women's Health Data Book* (1992), pp. 43ff.

Page 131. See studies in *PM* (1979, 1986, 1988) and *AHJ* (1972); J. E. Schwartz, et al., "Mood, Location, and Physical Position as Predictors of Ambulatory Blood Pressure and Heart Rate," *Annals of Behavioral Medicine*, 16 (1994), 210ff.; J. Markovitz, et al., "Psychological, Biological, and Health Predictors of Blood Pressure Changes in Middle-aged Women," *Journal of Hypertension (JH)*, 9 (1991), 399ff.; H. S. Goldstein, et al., "Relationship of Resting Blood Pressure and Heart Rate to Experienced Anger and Expressed Anger" *PM*, 50 (1988), 321ff.; C. Perini, et al., "Suppressed Aggression Accelerates Early Development of Essential Hypertension" *JH*, 9 (1991), 499ff.

Pages 131–32. See C. D. Spielberger, in Major Sources (1983, 1985); R. L. Rickman and C. D. Spielberger, "Gender Differences in the Experience and Expression of Anger in Persons with Essential Hypertension," paper presented at SBM, Chicago (1990); C. D. Spielberger and

P. London, *PT* (January–February 1990), 48ff; *HP*, 8 (1989), 557ff.; *Western Journal of Nursing Research (WJNR)*, 14 (1992), 754ff.

Page 132. H. Benson, "The Relaxation Response and Stress," in J. Matarazzo, et al., eds., *Behavioral Health* (1984), pp. 326ff.

Page 133. S. P. Thomas, *WA* (1993); S. P. Thomas, et al., paper presented at SBM, San Diego (March 1995).

CHAPTER 15

Page 135. C. B. Thomas, *Advances*, 5(2) (1988), 42ff.

Page 136. Grossarth-Maticek, et al. *Journal of Psychosomatic Research (JPR)*, 29 (1985), 167ff; L. Temoshok and H. Dreher, "The Type C Connection," *Noetic Sciences Review* (Spring 1993), pp. 21ff.

Page 136. Studies by Greer, et al., published in *JPR* in 1975, 1981, and 1984.

Page 137. D. Spiegel, et al, *The Lancet* (October 1989), 888ff.; S. Moorey and S. Greer, *Psychological Therapy for Patients with Cancer* (1989).

Page 138. P. Brohn, *The Bristol Program* (1987).

CHAPTER 16

Page 141. *Issues in Mental Health Nursing*, 14 (1993), 19ff.; S. P. Thomas, *WA* (1993).

Page 142. M. Leiker and B. J. Hailey, "A Link Between Hostility and Disease," *Behavioral Medicine (BM)*, 14 (1988), 129ff.; B. K. Houston and C. R. Vavak, "Cynical Hostility," *HP*, 10 (1991), 9ff.; see Friedman (1992), in Major Sources; B. W. Lex, "Some Gender Differences in Alcohol and Polysubstance Users," *HP*, 10 (1991), 121ff.; M. Frezza, et al., "High Blood Alcohol Levels in Women," *New England Journal of Medicine (NEJM)*, 322(2) (1990), 95ff.; J. Orford and A. Keddie, "Gender Differences in the Functions and Effects of Moderate and Excessive Drinking," *British Journal of Clinical Psychology*, 24 (1985), 265ff.

Page 143. M. Kilbey and J. Sobeck, "Epidemiology of Alcoholism," in C. B. Travis, ed., *Women and Health Psychology* (1988), pp. 91ff; R. Wilsnack, et al., "Women's Drinking and Drinking Problems," *American Journal of Public Health*, 74 (1984), 1231ff.; B. W. Lex, "Some Gender Differences in Alcohol and Polysubstance Users," *HP*, 10 (1991), 121ff.; L. J. Beckman and H. Amaro, "Personal and Social Difficulties Faced by Women and Men Entering Alcoholism Treatment," *Journal of Studies in Alcoholism*, 47 (1986), 135ff.

Page 145. *Journal of Social Issues*, 38 (1982), 1ff.

Page 147. R. O. Pihl, et al., *International Journal of the Addictions*, 17 (1982), 259ff.; K. Koumjian, *Social Science and Medicine (SSM)*, 15E (1981), 245ff.; C. B. Travis, ed., *Women and Health Psychology* (1988), pp. 67ff.

Page 147. G. Cafferata, et al., "Family Roles, Structure, and Stressors in Relation to Sex Differences in Obtaining Psychotropic Drugs," *JHSB,* 24 (1983), 132ff.; J. A. Horton, ed., *The Women's Health Data Book* (1992).

Page 147. J. A. Horton, op. cit.; M. Nellis, *The Female Fix* (1980); M. A. Schuckit, *Drug and Alcohol Abuse* (1989); R. Bell, "Over-the-counter Drugs," *Public Health Reports,* 99 (1984), 319ff.

Page 148. See studies in *AJE* (1978), *HP* (1989), *RINAH* (1989), *NR* (1991), and *JPSP* (1991); G. Witkin, *The Female Stress Syndrome* (1991).

Page 150. See Friedman (1992), in Major Sources; C. L. Macnee, "Perceived Well-being of Persons Quitting Smoking," *NR,* 40 (1991), 200ff.

Page 150. J. Hughes, Symposium presented at SBM, New Orleans (1985); See A. G. Christensen, and K. Cooper, *Strategic Withdrawal from Cigarette Smoking,* American Cancer Society, New York, 1979.

Page 151. In R. C. Barnett, et al., eds., *Gender and Stress* (1987); S. P. Thomas and M. W. Groër, "Relationship of Demographic, Life-style, and Stress Variables to Blood Pressure in Adolescents," *NR,* 35 (1986), 169ff.; A. Swan, et al., "Why Do More Girls Than Boys Smoke Cigarettes?" *Health Education Journal,* 48(2) (1989), 59ff.; G. Sorenson and T. Pechacek, "Occupational and Sex Differences in Smoking and Smoking Cessation," *Journal of Occupational Medicine,* 28 (1986), 360ff.; M. Chen, et al., "Tobacco Use Prevention in the National School Curricula," *Health Values,* 15(2) (1991), 3ff.; *Cancer Facts and Figures—1994,* American Cancer Society.

Page 152. Stanford Center for Research in Disease Prevention; R. C. Barnett, et al., op. cit.

Page 153. U.S. Department of Health and Human Services, *The Health Consequences of Smoking for Women* (1980).

CHAPTER 17

Page 154. F. X. Pi-Sunyer, "Health Implications of Obesity," *American Journal of Clinical Nutrition,* 1(53) (1991), 1595S ff.; T. Van Itallie, "Health Implications of Overweight and Obesity in the United States," *Annals of Internal Medicine (AIM)* 103(6, pt. 2) (1985), 983ff.

Page 155. E. M. Bennett, *American Journal of Clinical Nutrition,* 53 (1991), 1519S ff.; B. McFarland and T. Baker-Bauman, *Feeding the Empty Heart* (1988).

Page 155. See Siegman and Smith (1994), in Major Sources.

Page 156. Levonkron was cited in A. Katherine *Anatomy of a Food Addiction* (1991).

Page 158. See Friedman (1992), in Major Sources; D. M. Kagan and R. L. Squires, "Compulsive Eating, Dieting, Stress, and Hostility among College Students," *Journal of College Student Personnel,* 25 (1984),

213ff.; B. K. Houston and C. R. Vavak, *HP*, 10 (1991), 9ff.; S. P. Thomas, *WA* (1993).

Page 158. C. M. Grilo, et al., "Relapse Crisis and Coping Among Dieters," *Journal of Consulting and Clinical Psychology*, 57 (1989), 488ff.

Page 159. A. Olson, "Women and Weight Control," in B. J. McElmurry and R. S. Parker, eds., *Annual Review of Women's Health* (1993), pp. 199ff.; see studies reported in *American Journal of Clinical Nutrition* (1992), *International Journal of Obesity* (1991), *AIM* (1987).

Page 161. Studies reported in *Advances* (1985), *Journal of Chronic Disease* (1969), *PM* (1965), *SBM* (1993), *BJMP* (1991), *JPSP* (1987), *J: PM* (1993).

CHAPTER 18

Page 162. S. Adams, "The Role of Hostility in Women's Self-rated Health," paper presented at SBM, San Francisco (1993).

Page 163. M. T. Johnson-Saylor, "Psychosocial Predictors of Healthy Behaviors in Women," *Journal of Advanced Nursing*, 16 (1991), 1164ff.; M. Leiker and B. J. Hailey, "A Link Between Hostility and Disease," *BM*, 14 (1988), 129ff.; see Friedman (1992), in Major Sources; S. P. Thomas, *WA* (1993).

Page 163. The Commonwealth Fund Survey of Women's Health (July 14, 1993); S. P. Thomas and M. M. Donnellan, "Correlates of Anger Symptoms in Women in Middle Adulthood," *AJHP*, 5 (1991), 266ff.

Page 167. Statistics in this section from *The Commonwealth Fund Survey of Women's Health*, op. cit.

Page 167. J. Smith, *The Idea of Health* (1983).

Page 168. M. A. Newman, *Health as Expanding Consciousness* (1986). The five-dimensional model of optimal health was presented in *AJHP* (1986).

Page 170. R. S. Paffenbarger, et al., "Physical Activity, All-Cause Mortality, and Longevity of College Alumni," *NEJM*, 314 (1986), 605ff.; P. Choi, et al., "Mood Changes in Women After an Aerobics Class," *Health Care for Women International (HCWI)*, 14 (1993), 167ff.

Page 171. J. Moses, et al., "The Effects of Exercise Training on Mental Well-being in the Normal Population," *JPR*, 33 (1989), 47ff.; H. A. Wenger and G. J. Bell, "The Interactions of Intensity, Frequency, and Duration of Exercise Training in Altering Cardio-respiratory Fitness," *Sports Medicine*, 3 (1986), 346ff.; R. E. Thayer, "Energy Walks," *PT* (October 1988), 12ff.

Page 172. W. Fry, "Roundtable," *Mind-Body-Health Digest (MBHD)*, 4(2) (1990), 6; B. Graham, "The Healing Power of Humor," *MBHD*, 4(2) (1990), 1f.; see Siegman and Smith (1994), in Major Sources.

Page 173. P. Tournier, *The Healing of Persons* (1965).

Page 174. L. M. Verbrugge, "Gender and Health," *JHSB*, 26 (1985),

156ff.; L. Lempert, "Women's Health from a Woman's Point of View," *HCWI*, 7 (1986), 255ff.; L. M. Verbrugge, "An Epidemiological Profile of Older Women," in M. R. Haug, et al., eds., *The Physical and Mental Health of Aged Women* (1985), pp. 41ff.

CHAPTER 19

Page 178. Statistic from J. Bales, *APA Monitor*, 22(11) (1991), 32.

Page 179. C. M. DeVries and M. W. Vanderbilt, "DOL Women's Bureau Releases Results of 'Working Women Count!' Survey," *Capital Update*, 12(21) (November 11, 1994), 6; employed women study by D. Hughes and E. Galinsky, "Gender, Job, and Family Conditions, and Psychological Symptoms," *Psychology of Women Quarterly (PWQ)*, 18 (1994), 251ff.; see Jordan (1991), in Major Sources.

Page 180. Statistics from *Women's Research Network News* (Winter 1994), p. 5; see Taeuber (1991), in Major Sources.

Page 180. *Women's Research Network News*, op. cit.; C. M. DeVries and M. W. Vanderbilt, op. cit.; the demand/control model of job stress was developed by R. Karasek and T. Theorell, *Healthy Work* (1990); P. Stevens, et al., "Examining Vulnerability of Women Clerical Workers from Five Ethnic Racial Groups," *WJNR*, 14(6) (1992), 754ff.

Page 181. Research conducted by A. Riefman, et al., "Stress, Social Support, and Health in Married Professional Women with Small Children," *PWQ*, 15 (1991), 431ff.

Page 183. Report on the Governor's Task Force on the Glass Ceiling Initiative, Wisconsin (November 1993), pp. 7ff.

Page 183. Percentages cited in J. Hyde, "Some Thoughts on the Glass Ceiling," *Psychology of Women*, 21(1) (1994), 1f.; cited in S. Moses-Zirkes, "Women Bosses' Uphill Trek Not Due to Family Demands," *APA Monitor*, 24(8) (1993), 51.

Page 184. P. Cotten, *JAMA*, *268* (1992), 173.

Page 184. Catalyst, *Flexible Work Arrangements II: Succeeding with Part-Time Options*. Report highlighted in *Issues Quarterly*, 1(2) (1993) p. 19, a publication of the National Council for Research on Women.

Page 184. F. Crosby, *Juggling* (1991).

Page 187. Cited in L. Fitzgerald, "Sexual Harassment," *AP*, 48 (1993), 1070ff.

Page 188. M. Little, "AMA's New Smear Campaign—Fowl Play," *Tennessee Nurse*, 56(4) (Winter 1993), 12ff.

Page 191. S. Faludi, *Backlash* (1991).

CHAPTER 20

Page 193. M. Baker, *Women* (1991), p. 179.

Page 195. B. Houston and K. Kelly, "Hostility in Employed Women," *Personality and Social Psychology Bulletin* 15(2) (1989), 175ff.

Page 200. Study reported in L. A. Mainiero, "Coping with Powerlessness," *Administrative Science Quarterly* 31 (1986), 633ff.

Page 202. Reported in G. Sorenson, et al., *JHSB*, 26 (1985) 379ff.

CHAPTER 21

Page 208. R. Bly, "Where Are Men Now?" paper presented at APA, Los Angeles (August 1994); see J. B. Miller (1983), in Major Sources.

Page 209. M. Polster, *Eve's Daughter* (1992).

Page 210. J. Muff, *Women's Issues in Nursing* (1982); see J. B. Miller (1983), in Major Sources; A. Dillard, *An American Childhood* (1987).

Page 211. C. Jacklin and E. Maccoby, "Social Behavior at 33 Months in Same-Sex and Mixed-Sex Dyads," *Child Development, 49* (1978), 557ff.

Page 211. B. Thorne, *Gender Play* (1993).

Page 211. American Association of University Women, report entitled "Hostile Hallways" (1993).

Page 213. M. Marshment, in D. Richardson and V. Robinson, eds., *Thinking Feminist* (1993), pp. 123ff.

Page 213. J. Levine, *My Enemy, My Love* (1992); C. Tavris, *Anger,* 2nd ed. (1989).

CHAPTER 22

Page 214. See Taeuber (1991), in Major Sources.

Page 215. J. Bernard, *The Future of Marriage* (1982); G. Margolin and B. Wampold, "Sequential Analysis of Conflict and Accord in Distressed and Nondistressed Marital Partners," *Journal of Consulting and Clinical Psychology,* 49 (1981), 554ff.

Page 215. Poll conducted by Scripps Howard News Service and Ohio University (1993). Interview reported in H. Cosell, *Women on a Seesaw* (1985), p. 92.

Page 217. S. P. Thomas, et al., "Gender Differences in Anger Experience and Expression," presented at APA, New York (August 1995).

Pages 218–19. H. G. Lerner, *The Dance of Anger* (1985); M. Scarf, *Intimate Partners* (1987).

CHAPTER 23

Page 226. J. G. Goldberg, *The Dark Side of Love* (1993).

Page 227. H. G. Lerner, *The Dance of Intimacy* (1989); C. T. Fischer, "The Angry Outburst," paper presented at APA, Toronto (1993).

Page 229. J. R. Averill (1982), in Major Sources; A. T. Beck, *Love Is Never Enough* (1988).

Page 230. See W. Gaylin (1984), in Major Sources.

Page 232. D. W. Helmering, *Happily Ever After* (1986).

Page 232. See H. Weisinger (1985), in Major Sources.
Page 235. R. Driscoll, *The Binds That Tie* (1991).

CHAPTER 24

Page 242. S. P. Thomas, et al., *Family Relations (FR)*, 33 (1984), 513ff.; *Context*, 11(15) (May 27, 1994).
Page 243. H. Cosell, *Women on a Seesaw* (1985).
Page 244. M. C. Bateson, *Composing a Life* (1989); S. P. Thomas and K. Albrecht, *"Stressors and Coping Styles of American Dual-Career Professional Women,"* paper presented at 2nd International Congress on Women's Health, Nova Scotia (November 1986).
Page 244. E. Berscheid, et al., "The Relationship Closeness Inventory," *JPSP*, 57 (1989), 807ff.
Page 245. S. P. Thomas, et al., *FR*, 33 (1984), 513ff.
Page 245. P. White, et al., "Husbands' and Wives' Perceptions of Marital Intimacy and Wives' Stresses in Dual-Career Marriages," FP, 20 (1986), 27ff.
Page 246. H. I. Hartmann, "The Family as the Focus of Gender, Class and Political Struggle," *Signs*, 6(3) (1980), 366ff.
Page 247. Studies in *Journal of Marriage and the Family (JMF)* (1984), *Sloan Management Review* (1978), *Annals of Behavioral Medicine* (1991), and *Juggling*, 1991; S. P. Thomas, et al., *FR* 33 (1984), 513ff.
Page 248. F. Crosby, *Juggling* (1991).

CHAPTER 25

Page 251. H. S. Goldstein, et al., *PM* 50 (1988), 321ff.; M. Julius, et al., *AJE*, 124 (1986), 220ff.; see J. R. Averill (1982), in Major Sources; W. Riley, et al., "Anger and Hostility in Depression," *JNMD*, 177 (1989), 668ff.; G. Weidner, et al., "Clusters of Behavioral Coronary Risk Factors in Employed Women and Men," *Journal of Applied Social Psychology*, 19 (1989), 468ff.; G. Margolin and B. Wampold, "Sequential Analysis of Conflict and Accord in Distressed and Nondistressed Marital Partners," *Journal of Consulting and Clinical Psychology*, 49 (1981), 554ff.
Page 251. J. Hawkins, et al., "Spouse Differences in Communication Style," *JMF*, 42 (1980), 585ff.
Page 252. D. Tannen, *You Just Don't Understand* (1990).
Page 253. D. Bell, et al., "Marital Conflict Resolution," *Journal of Family Issues* (March 1982), 111ff.; P. Lind and H. Connole, "Sex Differences in Behavioral and Cognitive Aspects of Decision Control," *SR*, 12 (1985), 813ff.
Page 256. Adapted from N. Jacobson and E. Anderson, "The Effects of Behavior Rehearsal and Feedback on the Acquisition of Problem-Solving Skills in Distressed and Non-distressed Couples," *Behavior Re-*

search and Therapy, 18 (1980), 25ff.; N. Jacobson and M. Dallas, "Helping Married Couples Improve Their Relationships," in W. Craighead, et al., eds., *Behavior Modification* (1981), pp. 379ff.

Page 257. D. W. Helmering, *Happily Ever After* (1986).

Page 260. Quote in *Context,* 11(15) (May 27, 1994).

CHAPTER 26

Page 262. AMA, *Five Issues in American Health* (1991).

Page 263. M. P. Koss, "Rape," *AP,* 48 (1993), 1062ff.; E. Stark, et al., *Wife Abuse in the Medical Setting* (1981); U.S. Senate Judiciary Committee, *Violence Against Women* (October 1992); A. Novello, et al., "From the Surgeon General," *JAMA* 267(23) (1992), 3132; R. J. Gelles, "Violence and Pregnancy," *JMF* (August 1988) 841ff.; see J. Smolowe, (July 4, 1994), in *Time,* 18ff.

Page 263. A. Browne, "Violence Against Women by Male Partners," *AP,* 48 (1993), 1077ff.

Page 264. M. D. Pagelow, *Family Violence* (1984).

Pages 266–67. P. A. Langer, *Preventing Domestic Violence Against Women* (1986).

Pages 267–68. From a report by U.S. Advisory Board on Child Abuse and Neglect, cited in *Noetic Sciences Review* (Autumn 1995), 33.

Page 268. G. T. Hotaling and D. B. Sugarman, "An Analysis of Risk Markers in Husband-to-Wife Violence," *Violence and Victims,* 1 (1986), 101ff.

Page 269. *The Commonwealth Fund Survey of Women's Health* (July 14, 1993).

Page 270. P. Evans, *The Verbally Abusive Relationship* (1992), p. 11.

CHAPTER 27

Page 273. P. Thoits, "Multiple Identities," *American Sociological Review,* 51 (1986), 259ff.

Page 273. R. Barnett and G. Baruch, "Women's Involvement in Multiple Roles and Psychological Distress," *JPSP,* 51 (1985), 578ff.; F. Crosby, *Juggling* (1991); N. Bolger, et al., "The Contagion of Stress Across Multiple Roles," *JMF,* 51 (1989), 175ff.; P. Stevens and A. Meleis, "Maternal Role of Clerical Workers," *SSM,* 32 (1991), 1425ff.

Page 274. Studies reported in *AP* (1989) and *JHSB* (1983, 1988).

Page 275. P. Cowan and C. Cowan, *When Partners Become Parents* (1993); Statistic in *The Kiplinger Washington Letter,* 70(35) (August 27, 1993), 3; H. McCubbin and B. Dahl, *Marriage and Family* (1985).

CHAPTER 28

Page 286. D. Herman, "A Statutory Proposal to Limit the Infliction of Violence upon Children," *Family Law Quarterly,* 19 (1985), 1ff.; M. McKay, et al., *When Anger Hurts* (1989).

Page 288. R. Taffel, *Parenting by Heart* (1991).

Page 295. B. Rollins and H. Feldman, "Marital Satisfaction over the Life Cycle," *JMF* 32 (1970), 20ff.

Page 296. A. Miller, *For Your Own Good* (1983).

Page 297. G. Jacobson, "The Meaning of Stressful Life Experiences in Nine- to Eleven-year-old Children," *NR* 43 (1994), 98; J. H. Block, et al., "Parental Agreement–Disagreement on Child-rearing Orientations and Gender-related Personality Correlates in Children," *Child Development (CD),* 52 (1981), 965ff.; R. E. Emery, "Interparental Conflict and the Children of Discord and Divorce," *PB,* 92 (1982), 310ff.; E. M. Cummings and J. L. Cummings, "A Process-Oriented Approach to Children's Coping with Adults' Angry Behavior," *Developmental Review (DR),* 8 (1988), 296ff.

CHAPTER 29

Page 300. S. Sleek, "Struggles for Equality Lead to More Divorce," *APA Monitor,* 27(10) (October 1994), 20.

Pages 302–08. Phases of divorce taken from P. Bohannan, *In Divorce and After* (1970); R. Weiss, *Marital Separation* (1975).

Page 305. J. Wallerstein and S. Blakeslee, *Second Chances* (1989).

Page 309. S. P. Thomas, *Journal of Divorce (JD),* 5(3) (1982), 19ff.

Page 311. M. Colgrove, et al., *How to Survive the Loss of a Love* (1993), p. 121.

Page 315. S. P. Thomas, *JD,* 5(3) (1982), 19ff.

CHAPTER 30

Page 317. C. Garrity and M. Baris, *Caught in the Middle* (1994).

Page 318. H. McCubbin and B. Dahl, *Marriage and Family* (1985).

Page 318. E. Hetherington and R. Cox, "The Aftermath of Divorce," *Mother/Child, Father/Child Relationships* (1978).

Pages 320–21. R. A. Gardner, *The Parents' Book About Divorce* (1991); J. Wallerstein, "Children of Divorce," *American Journal of Orthopsychiatry* (April 1983), 230ff.

Page 321. J. Wallerstein and J. Kelly, "California's Children of Divorce," *PT,* 13(8) (1980), 67ff.; N. Peterson (December 5, 1983) *USA Today.*

CHAPTER 31

Page 324. H. McCubbin and B. Dahl, *Marriage and Family* (1985).

Page 327. See A. McRary, (February 21, 1988), *Knoxville News Sentinel.*

Page 327. R. A. Gardner, *The Parents' Book About Divorce* (1991); quote from H. McCubbin and B. Dahl.

Page 328. E. Visher and J. Visher, *How to Win as a Stepfamily* (1982).

Page 329. A. T. Beck, *Love Is Never Enough* (1988); J. Wallerstein and J. Kelly, *Surviving the Breakup* (1980).

CHAPTER 32

Page 336. M. C. Bateson, *Composing a Life* (1989).

Page 338. G. Stern, "Think About Thinking," *Revolution* 1(1) (1991), 78ff.

Page 339. Four steps outlined in R. Driscoll, *The Binds That Tie* (1991).

Page 340. J. Prochaska, et al., "In Search of How People Change," *AP*, 47 (1992), 1102ff.

Page 340. See J. B. Miller (1983), in Major Sources.

CHAPTER 33

Page 343. C. Goodenow and E. Gaier, "Best Friends," paper presented at APA, Washington, D.C. (1986); L. B. Rubin, *Just Friends* (1985).

Page 344. See C. Wallis, "Onward Woman!," *Time* (December 4, 1989), pp. 80–89.

Page 346. L. Browning, "Government Affairs," *Tennessee Nurse* 57(1) (Spring 1994), 9f.; J. L. Surrey, "Relationship and Empowerment," *Writings from the Stone Center;* see Jordan (1991), in Major Sources.

Pages 346–47. L. Montada and A. Schneider, *Social Justice Research,* 3 (1989), 313ff.; J. DeRivera, paper presented at APA, Toronto (August 1993).

Page 347. Quote from S. Henry's book, *The Deep Divide,* cited in "The Power Gap," *New Woman,* p. 22 (July 1994).

Pages 348–49. P. Freiberg, "Self-esteem Gender Gap Widens in Adolescence," *APA Monitor,* 22(4) (1991), p. 29; M. Sadker and D. Sadker, *Failing at Fairness* (1994).

Page 349. M. Gittell, et al., *Building Human Capital* (City University of New York, 1993).

PERMISSIONS AND TESTS

Page xiii. "A Just Anger" is from *Circles on the Water,* by Marge Piercy. Copyright © 1982 by Marge Piercy. Reprinted by permission of Alfred A. Knopf, Inc.

Pages 34–35. "Exercise: The Anger Proneness Assessment Test." J. M. Siegel, "The Multi-dimensional Anger Inventory," *Journal of Personality and Social Psychology,* 51(1) (1986), 191–200. Siegel tested college students and factory workers during development of the questionnaire, which contains other sections in addition to the questions on general anger. Two of the items in Siegel's scale were taken from the Edwards Personality Inventory (A. L. Edwards, *Edwards Personality Inventory,* Chicago: Science Research Association, 1966). Siegel also used one item from the Buss-Durkee Hostility Inventory (A. H. Buss and A. Durkee, "An Inventory for Assessing Different Kinds of Hostility," *Journal of Consulting Psychology,* 21 (1957) 343–349. Copyright © 1986 by the American Psychological Association. Reprinted by permission.

Pages 56–58. "The Stress Test . . ." This quiz, known in the scientific literature as the Perceived Stress Scale, is reprinted with the permission of the American Sociological Association. It first appeared in S. Cohen, T. Kamarck, and R. Mermelstein, "A Global Measure of Perceived Stress," *Journal of Health and Social Behavior,* 24 (1983), 385–396.

Pages 100–01. "The Self-esteem Test." This questionnaire was published in M. Rosenberg, *Society and the Adolescent Self-image* (Princeton, N.J.: Princeton University Press, 1965). According to correspondence received from the Princeton University Press, it is in the public domain and may be reprinted.

Pages 102–03. "Do some detective work . . ." Exercises #1 and #3 were adapted from suggestions for classroom exercises in D. M. Young and S. Y. Kepes, "Techniques for Exploring Self-concept and Self-esteem in the Undergraduate Classroom," paper presented at the meeting of the American Psychological Association, Atlanta, Georgia (August 1988).

Pages 110–11. "CES-D Scale of Depression." The test was developed by a researcher at the National Institute of Mental Health and has been used to assess depression in normal populations for nearly two decades. It was introduced in L. Radloff, "The CES-D Scale: A Self-report Depression Scale for Research in the General Population," *Applied Psychological Measurement,* 1 (1977), 385–401. Copyright © 1977 by West Publishing Company/Applied Psychological Measurement Inc. Reproduced by permission.

Pages 143–44. "The Problem Drinker's Test." These questions were derived mainly from the Michigan Alcoholism Screening Test, which appeared in M. Selzer, "The MAST: The Quest for a New Diagnostic Instrument," *American Journal of Psychiatry,* 127 (1971), 1653–1658. Questions that are more pertinent to men ("Have you gotten into fights when drinking?") or to more severe alcoholism ("Have you ever had DT's?") were omitted.

Page 164. "Anger/Health Habits Assessment Test." The quiz is adapted from *Staying Young,* copyright © 1994 by Rodale Press, Inc. Permission granted by Rodale Press, Inc., Emmaus, PA 18098.

Pages 174–75. "The Twelve Warning Signs of Health." Reprinted with permission from *Brain/Mind, A Bulletin of Breakthroughs,* Los Angeles, Calif. Subscription price, $45 from BRAIN/MIND, P.O. Box 42211, Los Angeles, CA 90042. Free sample available upon request.

Page 177. "Home and Workplace Anger Yardsticks." This quiz is taken from an article by Goldstein, Edelberg, Meier, and Davis, which appeared in *Psychosomatic Medicine,* 50 (1988), 321–329. Note that the quiz is scored differently when it is used for research purposes. It is included by permission of the copyright owner, Williams & Wilkins Company.

Pages 220–23. "The Relationship Adjustment Test." G. B. Spanier, "Measuring Dyadic Adjustment: New Scales for Assessing the Quality of Marriage and Similar Dyads," *Journal of Marriage and the Family,* 38(1) (1976), 15–28. In the scientific literature, this scale is known as the Dyadic Adjustment Scale, and it is one of the most widely used questionnaires in the world. Copyright © 1976 by the National Council on Family Relations, 3989 Central Avenue NE, Suite 550, Minneapolis, MN 55421. Reprinted by permission of the author and the copyright holder. Copies of the test may be ordered from Multi-Health Systems, Inc., 95 Thorncliffe Park Drive, Suite 100, Toronto, Ontario, Canada, M4H 1L7.

Pages 310–11. "Constructive Steps for Adjusting to Divorce." This list of strategies has been adapted from a chapter I wrote for the third edition of R. L. Williams and J. D. Long's *Toward a Self-Managed Life Style,* Third edition. Copyright © 1983 by Houghton Mifflin Company. Adapted with permission.

◇ INDEX ◇